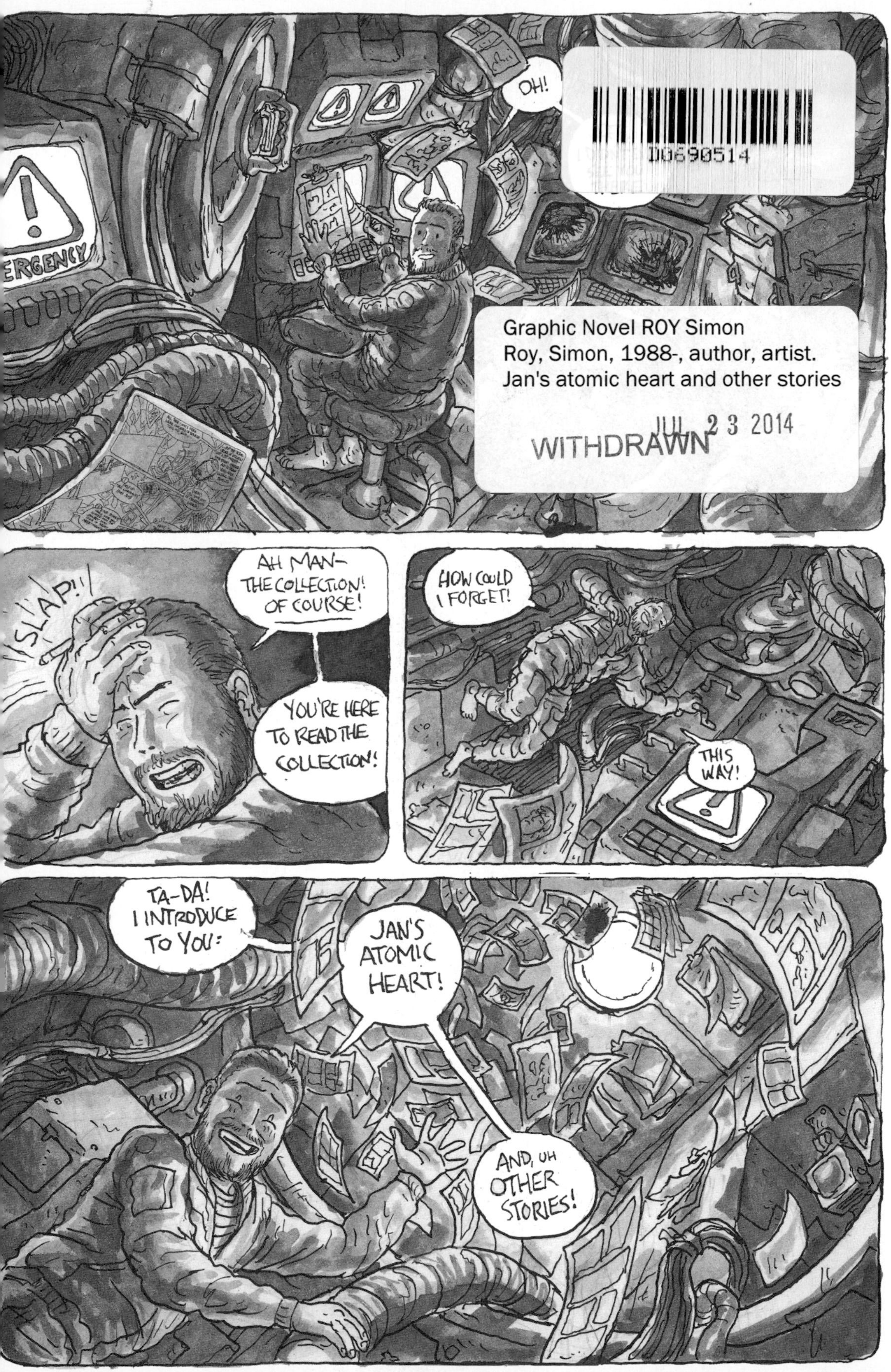
OH!
SLAP!!
AH MAN— THE COLLECTION! OF COURSE!
YOU'RE HERE TO READ THE COLLECTION!
HOW COULD I FORGET!
THIS WAY!
TA-DA! I INTRODUCE TO YOU:
JAN'S ATOMIC HEART!
AND, UH OTHER STORIES!

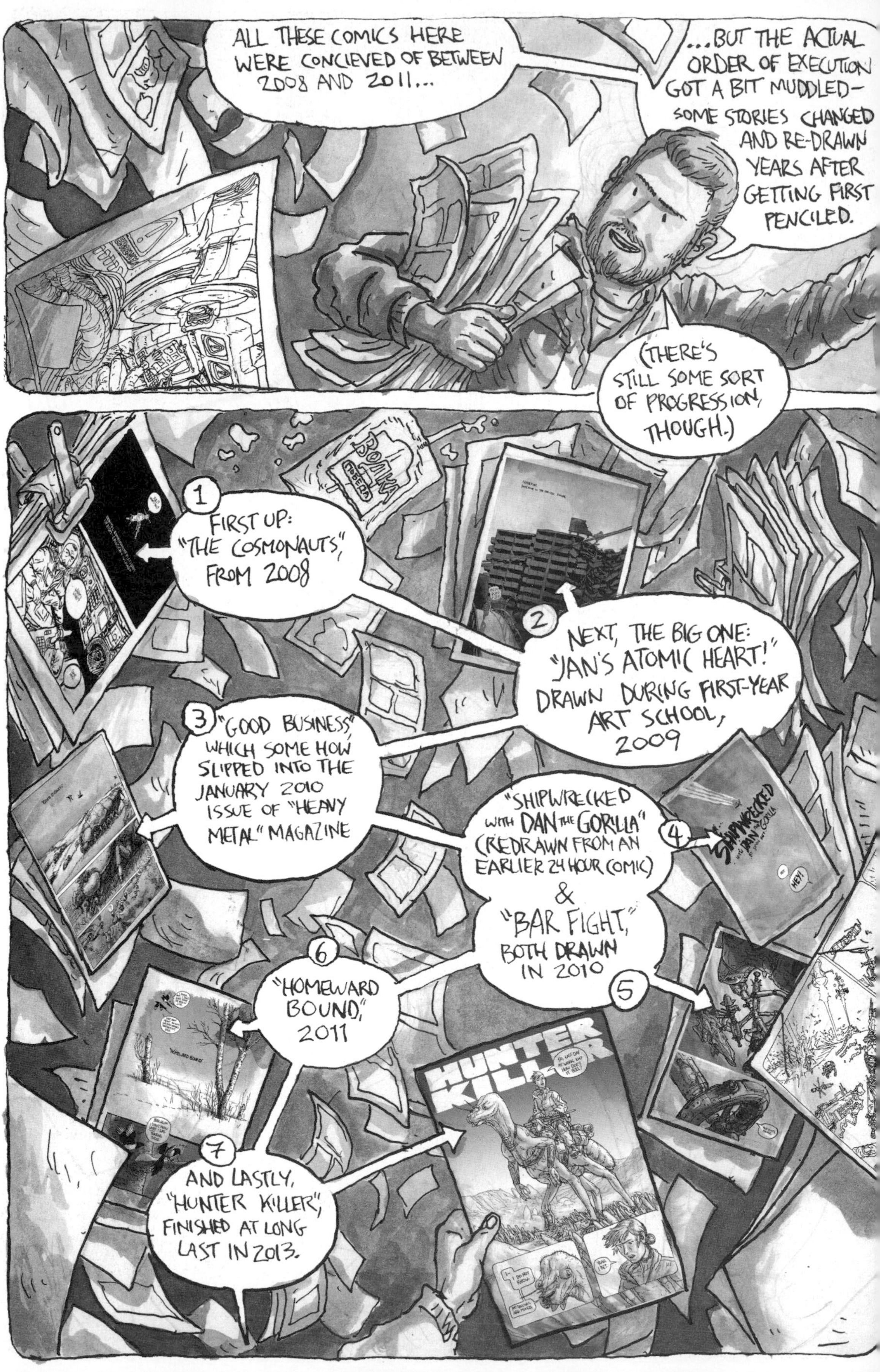

ALL THESE COMICS HERE WERE CONCIEVED OF BETWEEN 2008 AND 2011...
...BUT THE ACTUAL ORDER OF EXECUTION GOT A BIT MUDDLED– SOME STORIES CHANGED AND RE-DRAWN YEARS AFTER GETTING FIRST PENCILED.
(THERE'S STILL SOME SORT OF PROGRESSION, THOUGH.)
1 FIRST UP: "THE COSMONAUTS," FROM 2008
2 NEXT, THE BIG ONE: "JAN'S ATOMIC HEART!" DRAWN DURING FIRST-YEAR ART SCHOOL, 2009
3 "GOOD BUSINESS," WHICH SOME HOW SLIPPED INTO THE JANUARY 2010 ISSUE OF "HEAVY METAL" MAGAZINE
4 "SHIPWRECKED WITH DAN THE GORILLA" (REDRAWN FROM AN EARLIER 24 HOUR COMIC)
& 5 "BAR FIGHT," BOTH DRAWN IN 2010
6 "HOMEWARD BOUND," 2011
7 AND LASTLY, "HUNTER KILLER", FINISHED AT LONG LAST IN 2013.
HUNTER KILLER

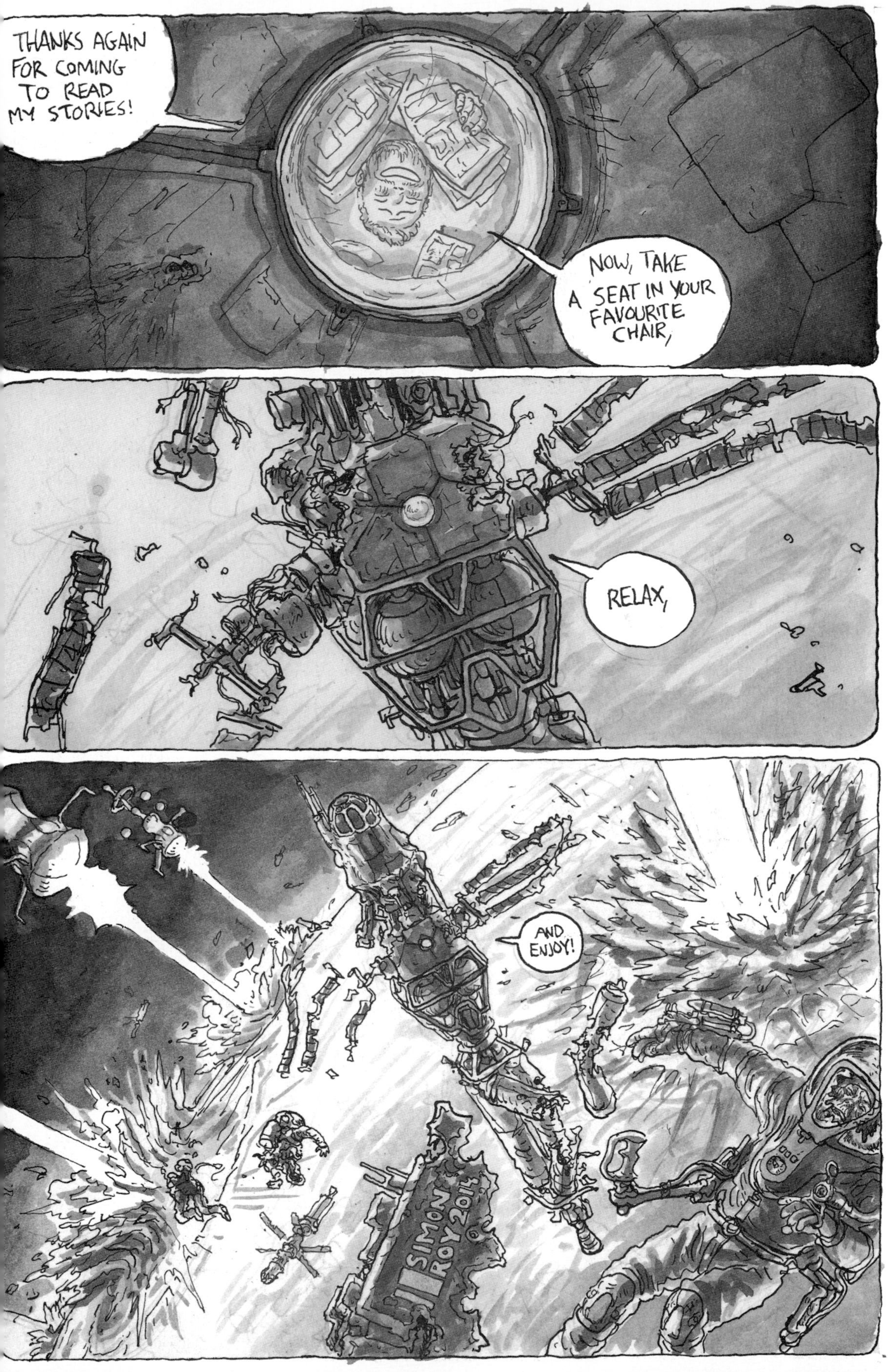
THANKS AGAIN FOR COMING TO READ MY STORIES!
NOW, TAKE A SEAT IN YOUR FAVOURITE CHAIR,
RELAX,
AND ENJOY!
SIMON ROY 2014 ©

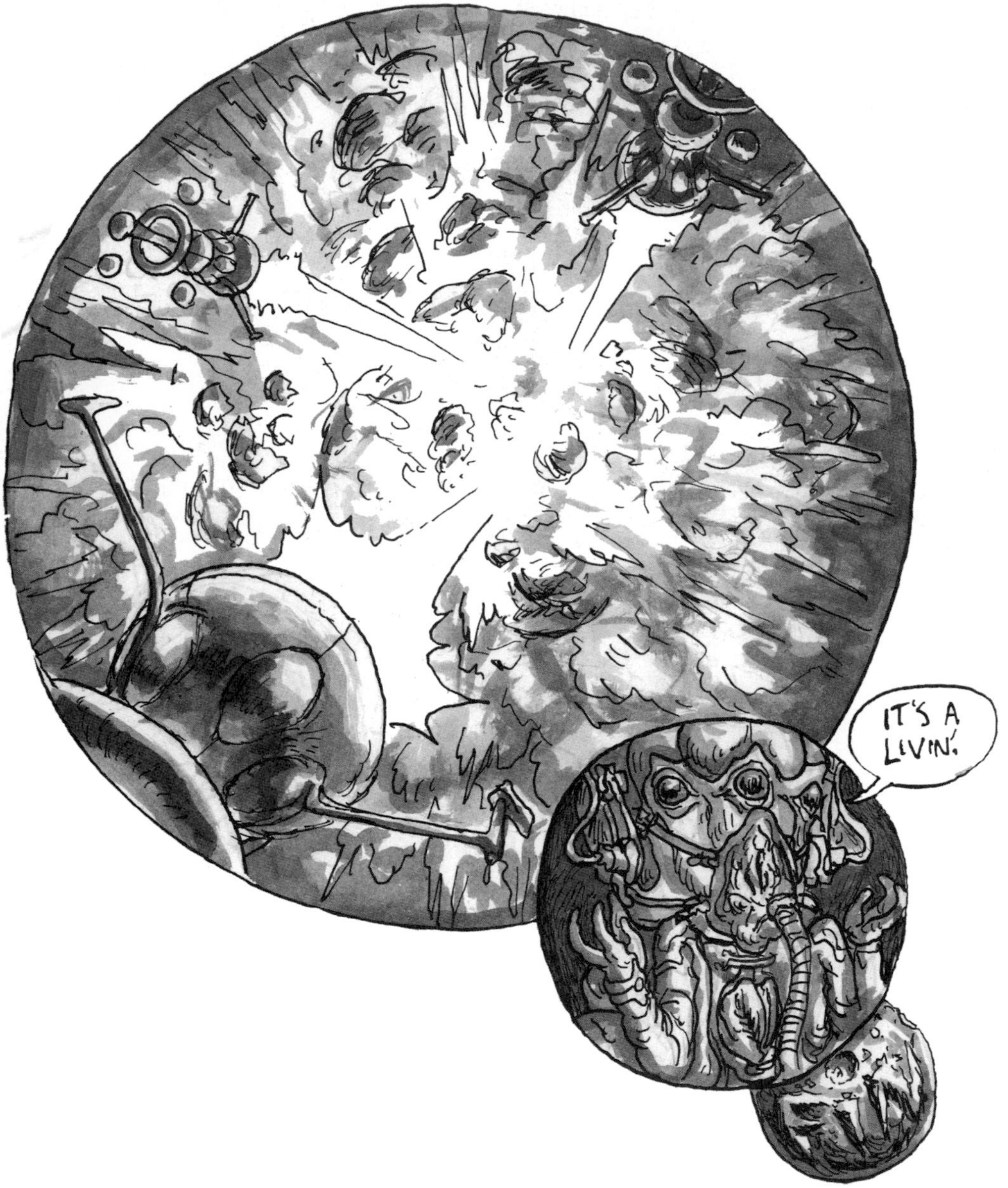
IT'S A LIVIN'.

JAN'S ATOMIC HEART
AND OTHER STORIES

SIMON ROY

JAN'S ATOMIC HEART
AND OTHER STORIES

IMAGE COMICS, INC.
Robert Kirkman – Chief Operating Officer
Erik Larsen – Chief Financial Officer
Todd McFarlane – President
Marc Silvestri – Chief Executive Officer
Jim Valentino – Vice-President

Eric Stephenson – Publisher
Ron Richards – Director of Business Development
Jennifer de Guzman – Director of Trade Book Sales
Kat Salazar – Director of PR & Marketing
Jeremy Sullivan – Director of Digital Sales
Emilio Bautista – Sales Assistant
Branwyn Bigglestone – Senior Accounts Manager
Emily Miller – Accounts Manager
Jessica Ambriz – Administrative Assistant
Tyler Shainline – Events Coordinator
David Brothers – Content Manager
Jonathan Chan – Production Manager
Drew Gill – Art Director
Meredith Wallace – Print Manager
Monica Garcia – Senior Production Artist
Jenna Savage – Production Artist
Addison Duke – Production Artist
Tricia Ramos – Production Assistant
IMAGECOMICS.COM

JAN'S ATOMIC HEART AND OTHER STORIES. FIRST PRINTING. MARCH 2014.
ISBN: 978-1-60706-936-2
Published by Image Comics, Inc. Office of publication: 2001 Center Street, 6th Floor, Berkeley, CA 94704. Copyright © 2014 Simon Roy. All rights reserved. JAN'S ATOMIC HEART AND OTHER STORIES™ (including all prominent characters featured herein), its logo and all character likenesses are trademarks of Simon Roy, unless otherwise noted. Image Comics® and its logos are registered trademarks of Image Comics, Inc. No part of this publication may be reproduced or transmitted, in any form or by any means (except for short excerpts for review purposes) without the express written permission of Image Comics, Inc. All names, characters, events and locales in this publication are entirely fictional. Any resemblance to actual persons (living or dead), events or places, without satiric intent, is coincidental. PRINTED IN THE U.S.A. For information regarding the CPSIA on this printed material call: 203-595-3636 and provide reference # RICH – 552264. For international rights, contact: foreignlicensing@imagecomics.com

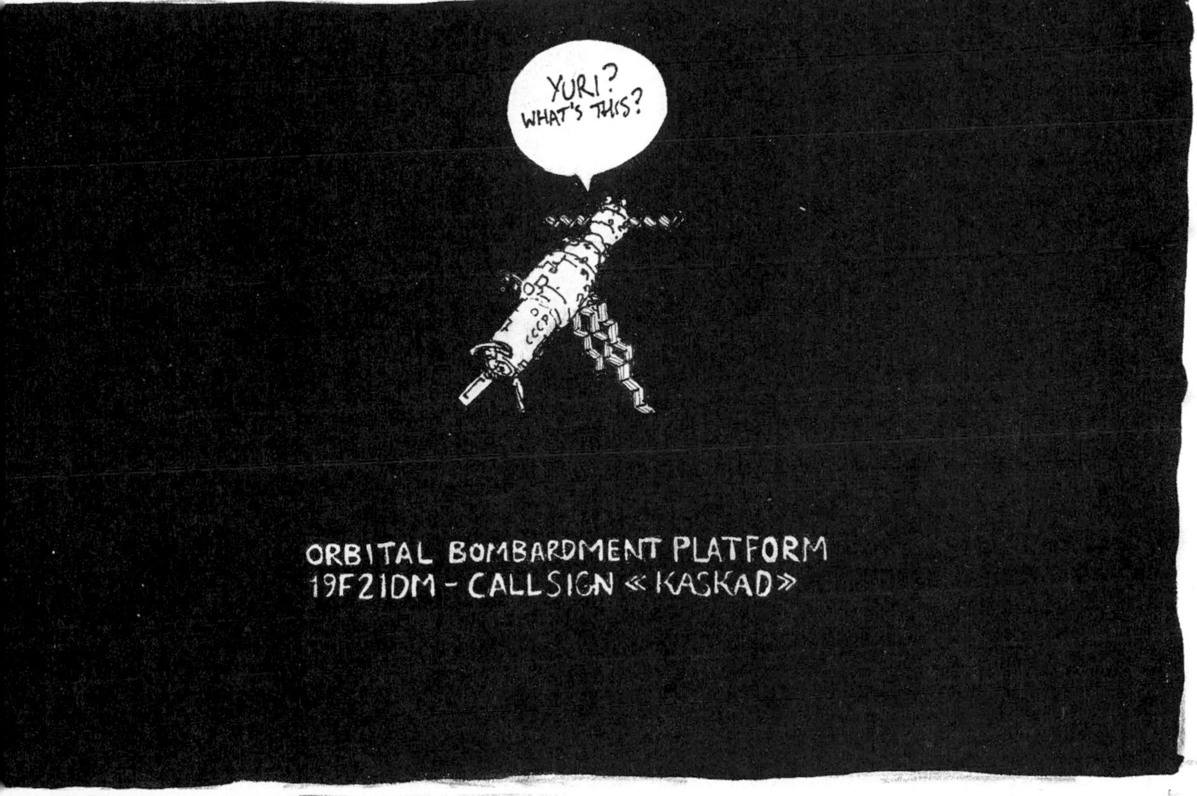
YURI? WHAT'S THIS?
ORBITAL BOMBARDMENT PLATFORM
19F21DM - CALLSIGN «KASKAD»

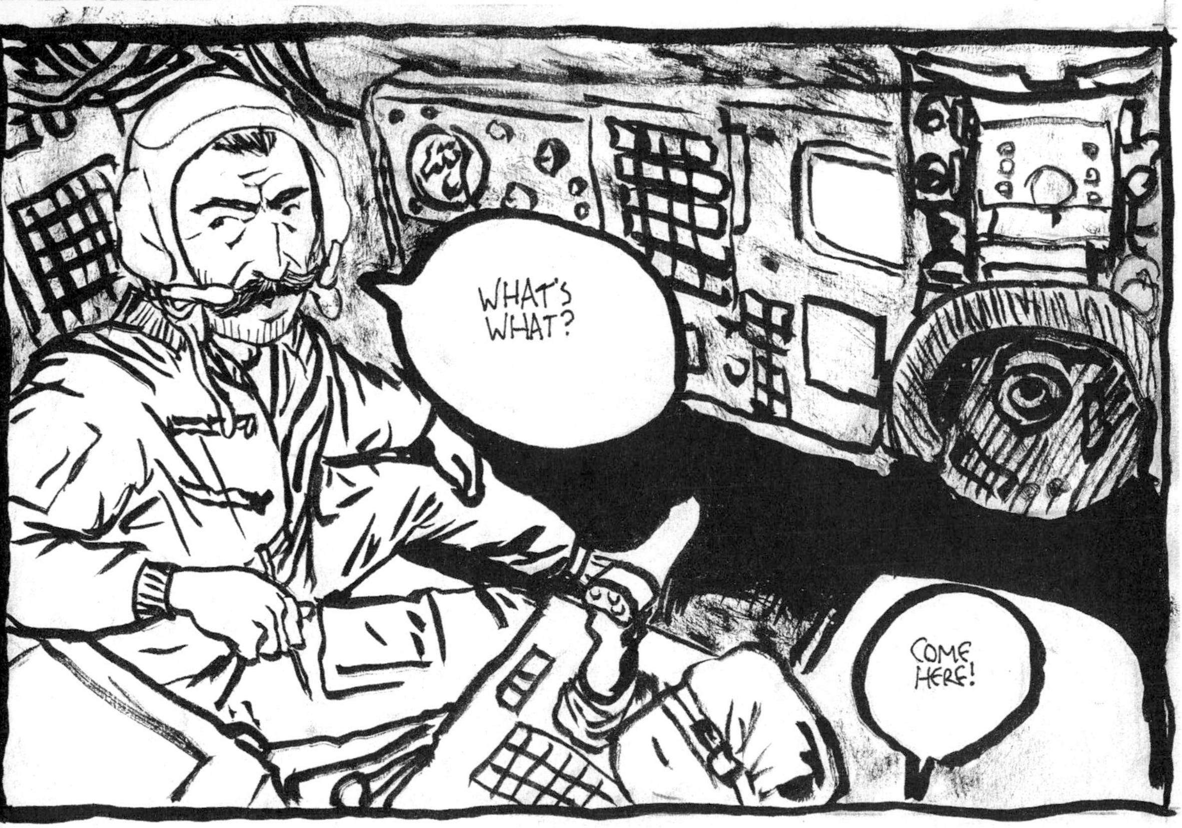
WHAT'S WHAT?
COME HERE!

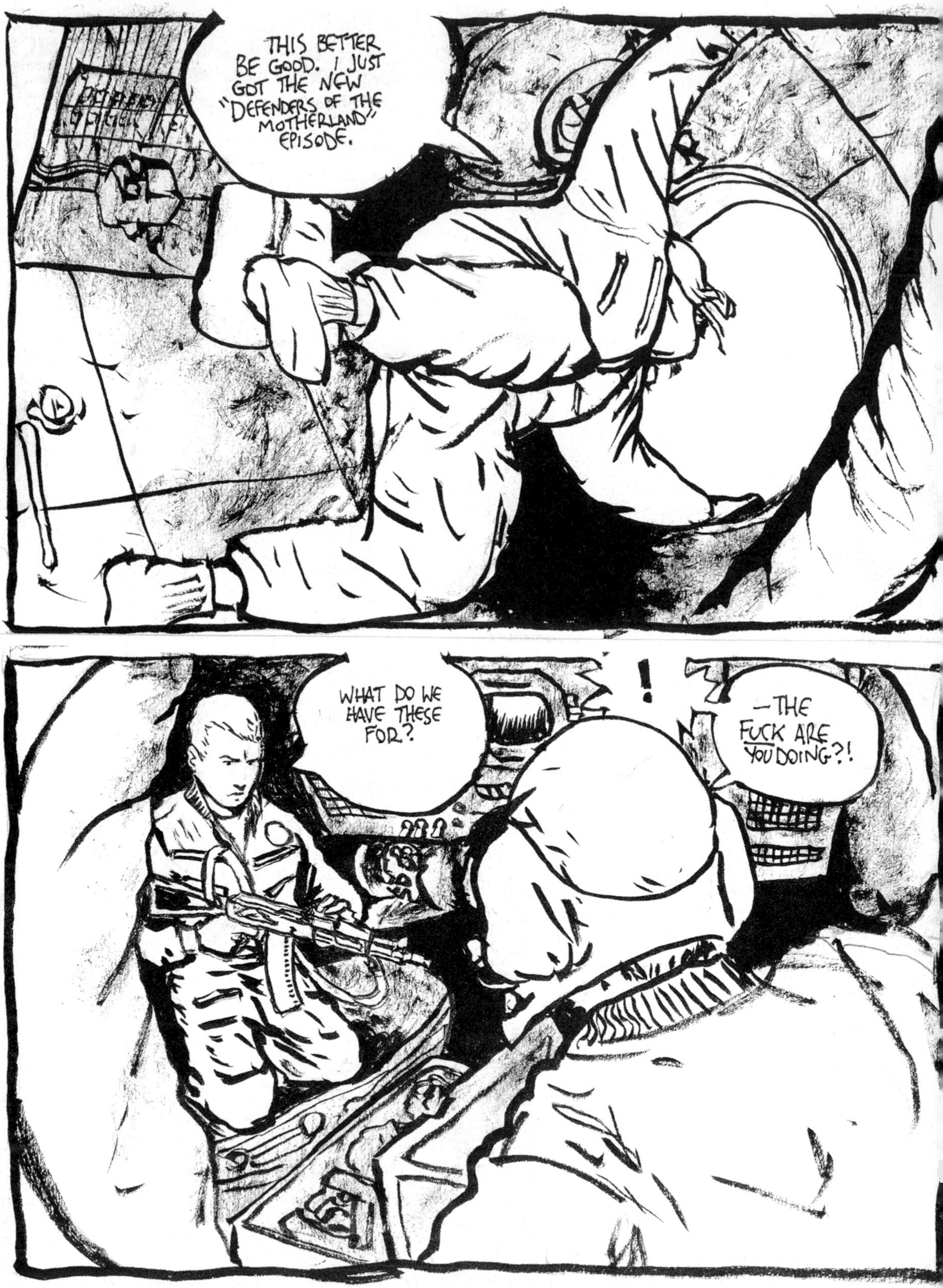
THIS BETTER BE GOOD. I JUST GOT THE NEW "DEFENDERS OF THE MOTHERLAND" EPISODE.
WHAT DO WE HAVE THESE FOR?
!
—THE FUCK ARE YOU DOING?!

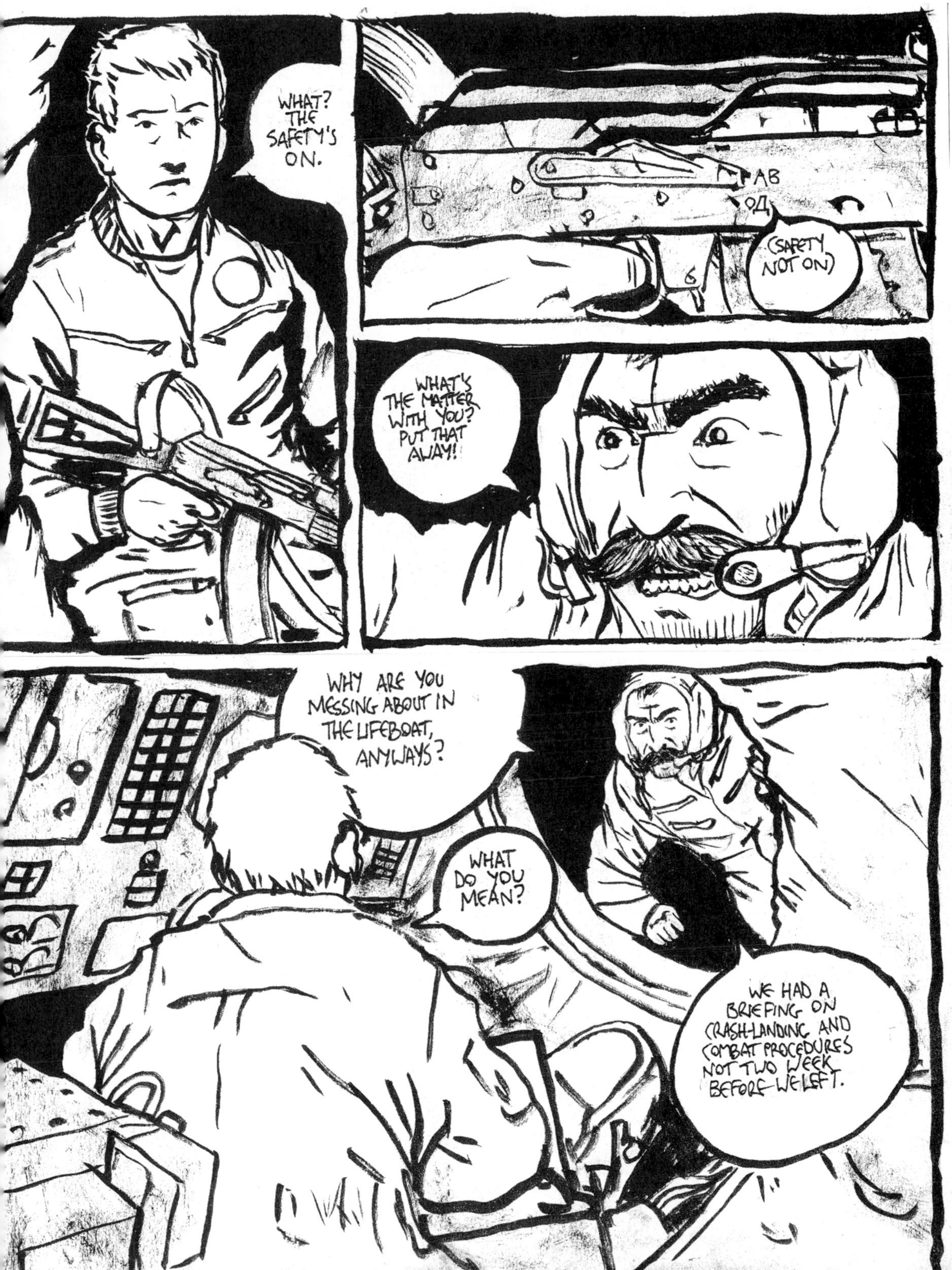
WHAT? THE SAFETY'S ON.
АВ
ОД
(SAFETY NOT ON)
WHAT'S THE MATTER WITH YOU? PUT THAT AWAY!
WHY ARE YOU MESSING ABOUT IN THE LIFEBOAT, ANYWAYS?
WHAT DO YOU MEAN?
WE HAD A BRIEFING ON CRASH-LANDING AND COMBAT PROCEDURES NOT TWO WEEK BEFORE WE LEFT.

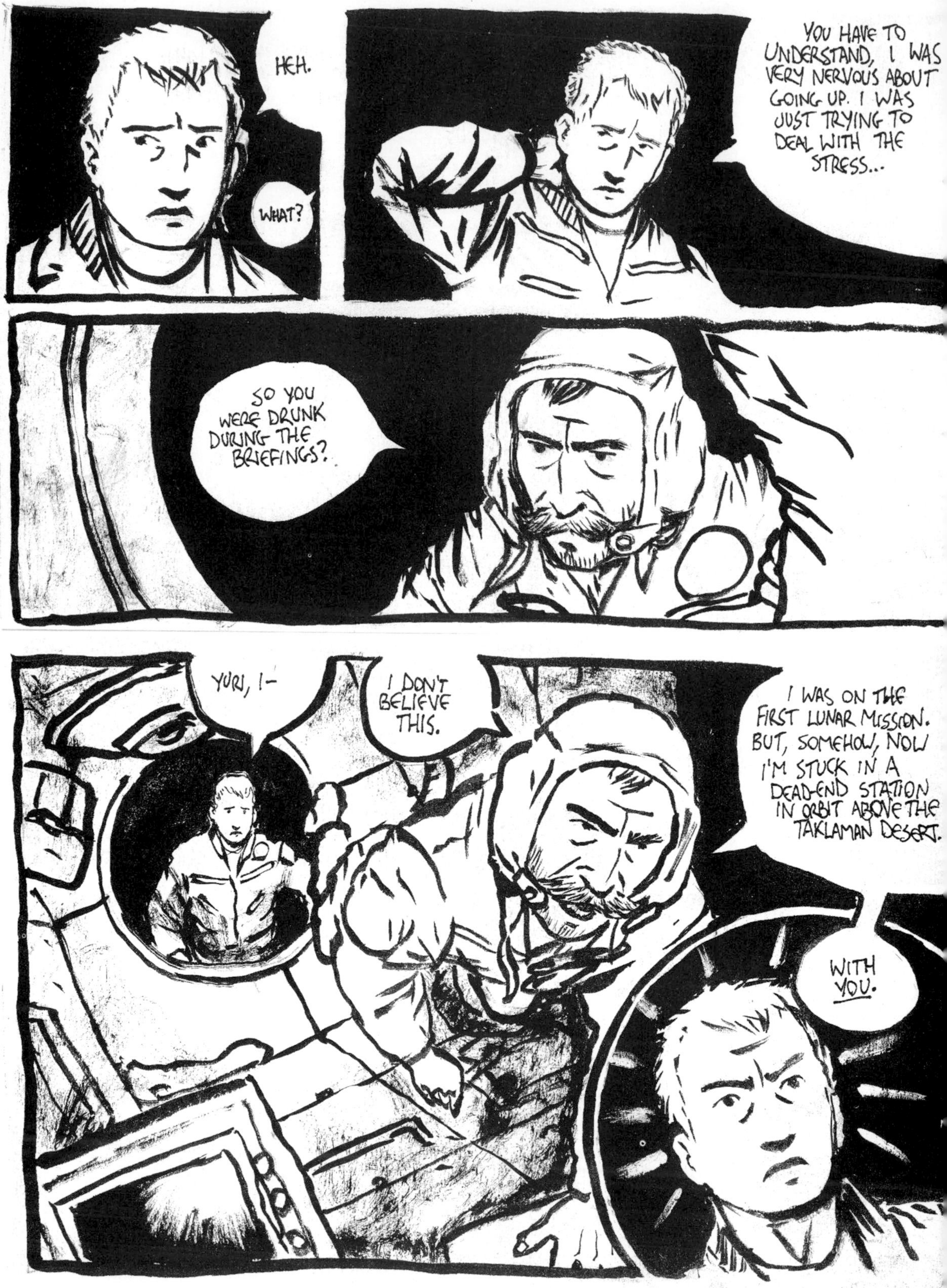
HEH.
WHAT?
YOU HAVE TO UNDERSTAND, I WAS VERY NERVOUS ABOUT GOING UP. I WAS JUST TRYING TO DEAL WITH THE STRESS...
SO YOU WERE DRUNK DURING THE BRIEFINGS?
YURI, I-
I DON'T BELIEVE THIS.
I WAS ON THE FIRST LUNAR MISSION. BUT, SOMEHOW, NOW I'M STUCK IN A DEAD-END STATION IN ORBIT ABOVE THE TAKLAMAN DESERT.
WITH YOU.

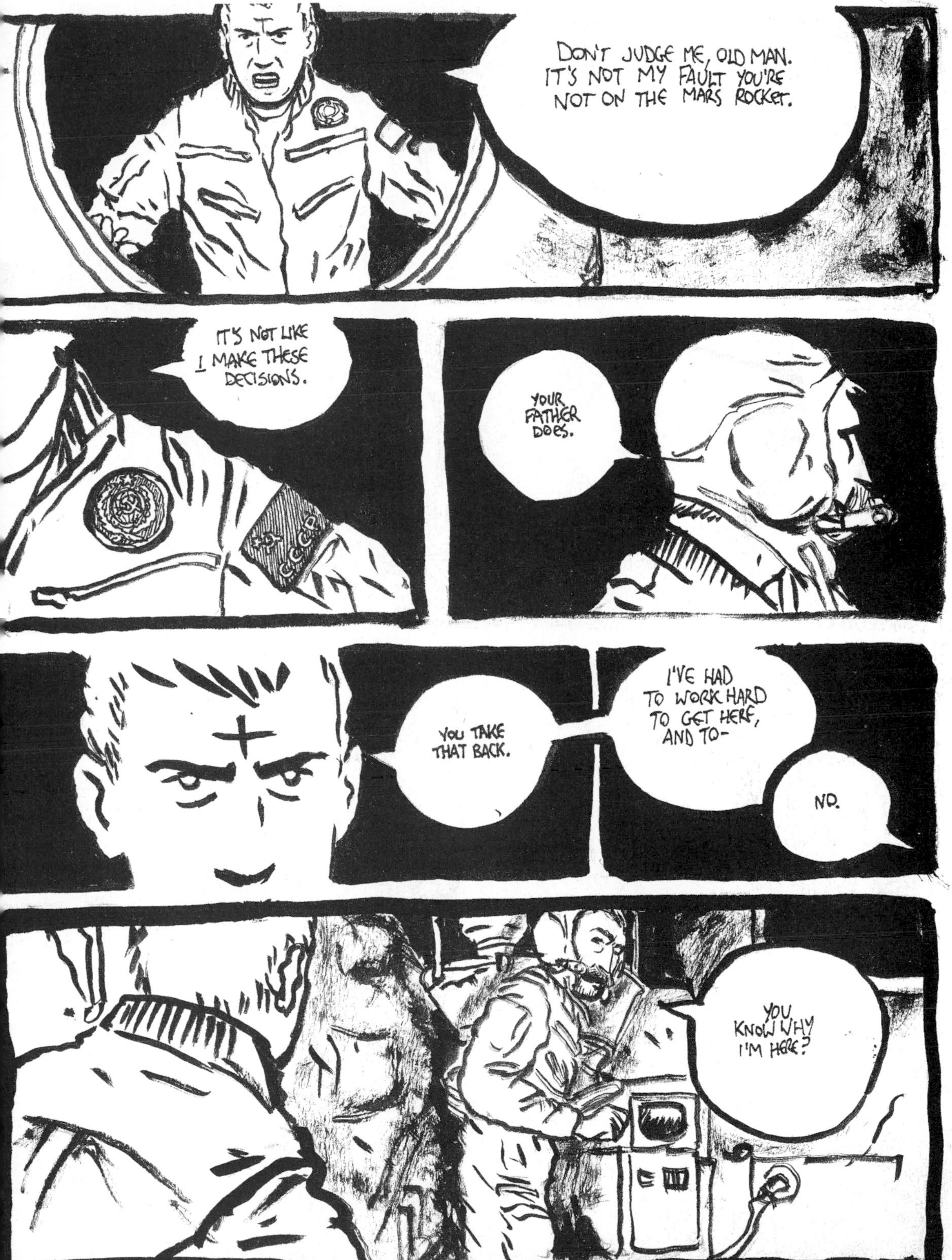
DON'T JUDGE ME, OLD MAN. IT'S NOT MY FAULT YOU'RE NOT ON THE MARS ROCKET.
IT'S NOT LIKE I MAKE THESE DECISIONS.
YOUR FATHER DOES.
YOU TAKE THAT BACK.
I'VE HAD TO WORK HARD TO GET HERE, AND TO-
NO.
YOU KNOW WHY I'M HERE?

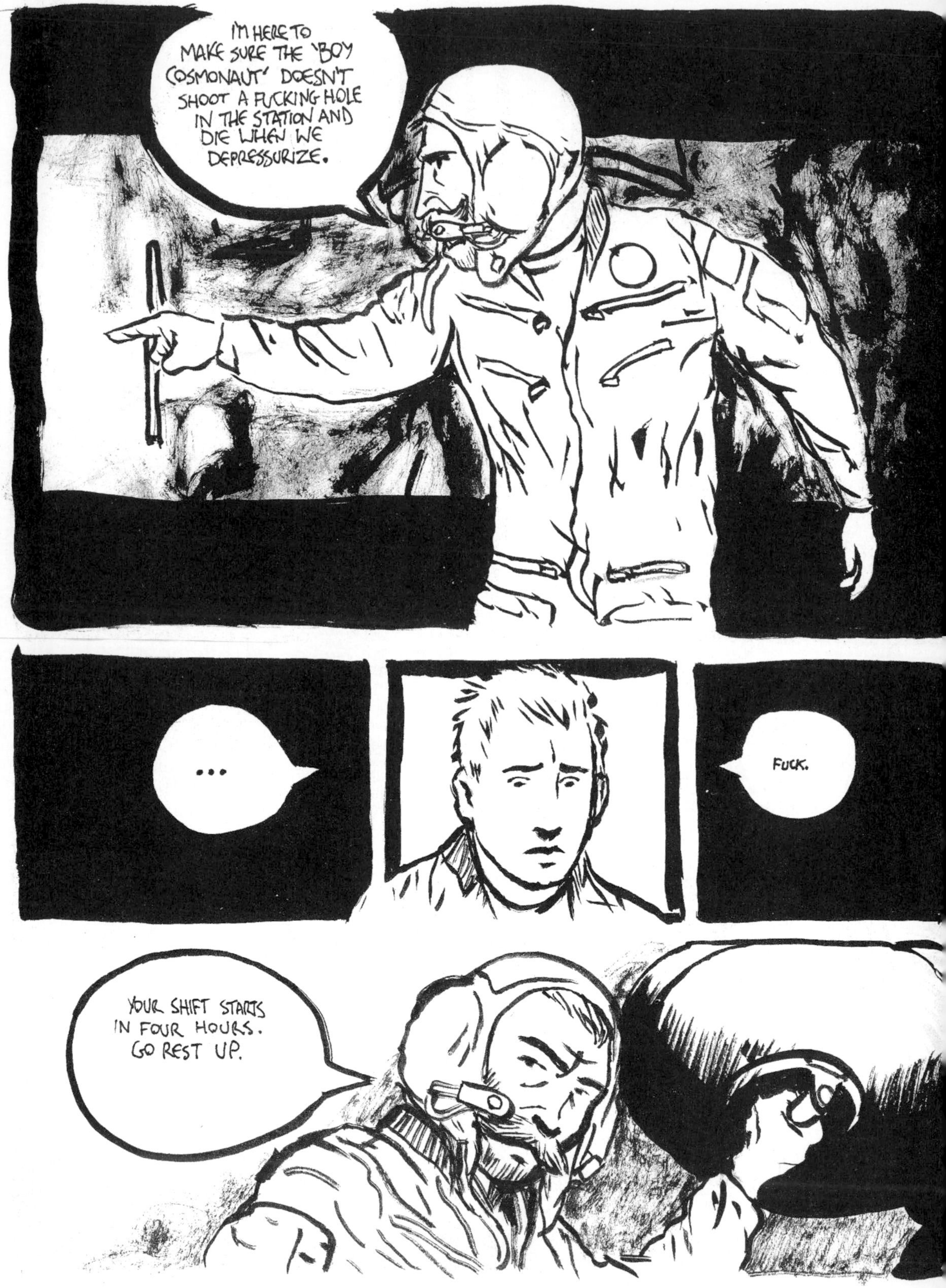
I'M HERE TO MAKE SURE THE 'BOY COSMONAUT' DOESN'T SHOOT A FUCKING HOLE IN THE STATION AND DIE WHEN WE DEPRESSURIZE.
...
FUCK.
YOUR SHIFT STARTS IN FOUR HOURS. GO REST UP.

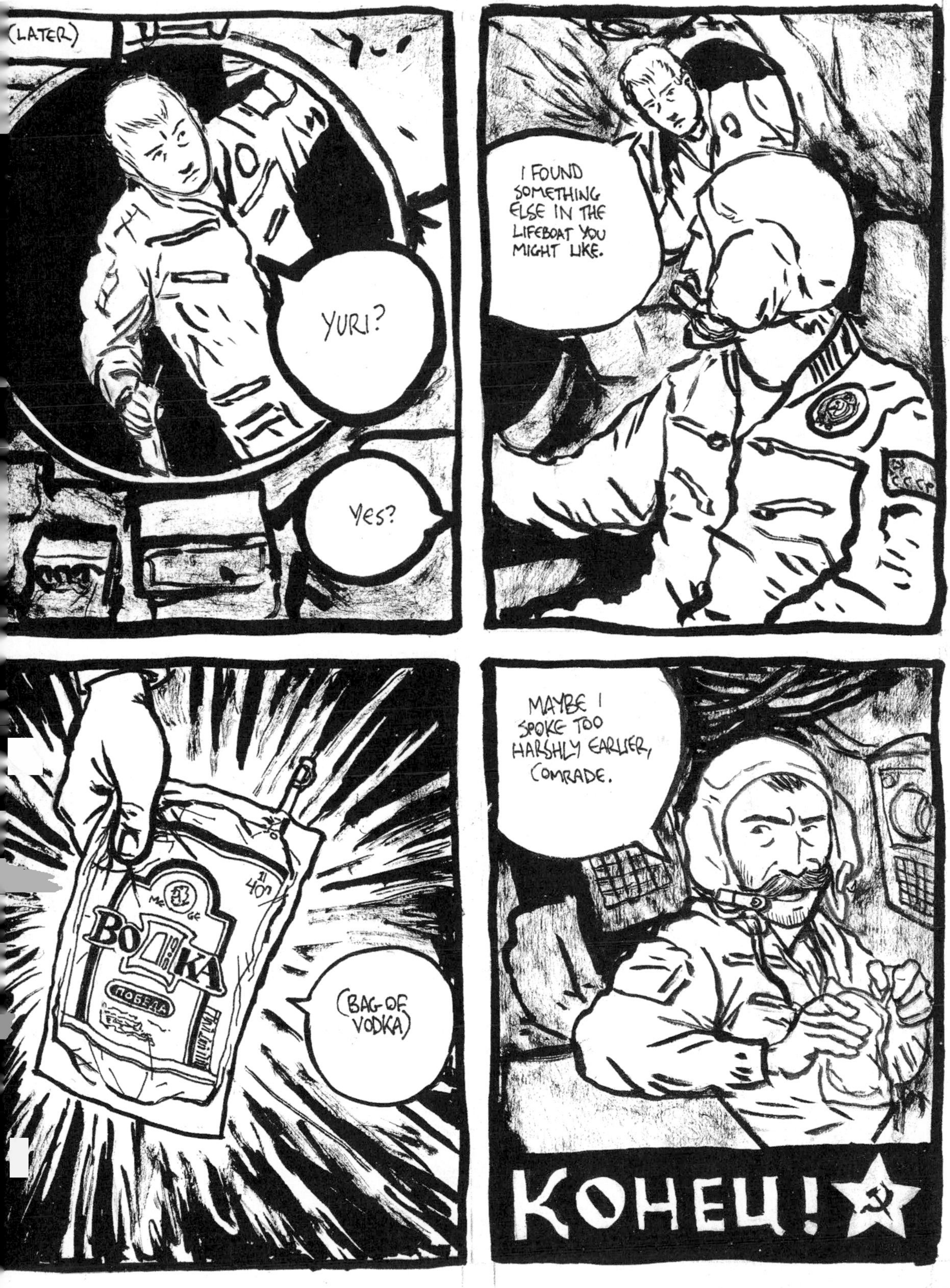
(LATER)
YURI?
YES?
I FOUND SOMETHING ELSE IN THE LIFEBOAT YOU MIGHT LIKE.
ВОДКА
ПОБЕДА
(BAG OF VODKA)
MAYBE I SPOKE TOO HARSHLY EARLIER, COMRADE.
КОНЕЦ!

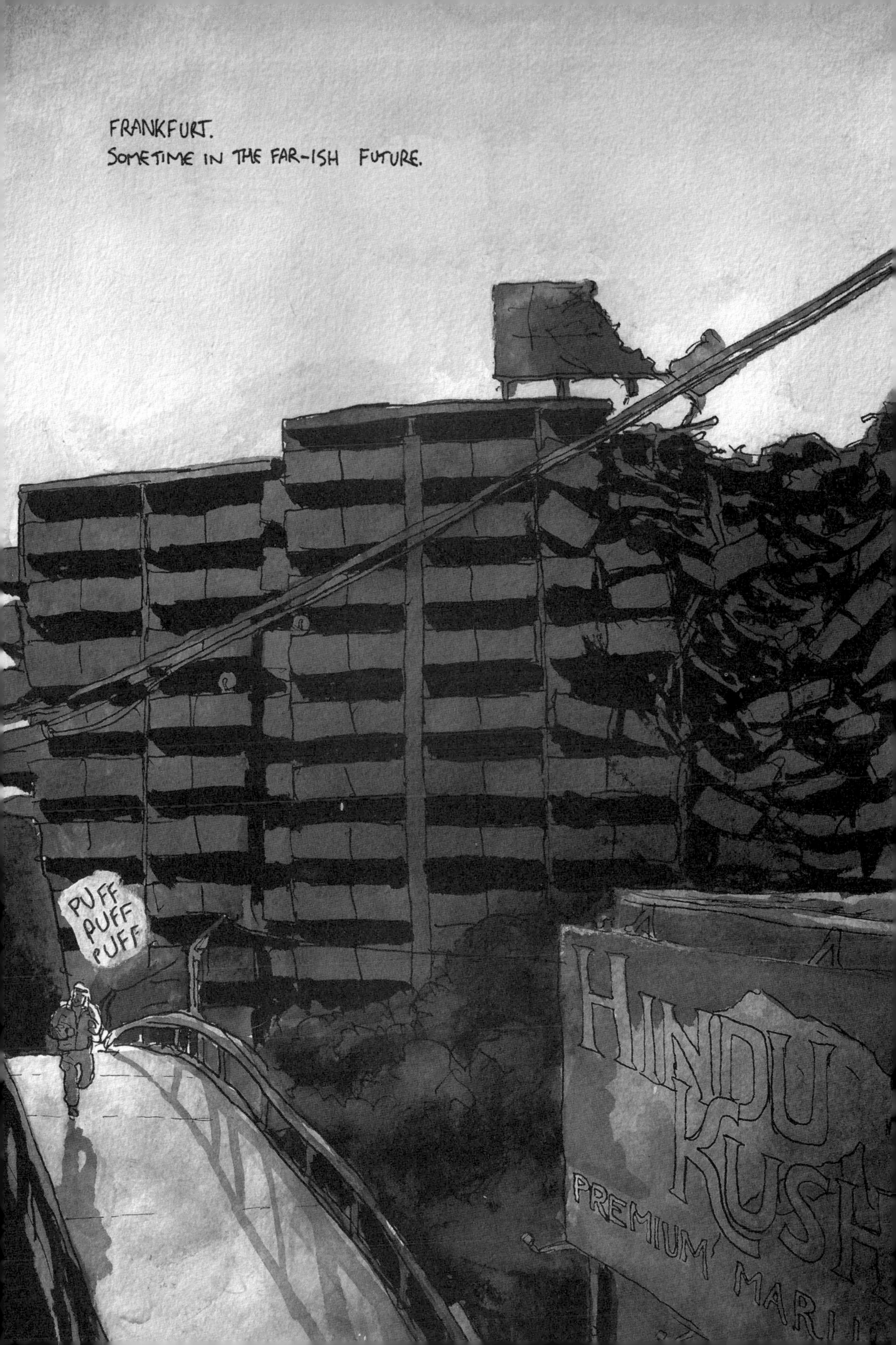
FRANKFURT.
SOMETIME IN THE FAR-ISH FUTURE.
PUFF PUFF PUFF
HINDU KUSH
PREMIUM
MARI

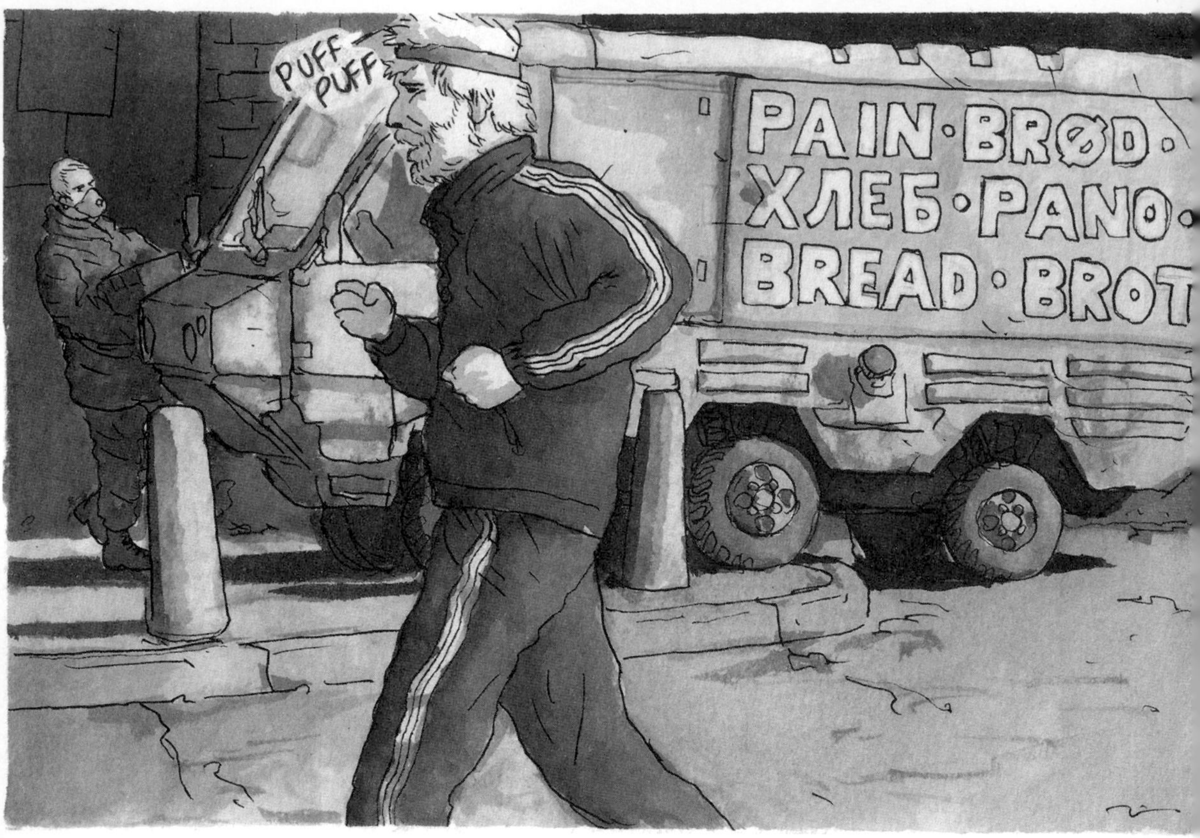
PUFF PUFF
PAIN·BRØD·
ХЛЕБ·PANO·
BREAD·BROT

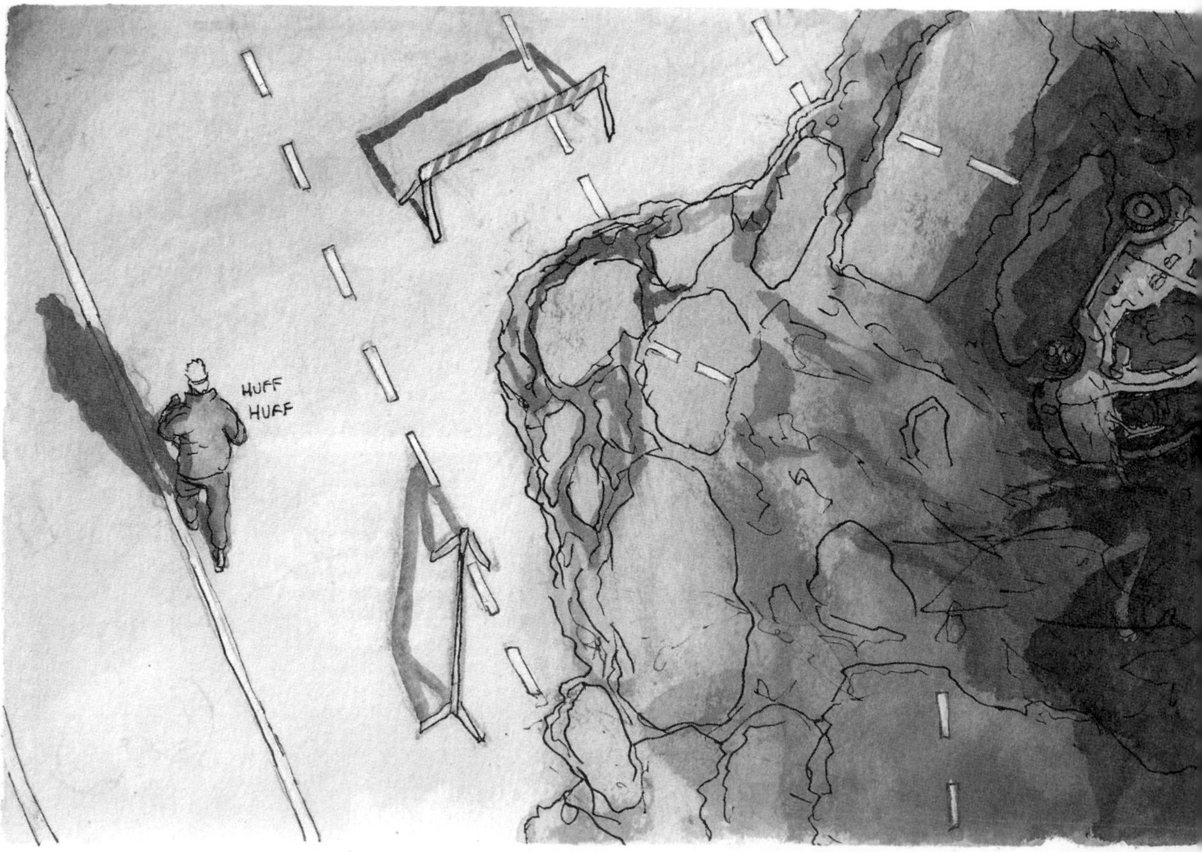
HUFF HUFF

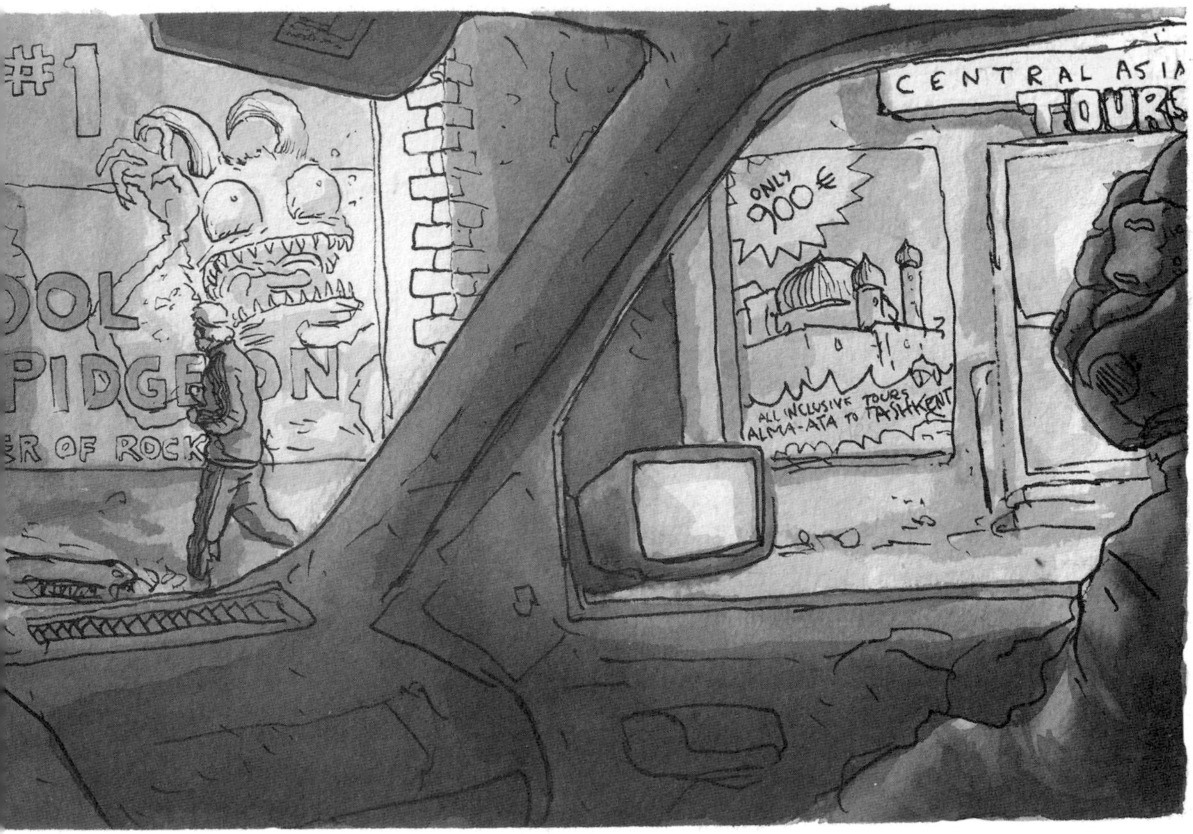
#1
OOL
PIDGEON
ER OF ROCK
ONLY 900 €
ALL INCLUSIVE TOURS
ALMA-ATA TO TASHKENT
CENTRAL ASIA
TOUR

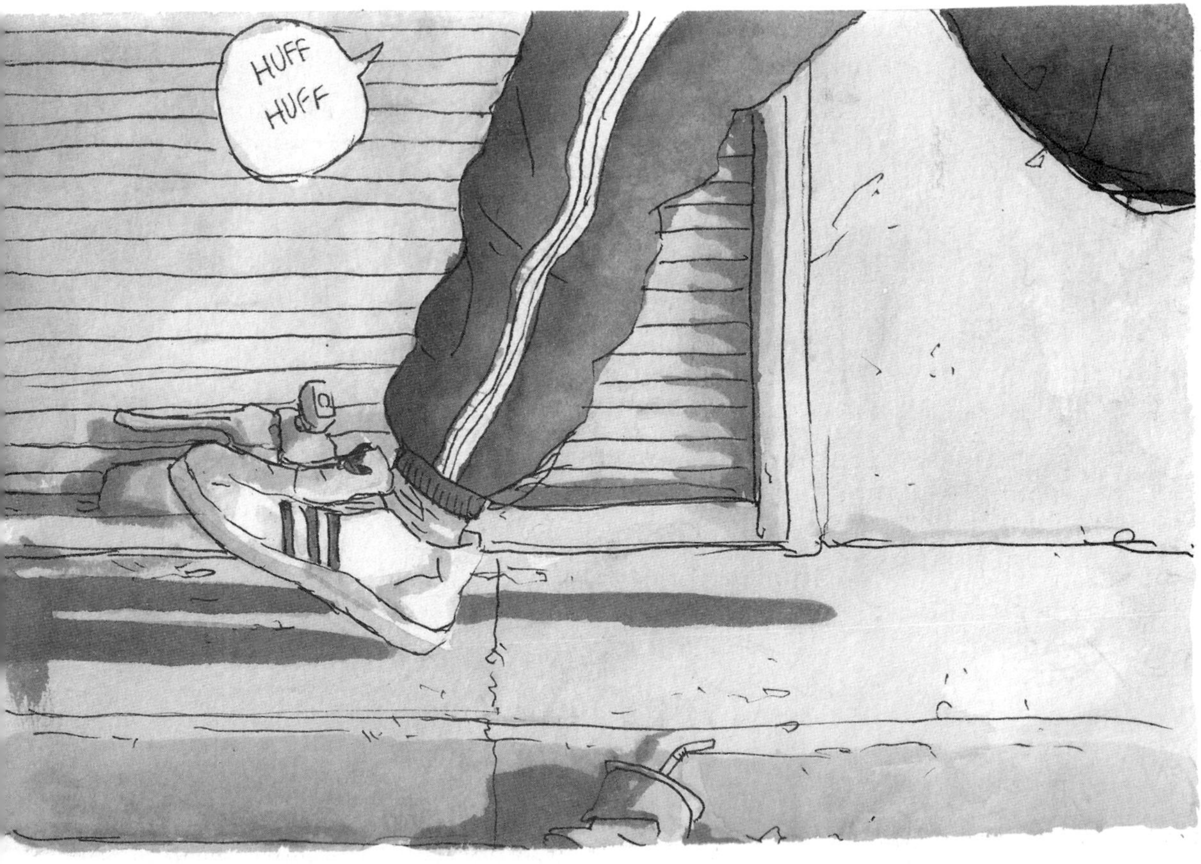
HUFF
HUFF

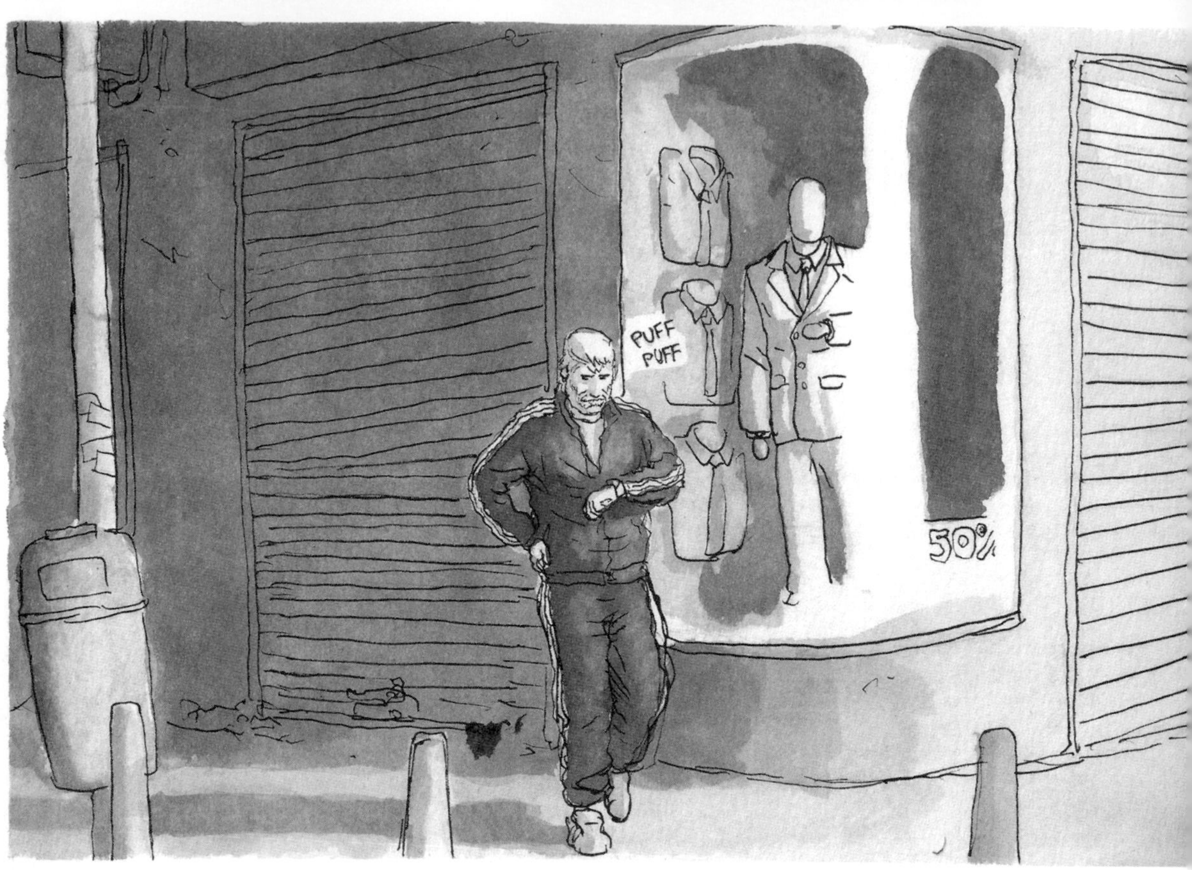
PUFF
PUFF
50%

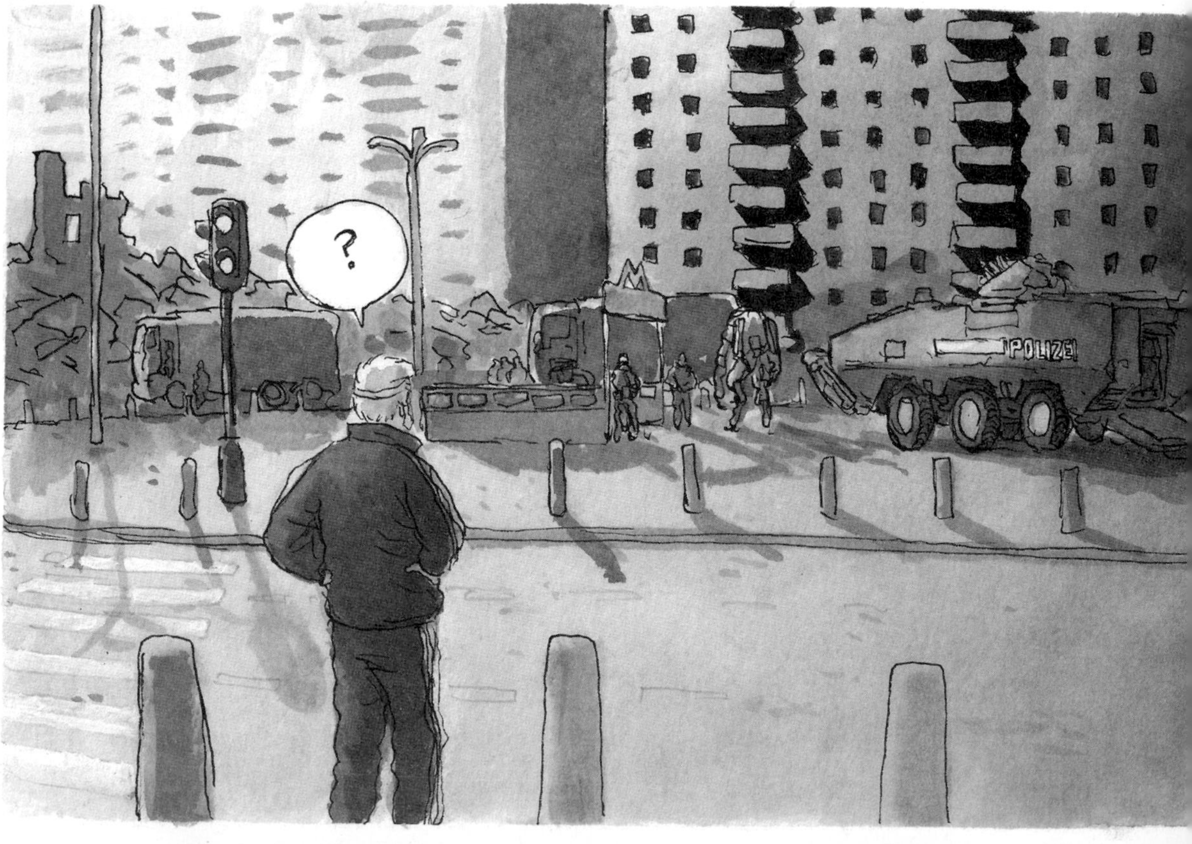
?
POLIZEI

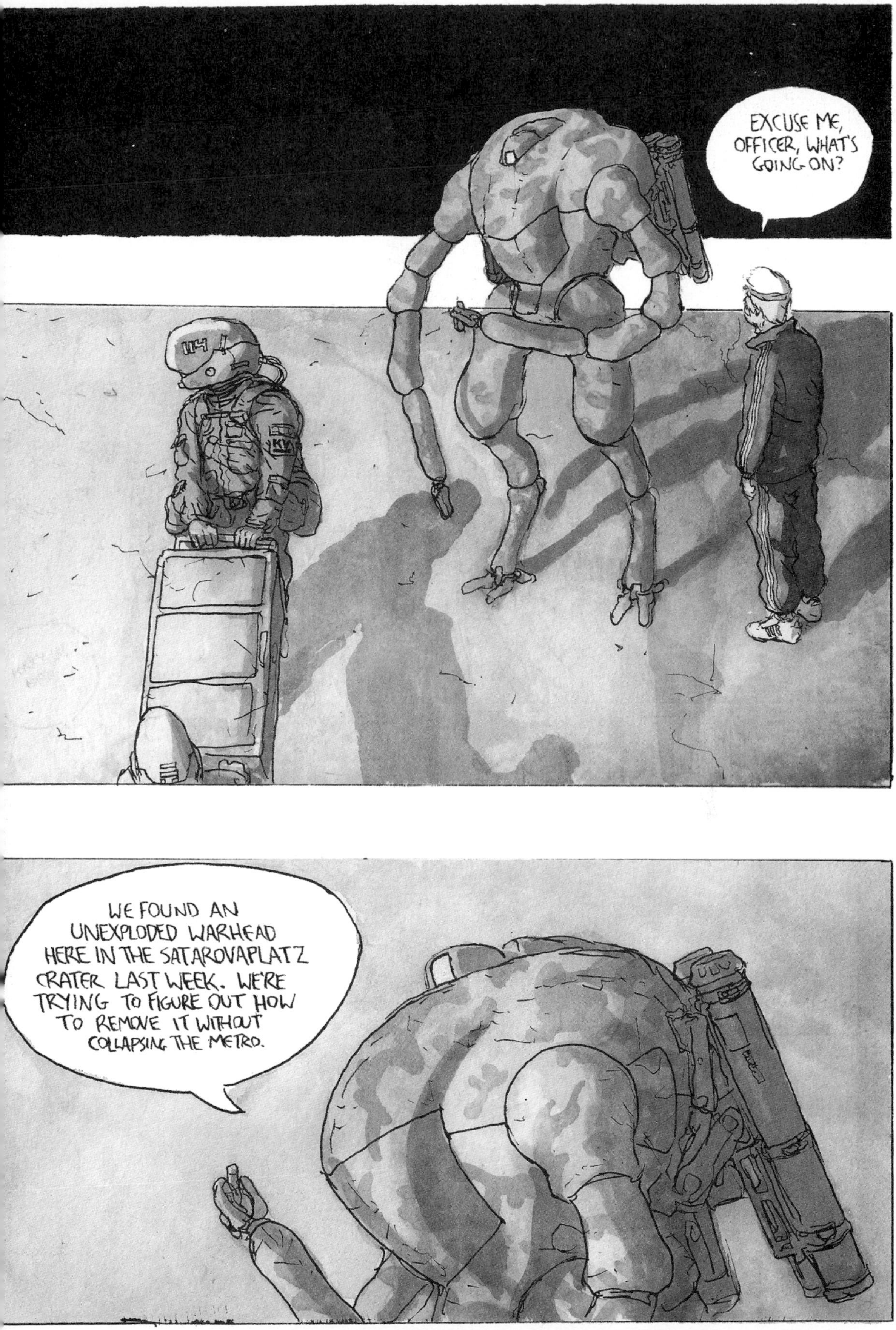
EXCUSE ME, OFFICER, WHAT'S GOING ON?
WE FOUND AN UNEXPLODED WARHEAD HERE IN THE SATAROVAPLATZ CRATER LAST WEEK. WE'RE TRYING TO FIGURE OUT HOW TO REMOVE IT WITHOUT COLLAPSING THE METRO.

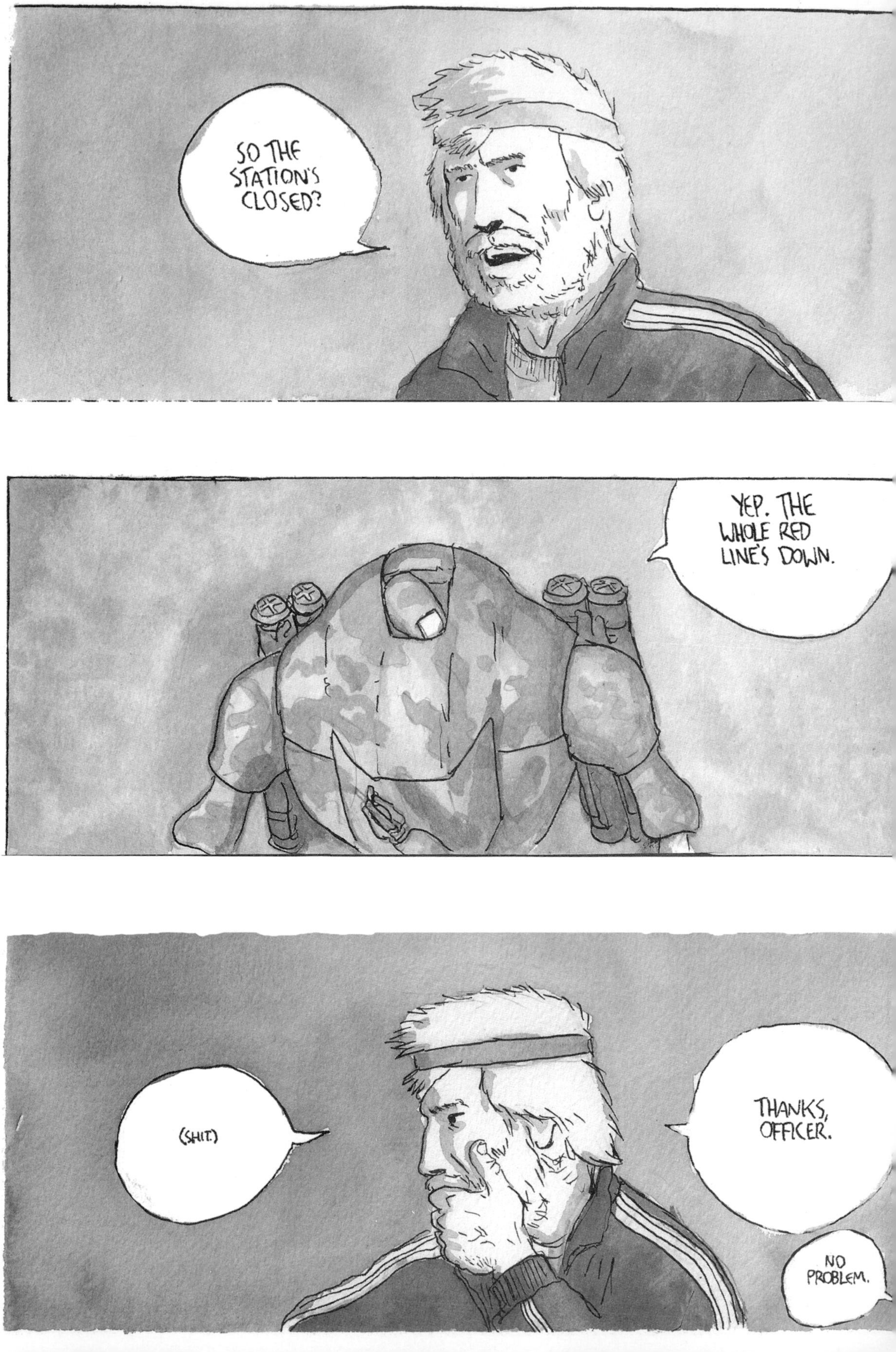
SO THE STATION'S CLOSED?
YEP. THE WHOLE RED LINE'S DOWN.
(SHIT.)
THANKS, OFFICER.
NO PROBLEM.

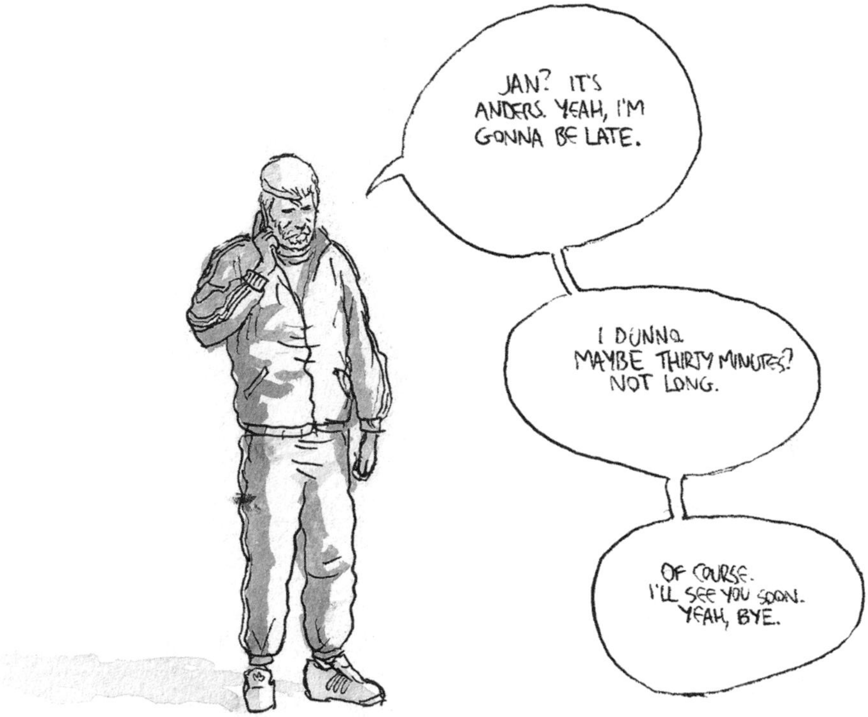
JAN? IT'S ANDERS. YEAH, I'M GONNA BE LATE.
I DUNNO. MAYBE THIRTY MINUTES? NOT LONG.
OF COURSE. I'LL SEE YOU SOON. YEAH, BYE.

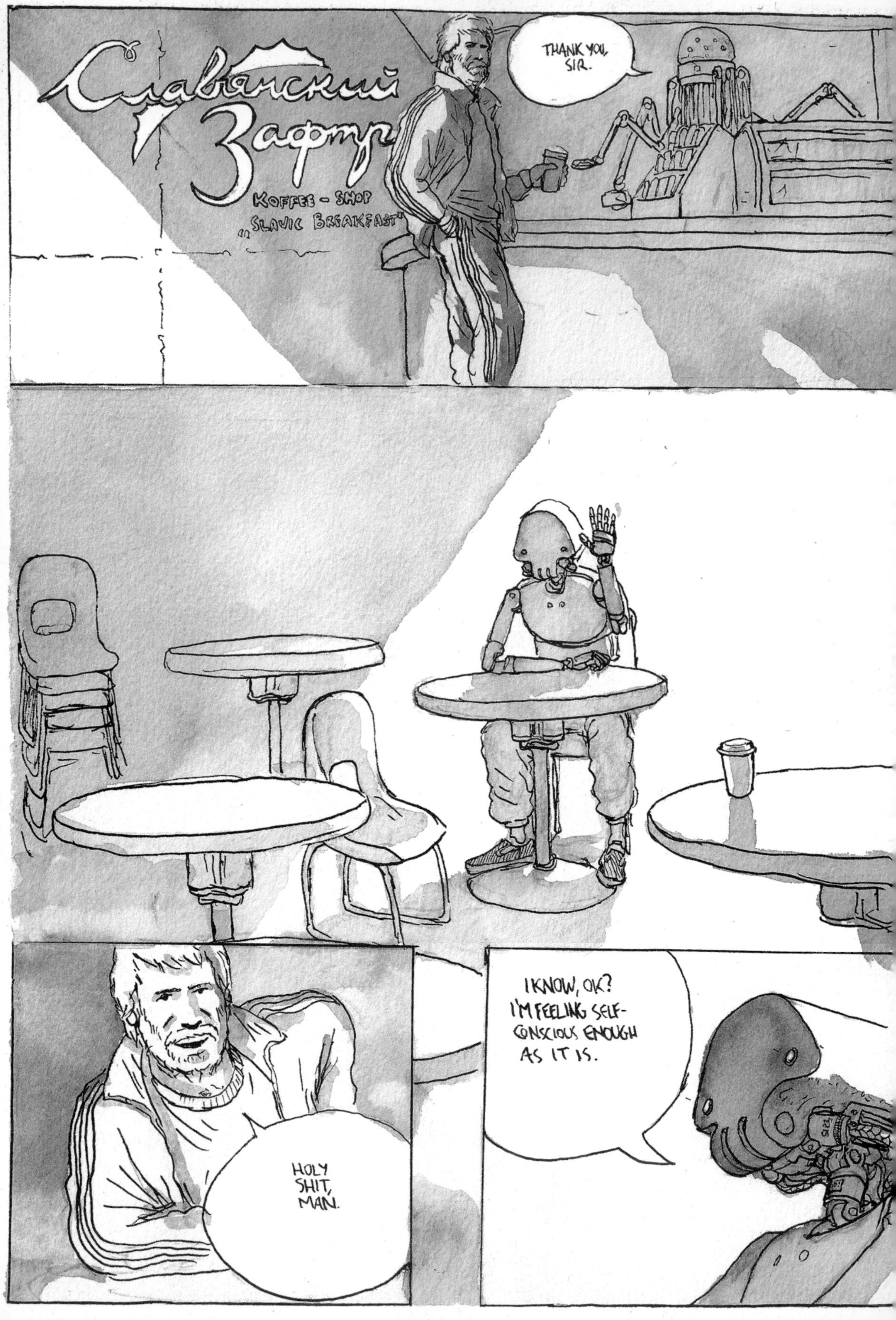
Славянский Зафтр
KOFFEE - SHOP
„SLAVIC BREAKFAST"
THANK YOU, SIR.
HOLY SHIT, MAN.
I KNOW, OK? I'M FEELING SELF-CONSCIOUS ENOUGH AS IT IS.

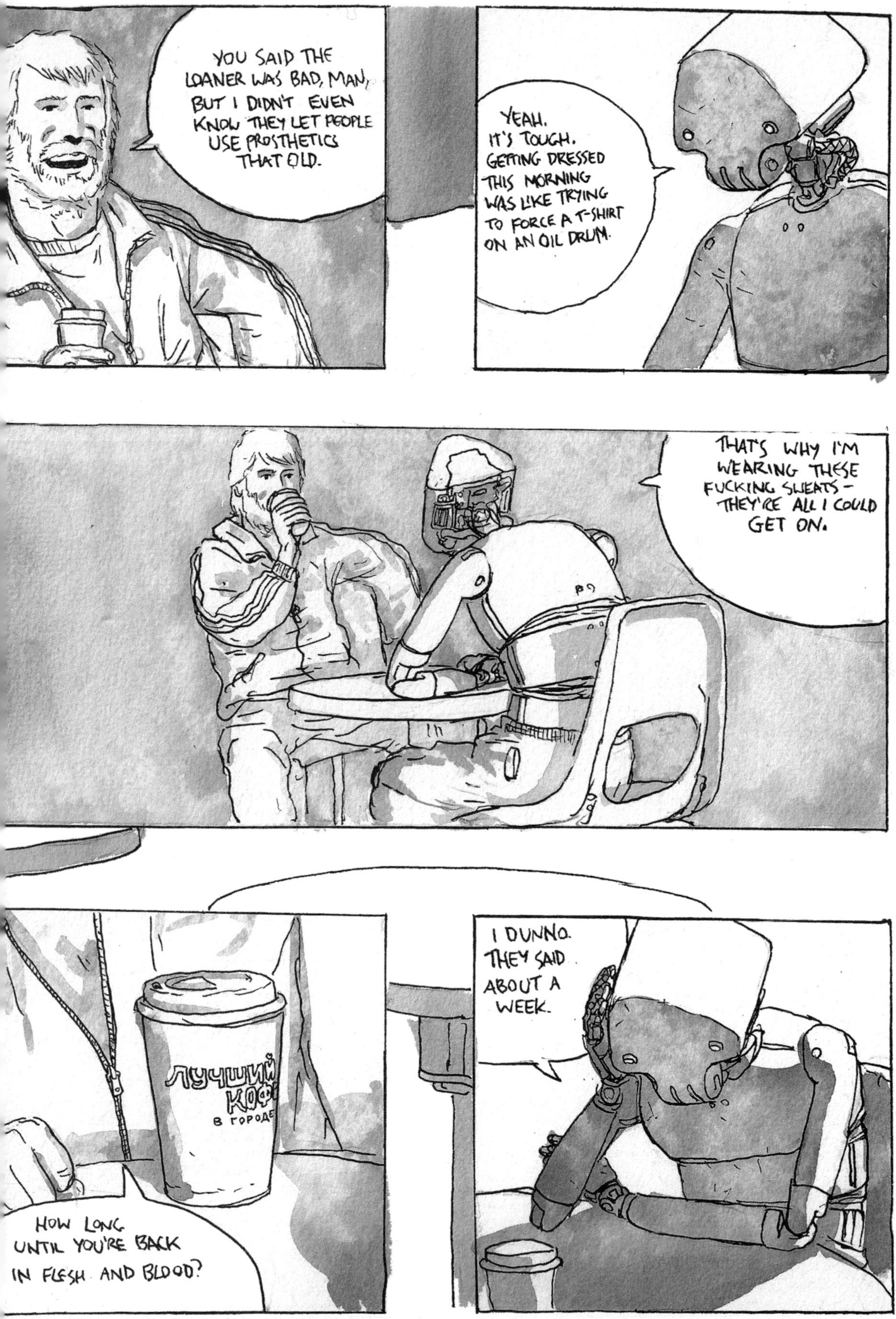
YOU SAID THE LOANER WAS BAD, MAN, BUT I DIDN'T EVEN KNOW THEY LET PEOPLE USE PROSTHETICS THAT OLD.
YEAH. IT'S TOUGH. GETTING DRESSED THIS MORNING WAS LIKE TRYING TO FORCE A T-SHIRT ON AN OIL DRUM.
THAT'S WHY I'M WEARING THESE FUCKING SWEATS — THEY'RE ALL I COULD GET ON.
ЛУЧШИЙ
КОФ
В ГОРОДЕ
HOW LONG UNTIL YOU'RE BACK IN FLESH AND BLOOD?
I DUNNO. THEY SAID ABOUT A WEEK.

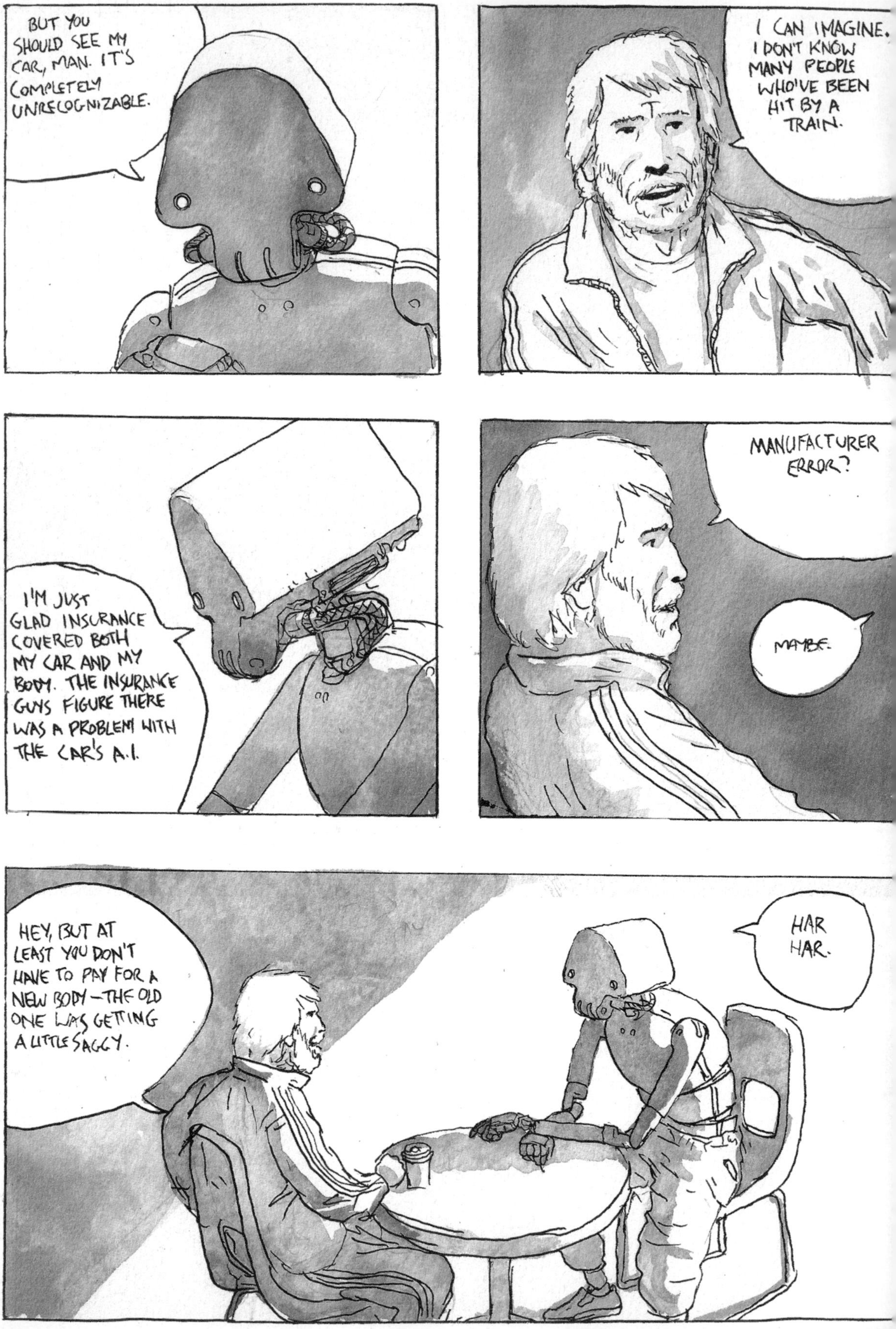
BUT YOU SHOULD SEE MY CAR, MAN. IT'S COMPLETELY UNRECOGNIZABLE.
I CAN IMAGINE. I DON'T KNOW MANY PEOPLE WHO'VE BEEN HIT BY A TRAIN.
I'M JUST GLAD INSURANCE COVERED BOTH MY CAR AND MY BODY. THE INSURANCE GUYS FIGURE THERE WAS A PROBLEM WITH THE CAR'S A.I.
MANUFACTURER ERROR?
MAYBE.
HEY, BUT AT LEAST YOU DON'T HAVE TO PAY FOR A NEW BODY—THE OLD ONE WAS GETTING A LITTLE SAGGY.
HAR HAR.

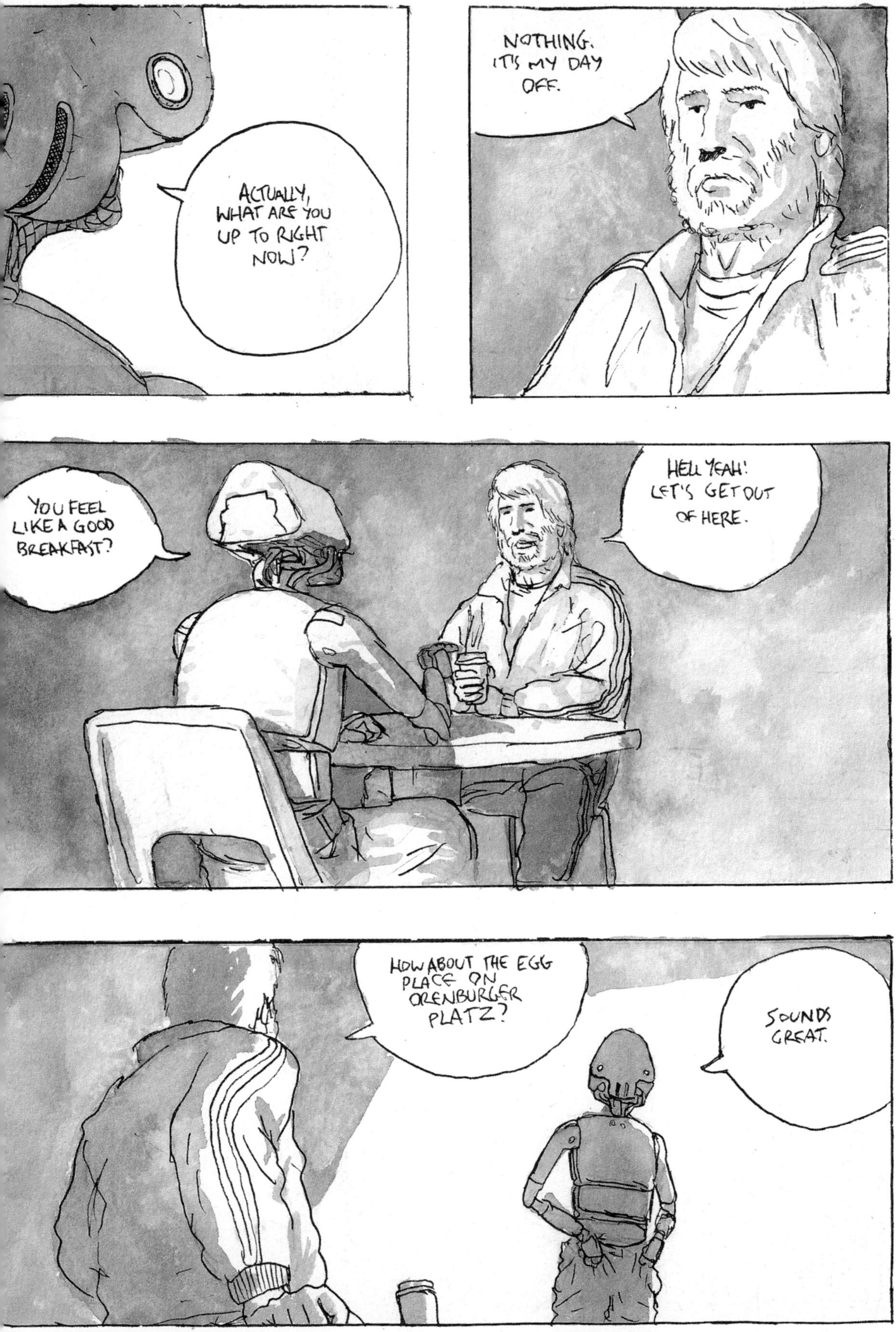
ACTUALLY, WHAT ARE YOU UP TO RIGHT NOW?
NOTHING. IT'S MY DAY OFF.
YOU FEEL LIKE A GOOD BREAKFAST?
HELL YEAH! LET'S GET OUT OF HERE.
HOW ABOUT THE EGG PLACE ON ORENBURGER PLATZ?
SOUNDS GREAT.

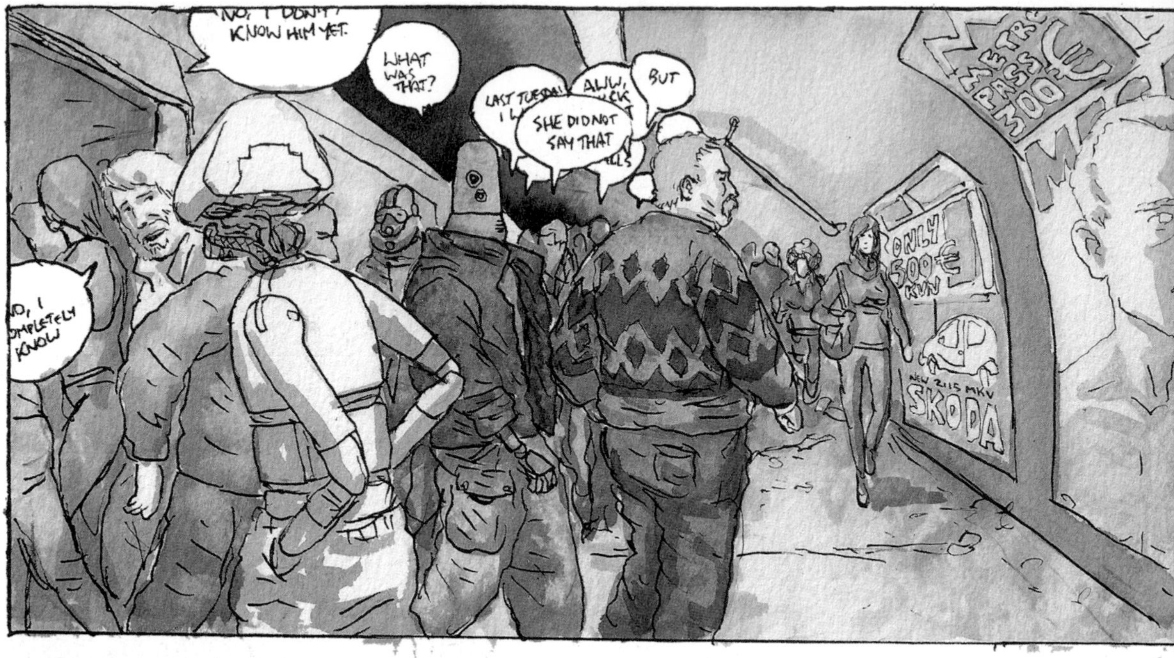
KNOW HIM YET.
WHAT WAS THAT?
BUT
SHE DID NOT SAY THAT
ONLY 500€
SKODA

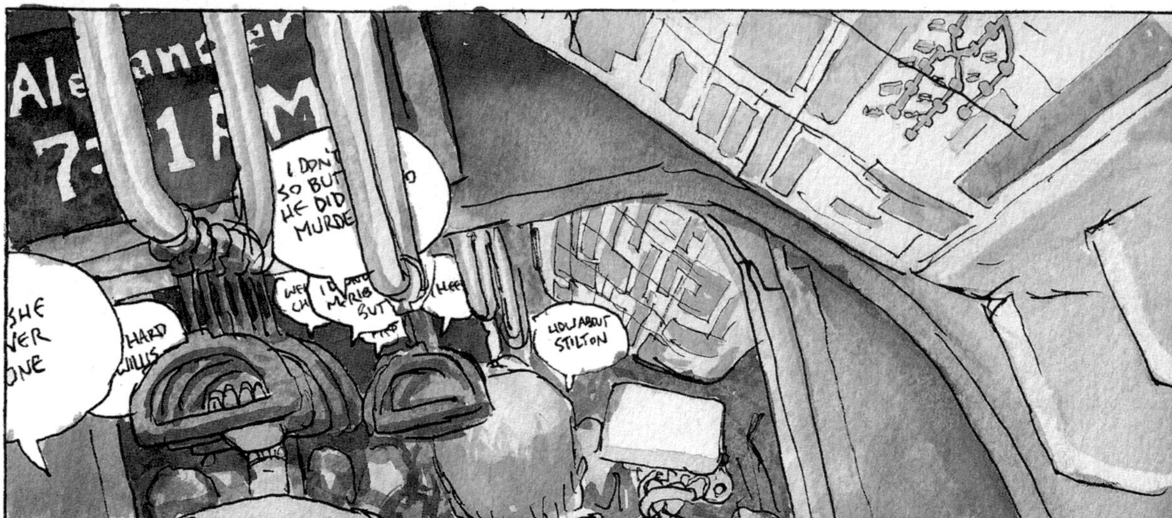

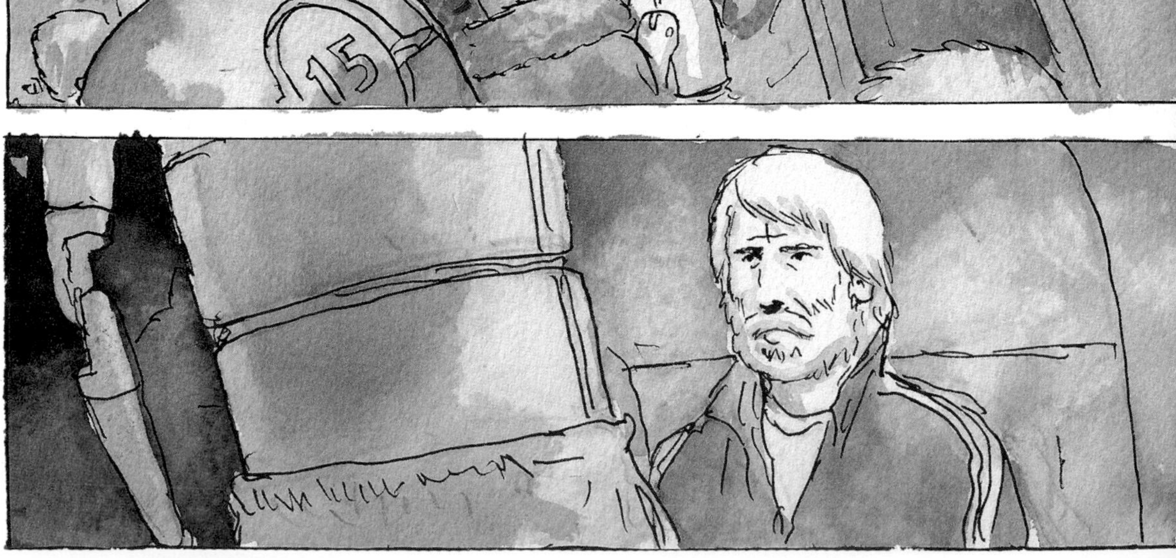

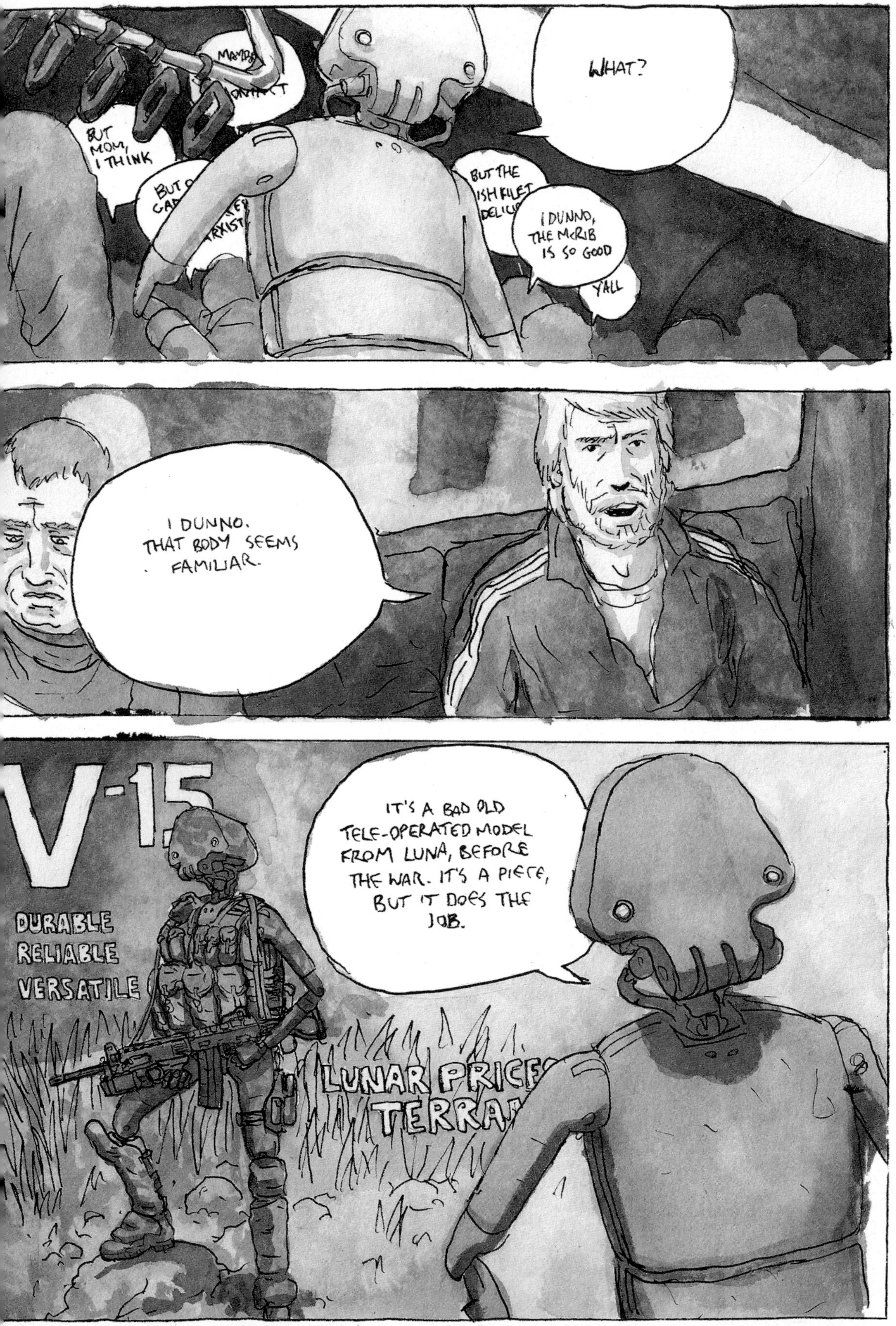
BUT MOM, I THINK
BUT THE
WHAT?
I DUNNO, THE McRIB IS SO GOOD
Y'ALL
I DUNNO. THAT BODY SEEMS FAMILIAR.
V-15
DURABLE
RELIABLE
VERSATILE
IT'S A BAD OLD TELE-OPERATED MODEL FROM LUNA, BEFORE THE WAR. IT'S A PIECE, BUT IT DOES THE JOB.

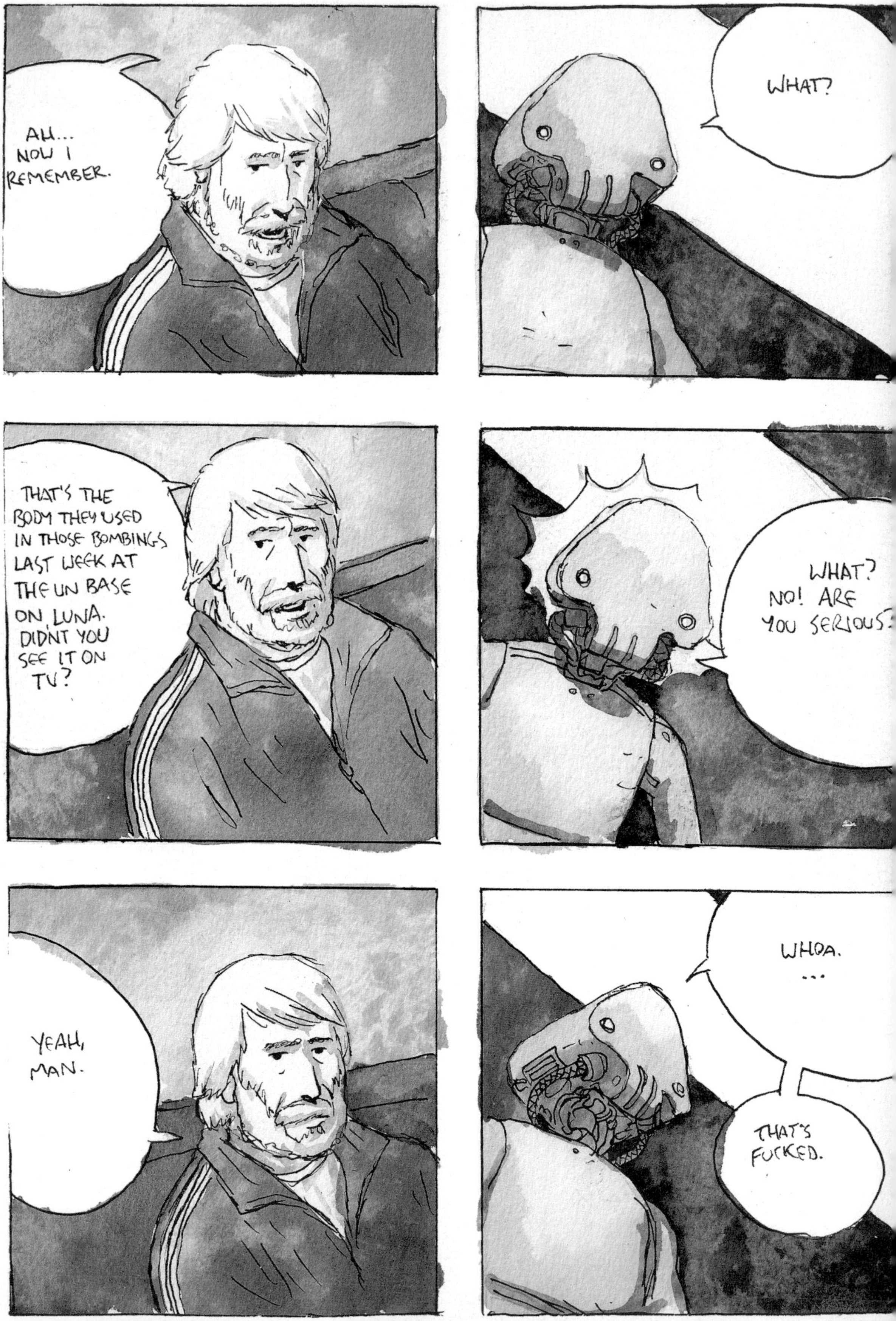
AH... NOW I REMEMBER.
WHAT?
THAT'S THE BODY THEY USED IN THOSE BOMBINGS LAST WEEK AT THE UN BASE ON LUNA. DIDN'T YOU SEE IT ON TV?
WHAT? NO! ARE YOU SERIOUS?
YEAH, MAN.
WHOA. ...
THAT'S FUCKED.

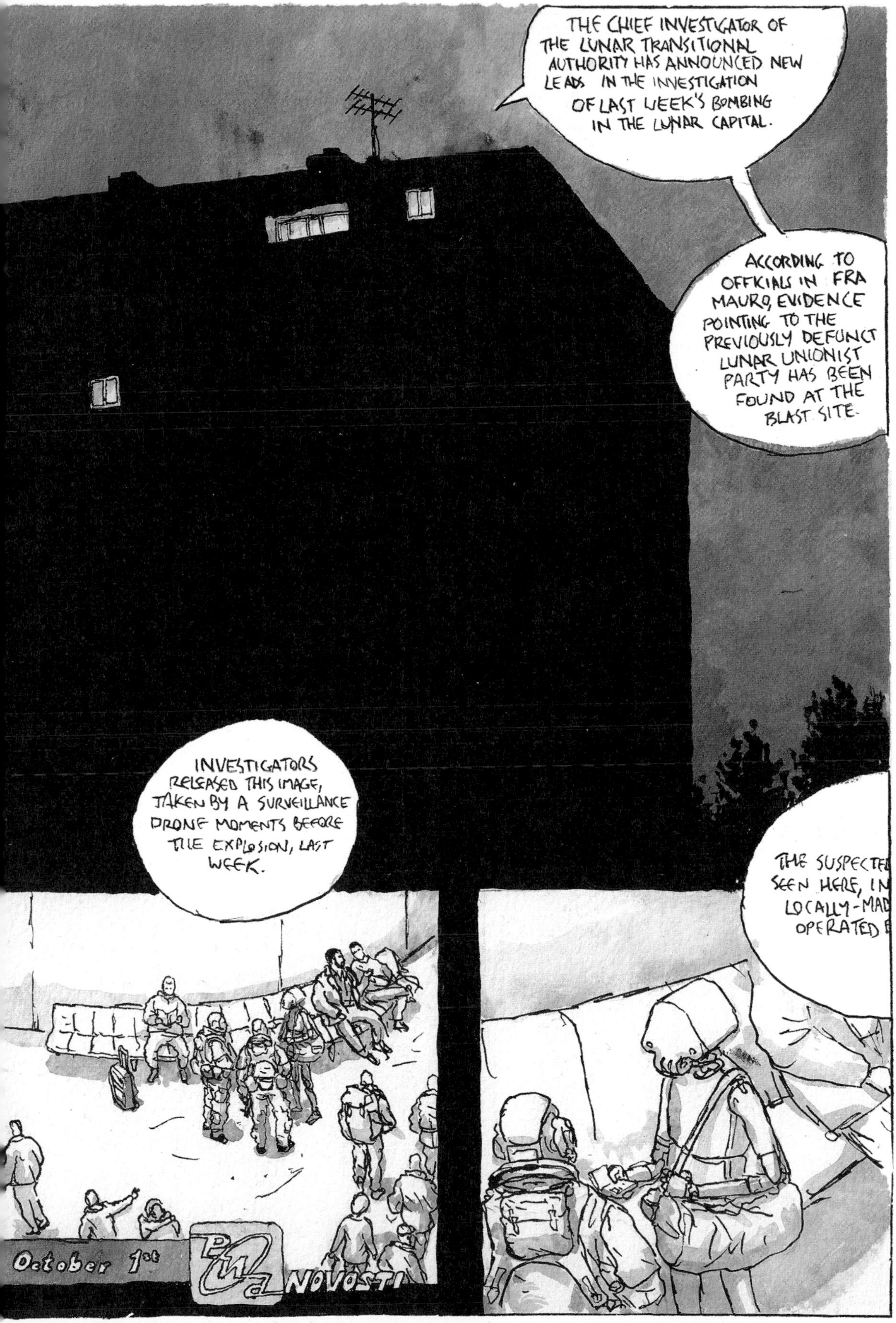
THE CHIEF INVESTIGATOR OF THE LUNAR TRANSITIONAL AUTHORITY HAS ANNOUNCED NEW LEADS IN THE INVESTIGATION OF LAST WEEK'S BOMBING IN THE LUNAR CAPITAL.
ACCORDING TO OFFICIALS IN FRA MAURO, EVIDENCE POINTING TO THE PREVIOUSLY DEFUNCT LUNAR UNIONIST PARTY HAS BEEN FOUND AT THE BLAST SITE.
INVESTIGATORS RELEASED THIS IMAGE, TAKEN BY A SURVEILLANCE DRONE MOMENTS BEFORE THE EXPLOSION, LAST WEEK.
October 1st
NOVOSTI
THE SUSPECTE
SEEN HERE, IN
LOCALLY-MAD
OPERATED

ELIEVED TO BE LEAD BY
ILSSEN, A FORMER
EBEL LEADER WHO

PAUSE.

ENHANCE
12 TO 21.

11:56 PM

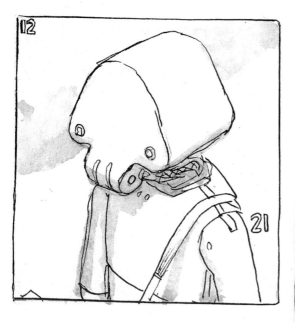

12

21

...

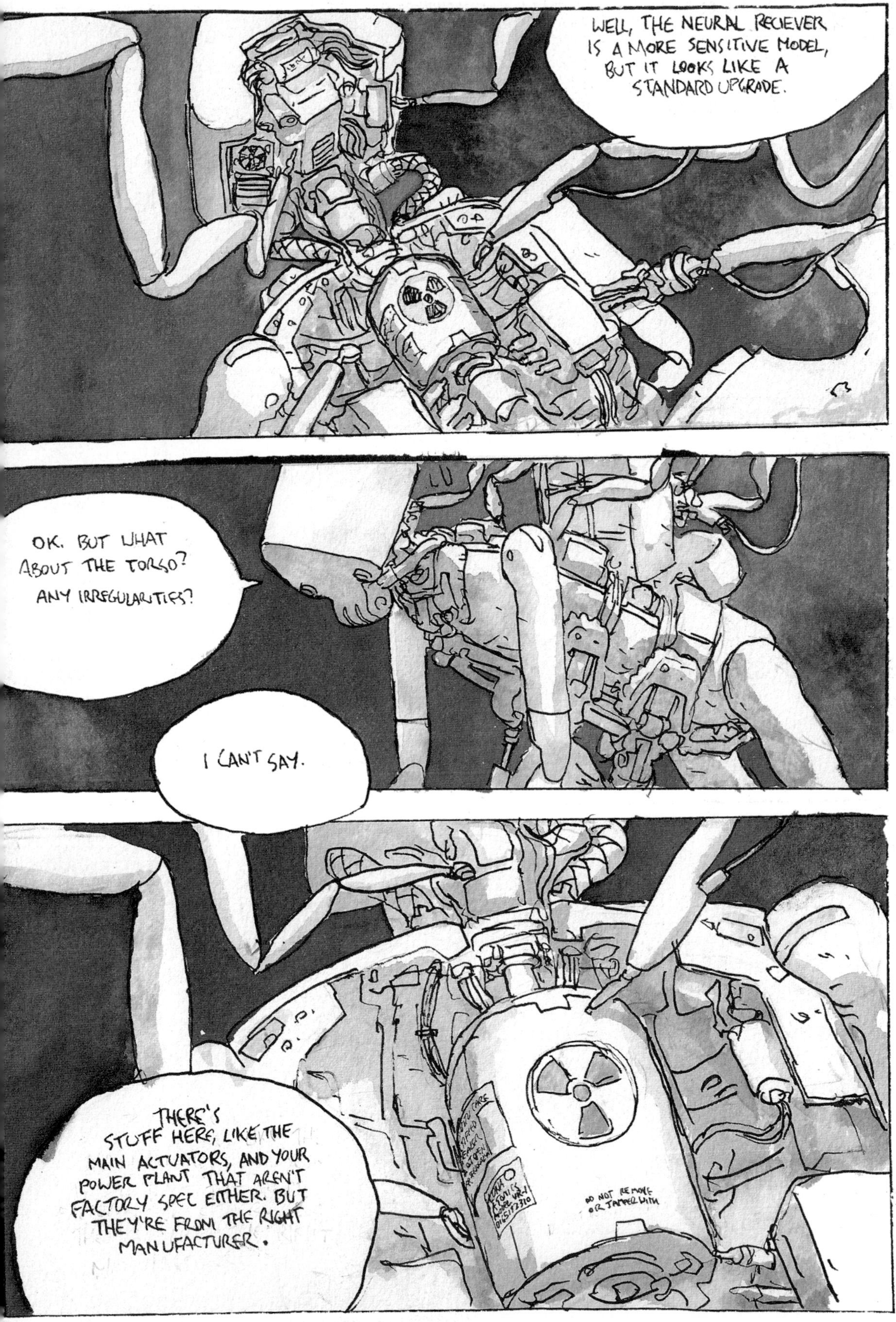
WELL, THE NEURAL RECIEVER IS A MORE SENSITIVE MODEL, BUT IT LOOKS LIKE A STANDARD UPGRADE.
OK. BUT WHAT ABOUT THE TORSO? ANY IRREGULARITIES?
I CAN'T SAY.
THERE'S STUFF HERE, LIKE THE MAIN ACTUATORS, AND YOUR POWER PLANT THAT AREN'T FACTORY SPEC EITHER. BUT THEY'RE FROM THE RIGHT MANUFACTURER.
DO NOT REMOVE OR TAMPER WITH

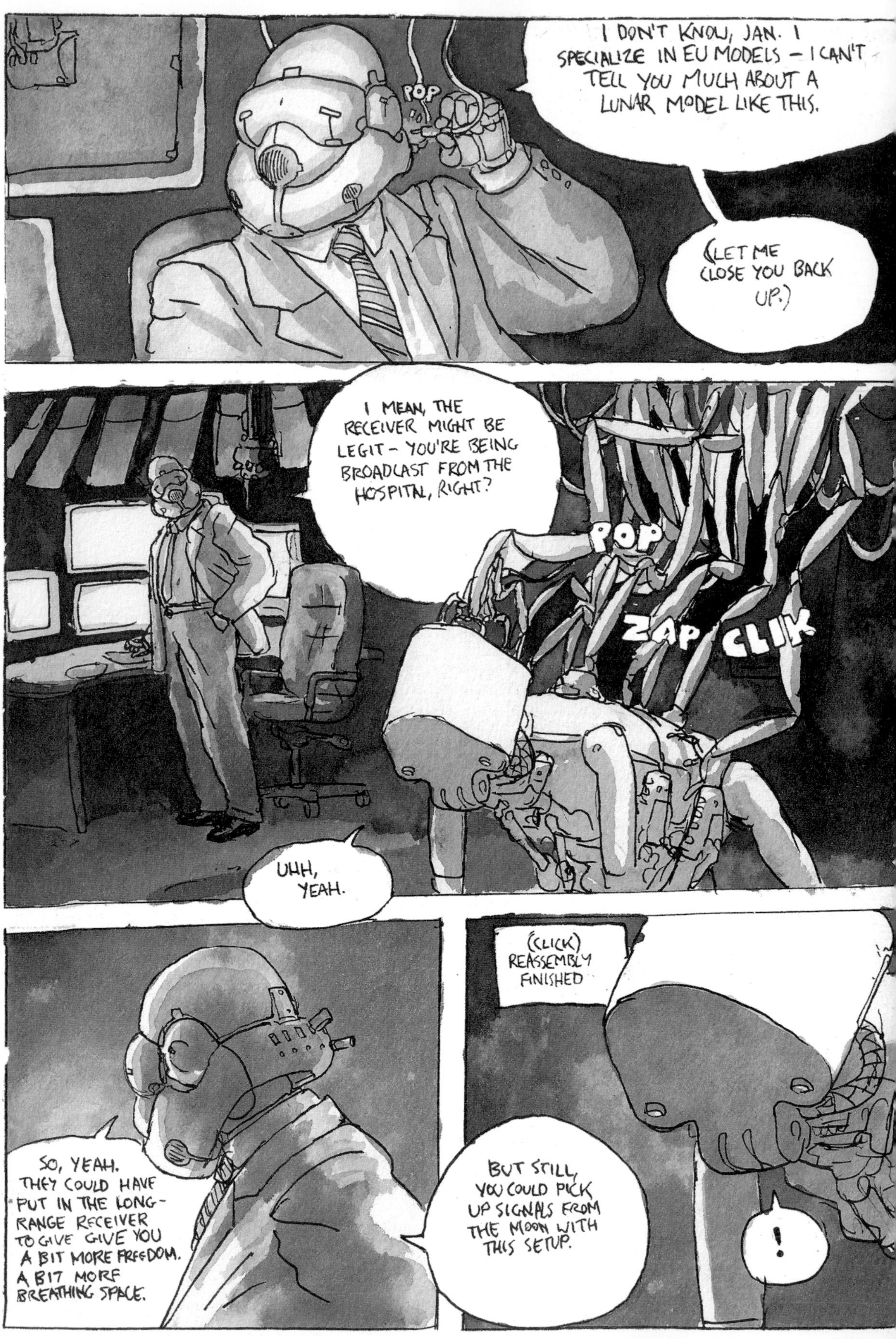
I DON'T KNOW, JAN. I SPECIALIZE IN EU MODELS – I CAN'T TELL YOU MUCH ABOUT A LUNAR MODEL LIKE THIS.
POP
(LET ME CLOSE YOU BACK UP.)
I MEAN, THE RECEIVER MIGHT BE LEGIT – YOU'RE BEING BROADCAST FROM THE HOSPITAL, RIGHT?
POP
ZAP
CLIK
UHH, YEAH.
SO, YEAH. THEY COULD HAVE PUT IN THE LONG-RANGE RECEIVER TO GIVE GIVE YOU A BIT MORE FREEDOM. A BIT MORE BREATHING SPACE.
(CLICK) REASSEMBLY FINISHED
BUT STILL, YOU COULD PICK UP SIGNALS FROM THE MOON WITH THIS SETUP.
!

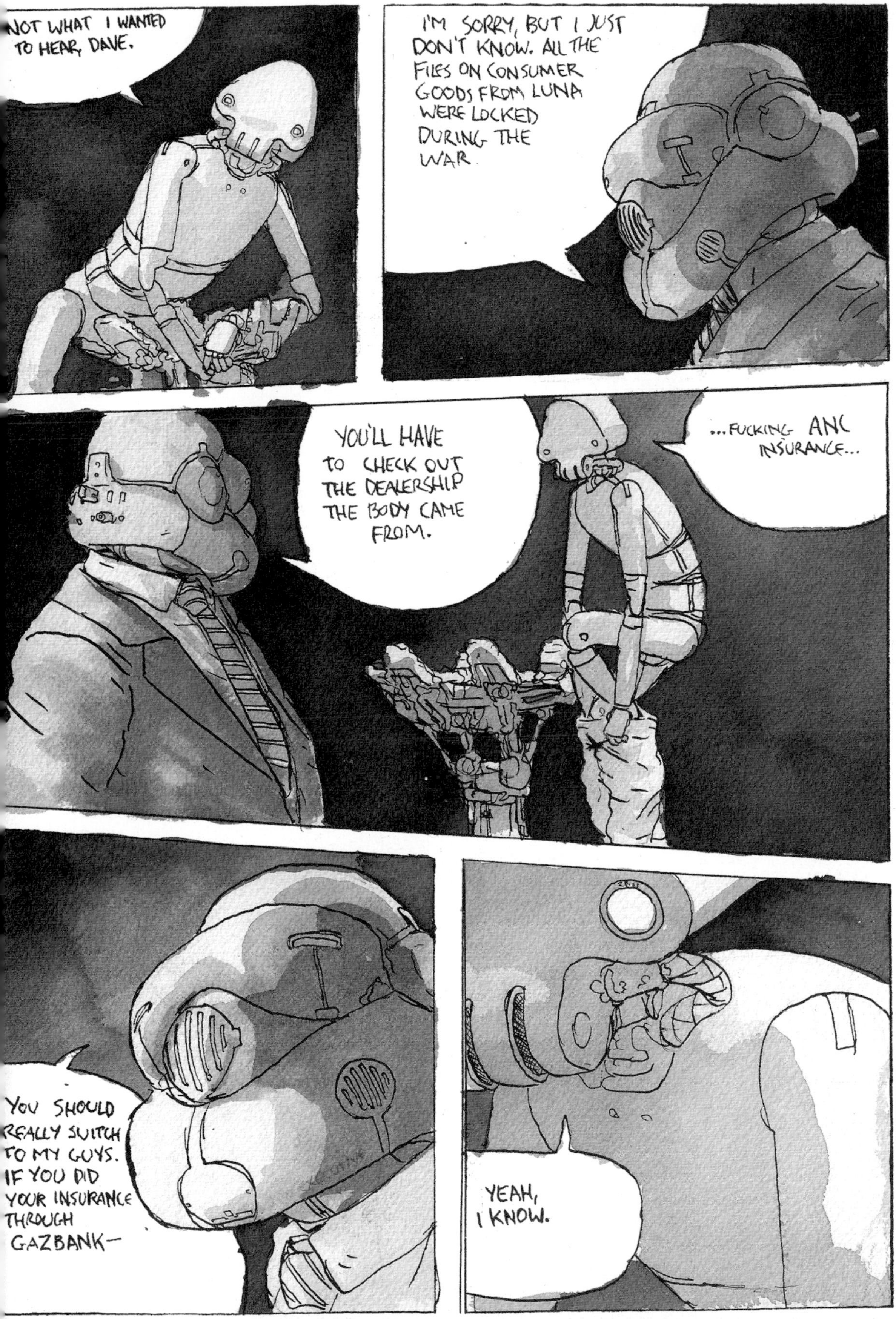
NOT WHAT I WANTED TO HEAR, DAVE.
I'M SORRY, BUT I JUST DON'T KNOW. ALL THE FILES ON CONSUMER GOODS FROM LUNA WERE LOCKED DURING THE WAR
YOU'LL HAVE TO CHECK OUT THE DEALERSHIP THE BODY CAME FROM.
...FUCKING ANC INSURANCE...
YOU SHOULD REALLY SWITCH TO MY GUYS. IF YOU DID YOUR INSURANCE THROUGH GAZBANK—
YEAH, I KNOW.

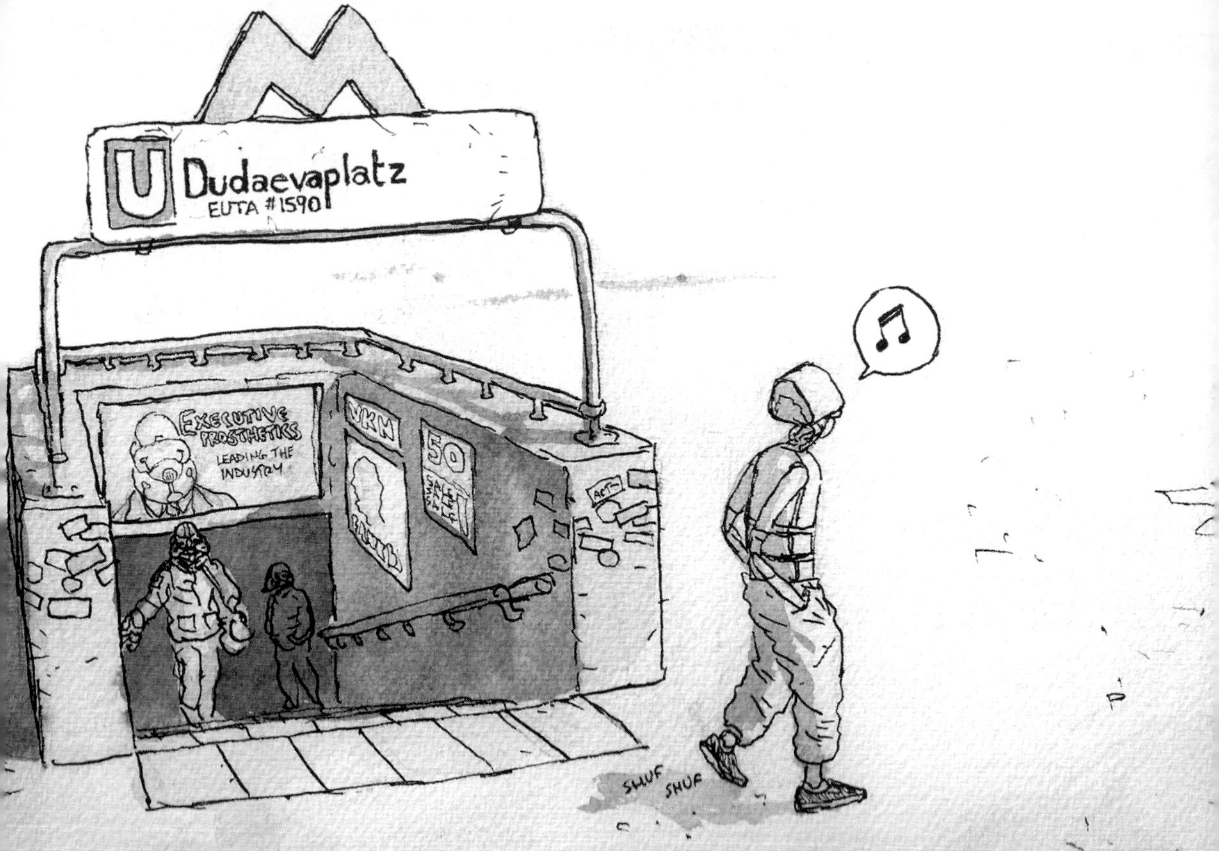
U
Dudaevaplatz
EUTA #1590
EXECUTIVE PROSTHETICS
LEADING THE INDUSTRY
50
SHUF
SHUF

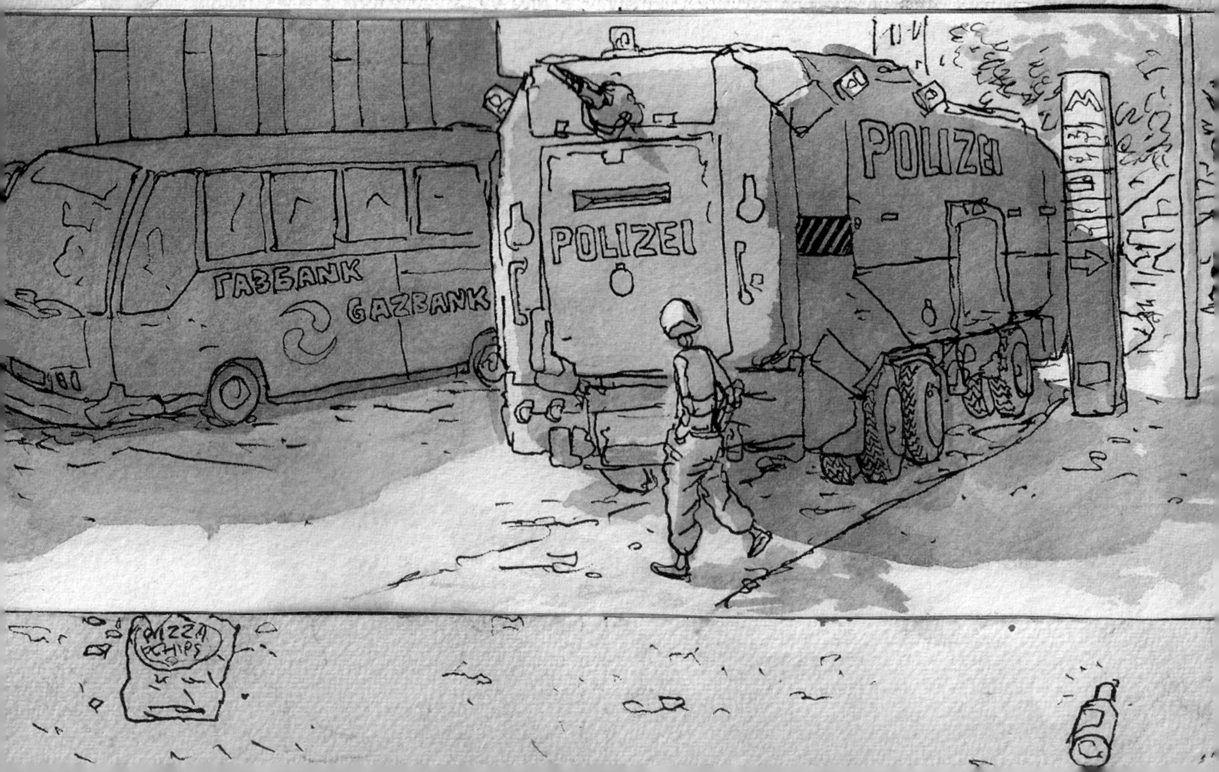
ГАЗБАНК
GAZBANK
POLIZEI
POLIZEI
PIZZA
CHIPS

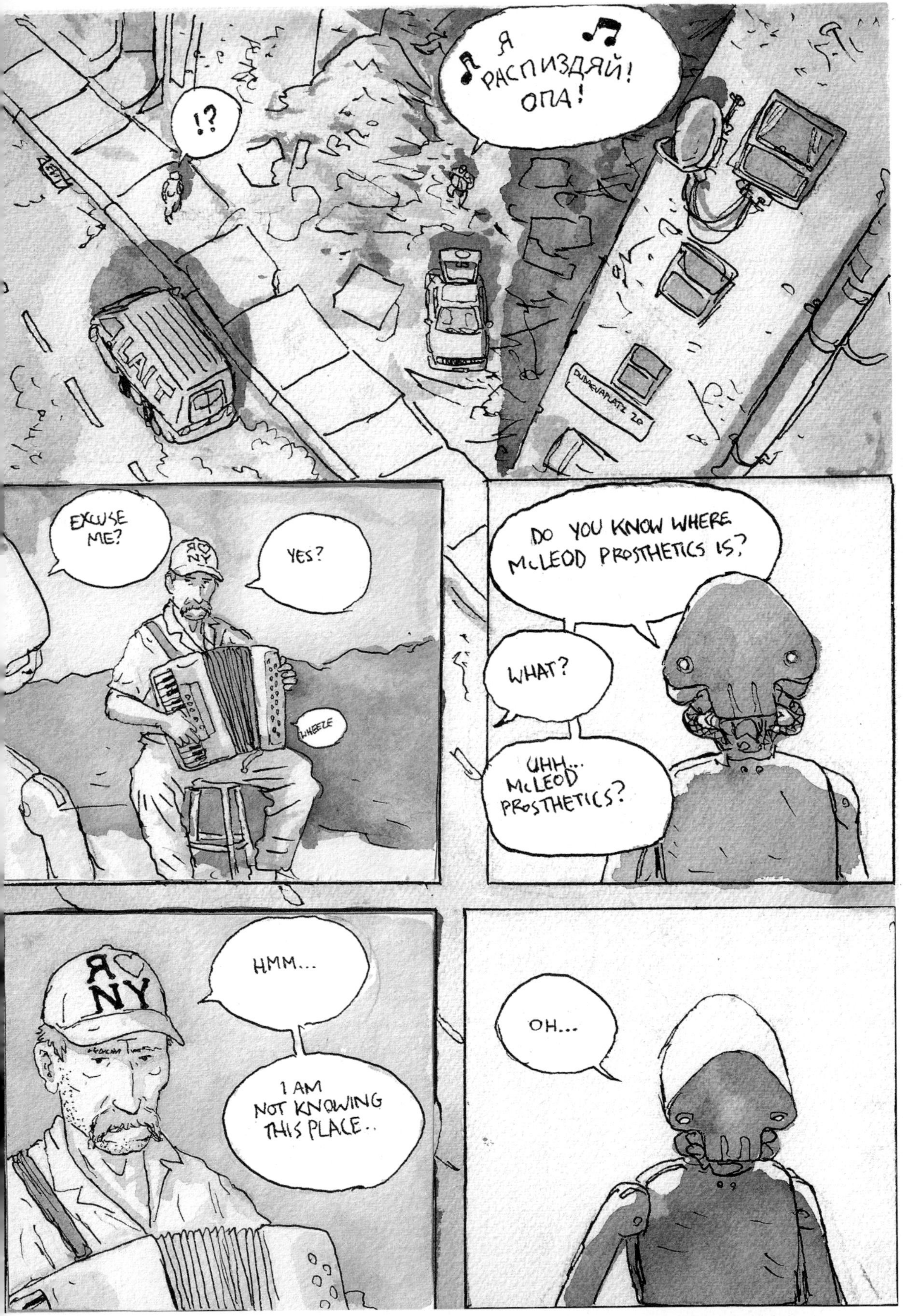

!?
♪ Я РАСПИЗДЯЙ! ОПА! ♪
LAIT
DUDAEVAPLATZ 20
EXCUSE ME?
YES?
WHEEZE
DO YOU KNOW WHERE McLEOD PROSTHETICS IS?
WHAT?
UHH... McLEOD PROSTHETICS?
Я NY
HMM...
I AM NOT KNOWING THIS PLACE..
OH...

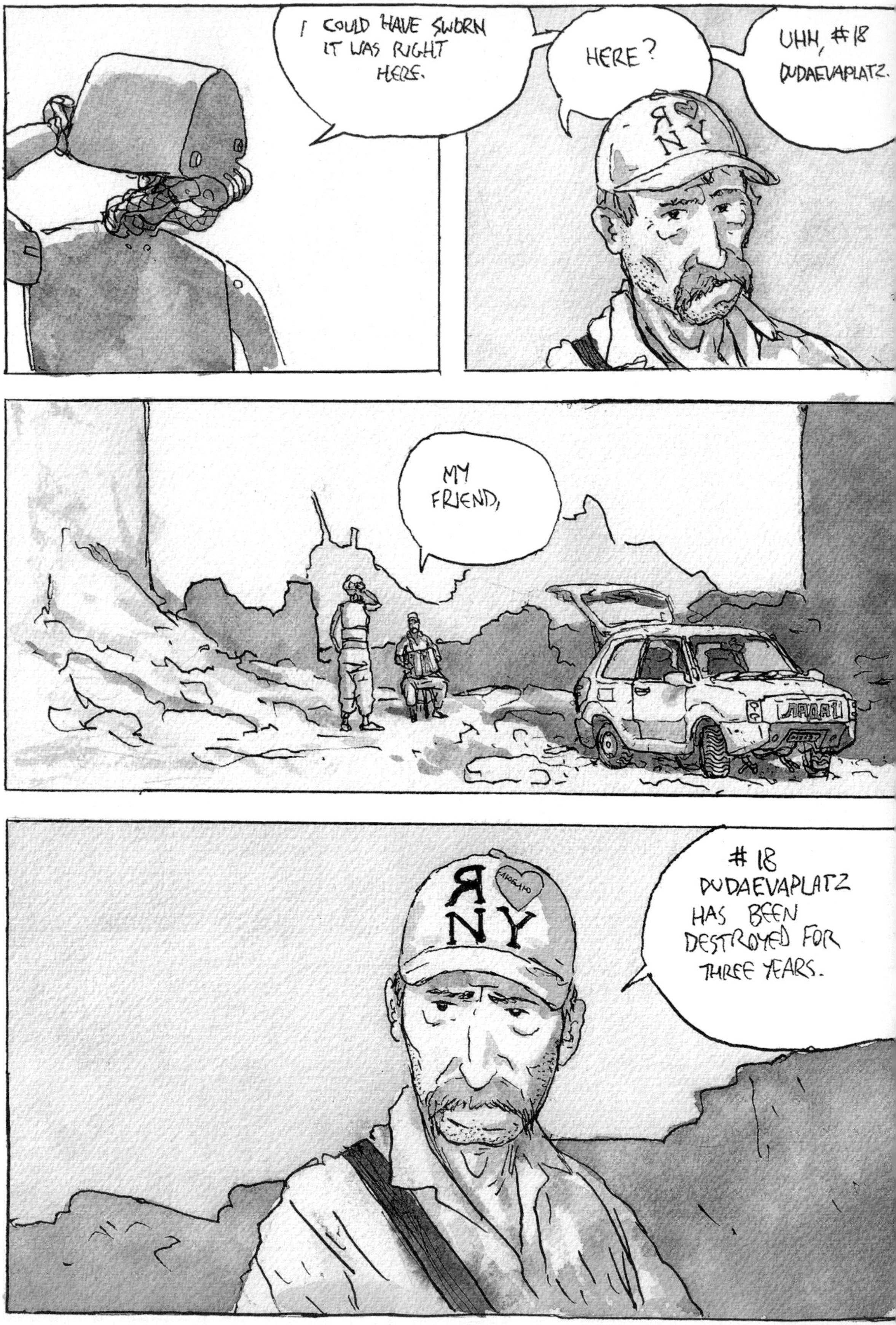
I COULD HAVE SWORN IT WAS RIGHT HERE.
HERE?
UHH, #18 DUDAEVAPLATZ.
MY FRIEND,
#18 DUDAEVAPLATZ HAS BEEN DESTROYED FOR THREE YEARS.

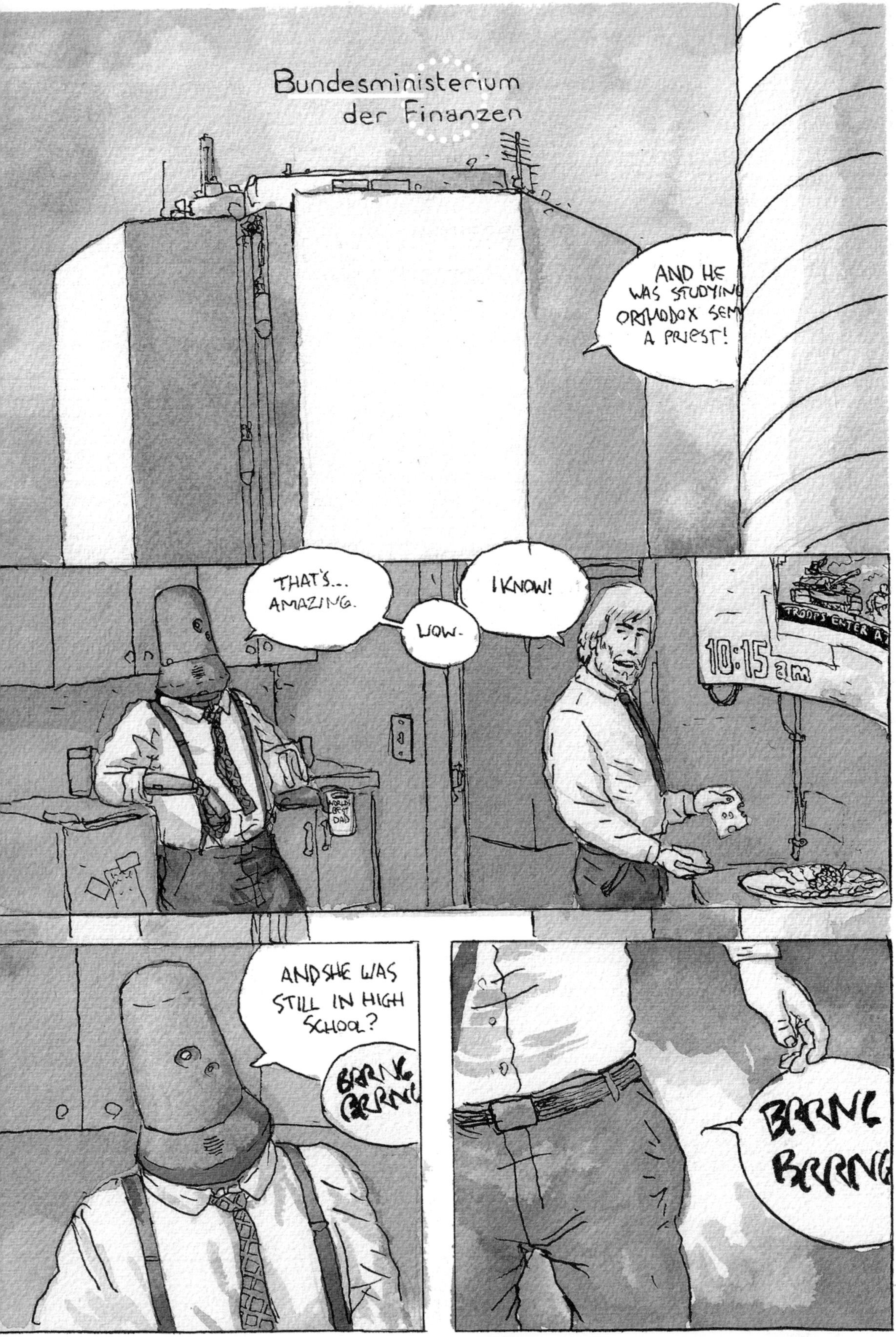
Bundesministerium
der Finanzen
AND HE
WAS STUDYIN
ORTHODOX SEM
A PRIEST!
THAT'S... AMAZING.
I KNOW!
WOW.
WORLD'S BEST DAD
TROOPS ENTER A
10:15 am
AND SHE WAS STILL IN HIGH SCHOOL?
BRRNG BRRNG
BRRNG BRRNG

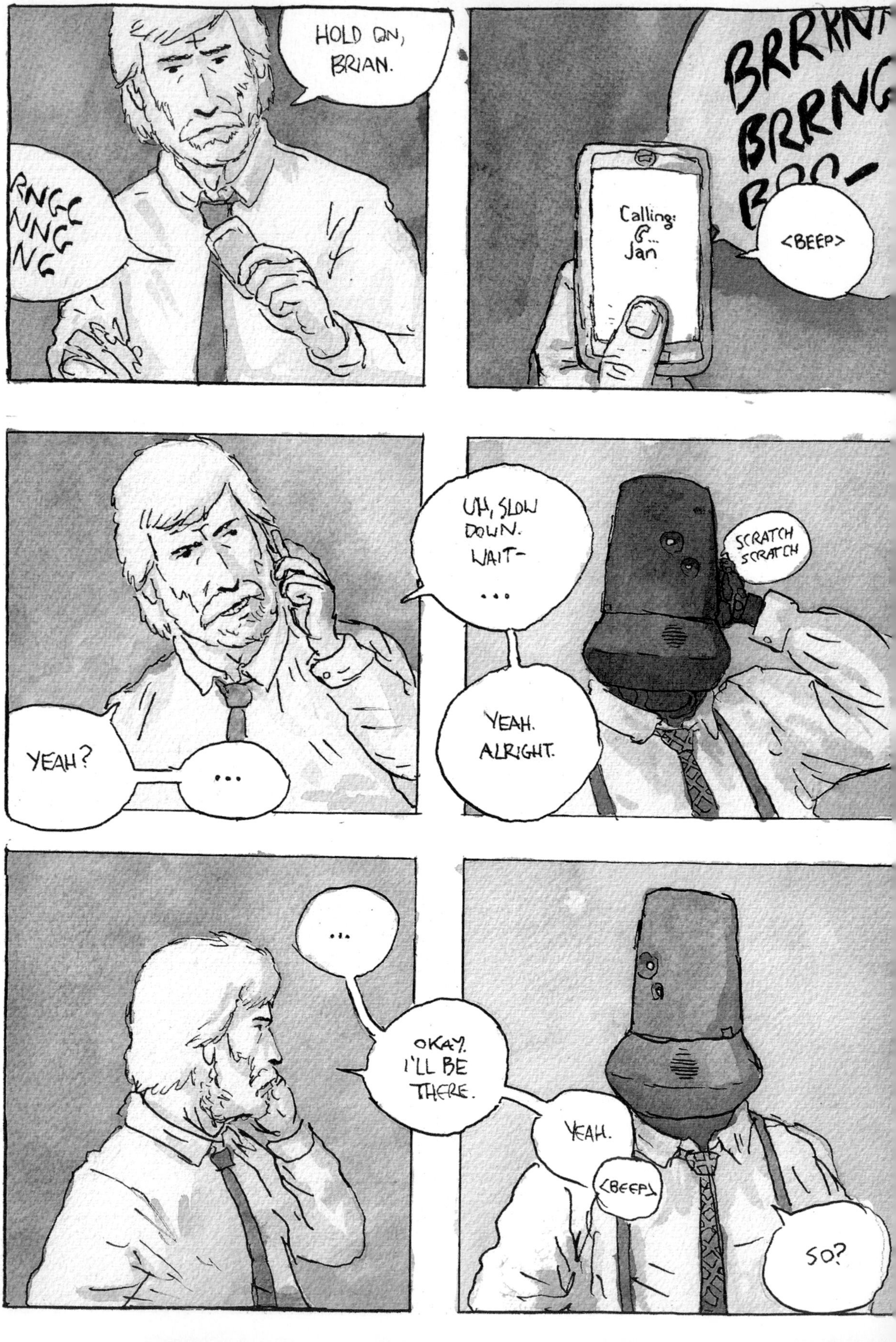
RNGC NNG NG
HOLD ON, BRIAN.
BRRRN BRRNG
Calling: Jan
<BEEP>
YEAH?
...
UH, SLOW DOWN. WAIT-
...
YEAH. ALRIGHT.
SCRATCH SCRATCH
...
OKAY. I'LL BE THERE.
YEAH.
<BEEP>
SO?

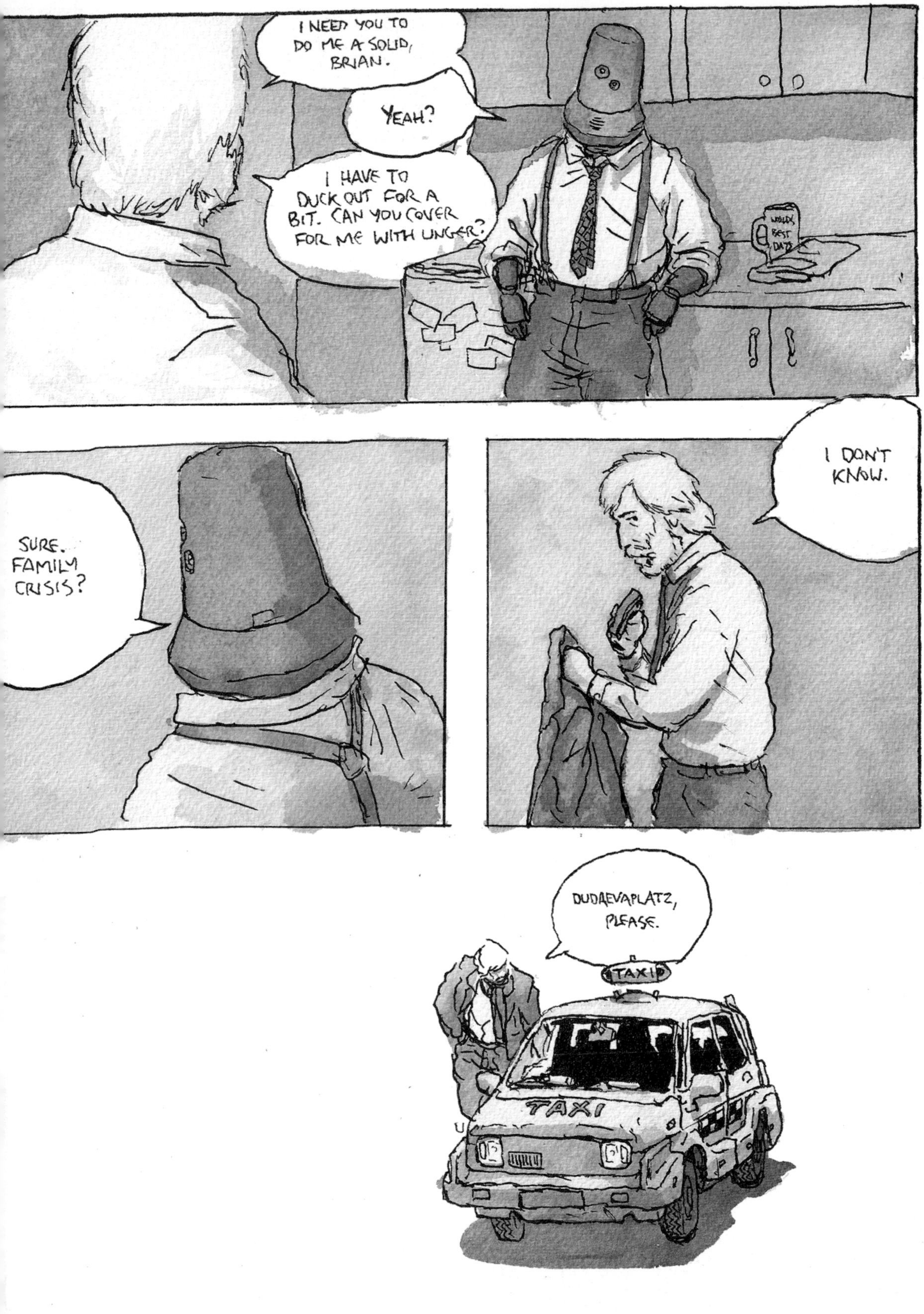
I NEED YOU TO DO ME A SOLID, BRIAN.
YEAH?
I HAVE TO DUCK OUT FOR A BIT. CAN YOU COVER FOR ME WITH UNGER?
SURE. FAMILY CRISIS?
I DON'T KNOW.
DUDAEVAPLATZ, PLEASE.
TAXI
TAXI

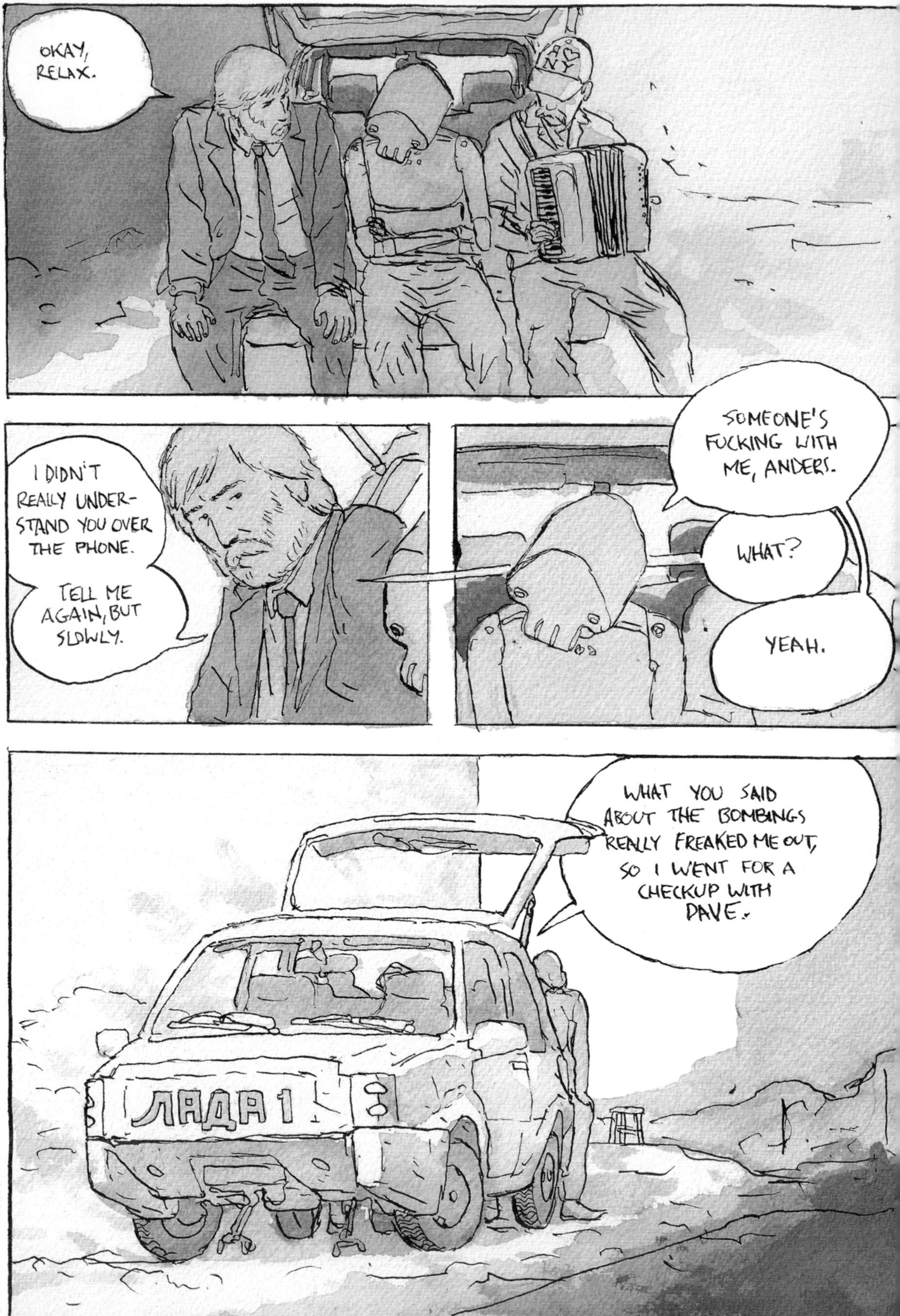
OKAY, RELAX.
I DIDN'T REALLY UNDERSTAND YOU OVER THE PHONE.
TELL ME AGAIN, BUT SLOWLY.
SOMEONE'S FUCKING WITH ME, ANDERS.
WHAT?
YEAH.
ЛАДА 1
WHAT YOU SAID ABOUT THE BOMBINGS REALLY FREAKED ME OUT, SO I WENT FOR A CHECKUP WITH DAVE.

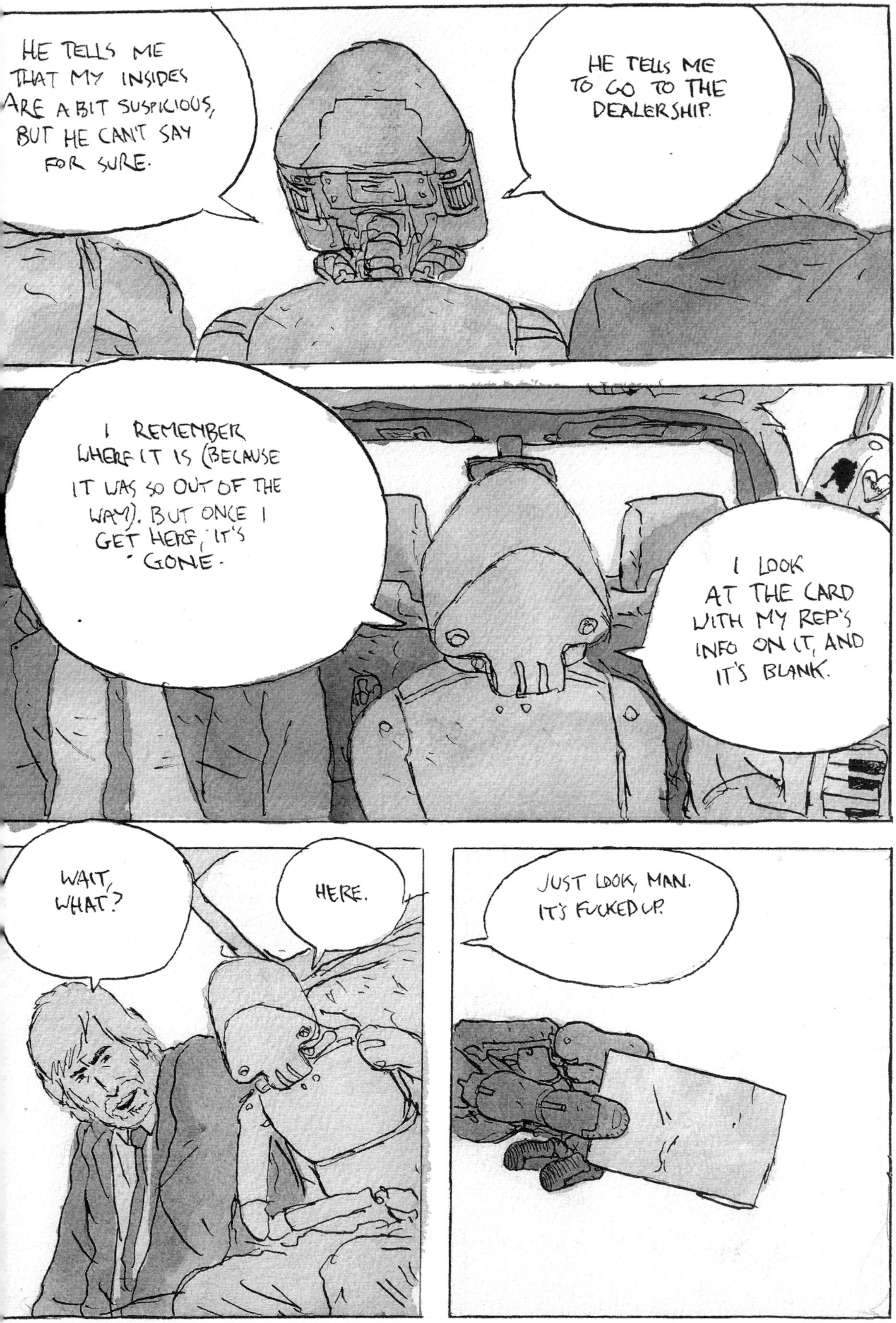

HE TELLS ME THAT MY INSIDES ARE A BIT SUSPICIOUS, BUT HE CAN'T SAY FOR SURE.
HE TELLS ME TO GO TO THE DEALERSHIP.
I REMEMBER WHERE IT IS (BECAUSE IT WAS SO OUT OF THE WAY). BUT ONCE I GET HERE, IT'S GONE.
I LOOK AT THE CARD WITH MY REP'S INFO ON IT, AND IT'S BLANK.
WAIT, WHAT?
HERE.
JUST LOOK, MAN. IT'S FUCKED UP.

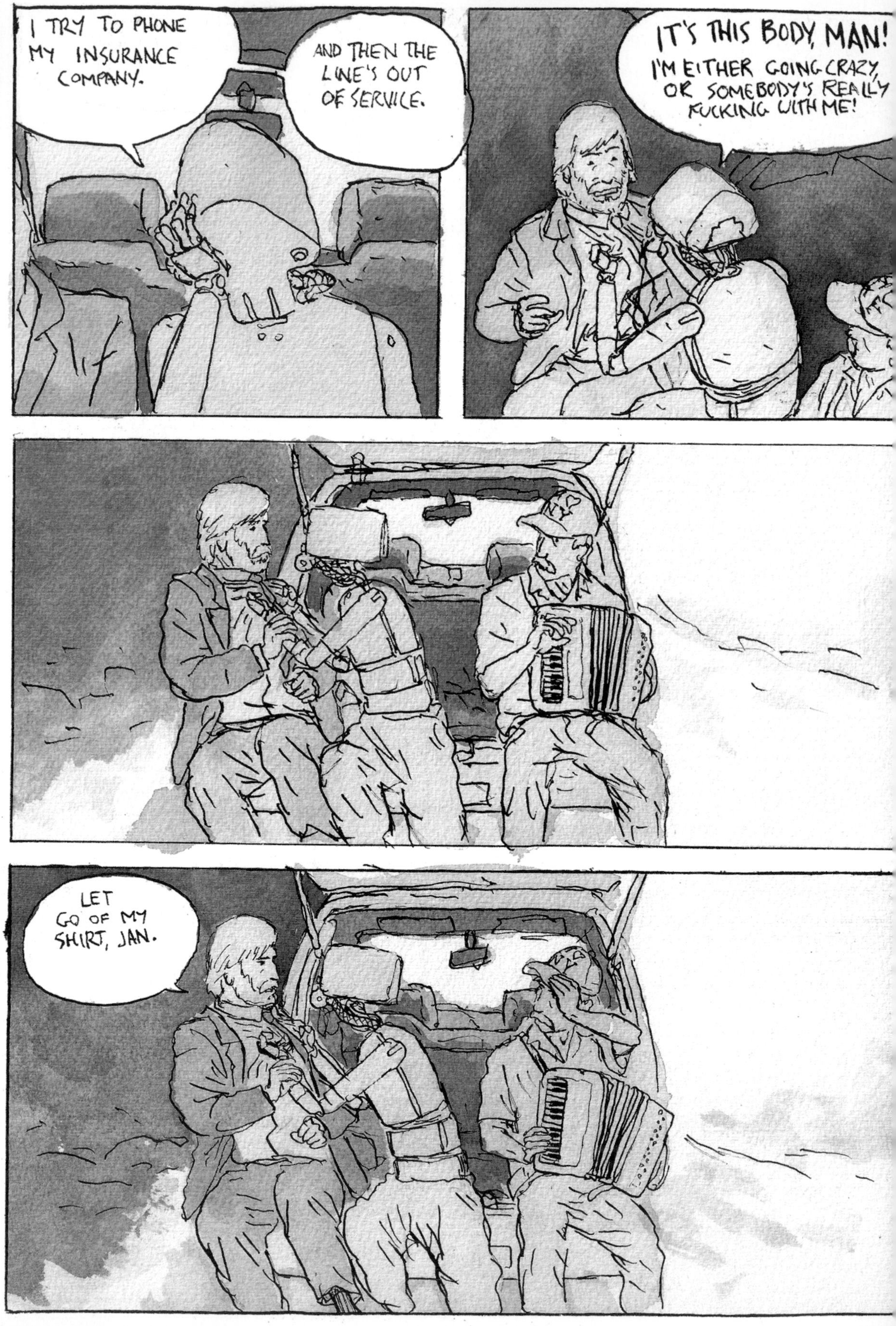
I TRY TO PHONE MY INSURANCE COMPANY.
AND THEN THE LINE'S OUT OF SERVICE.
IT'S THIS BODY, MAN!
I'M EITHER GOING CRAZY, OR SOMEBODY'S REALLY FUCKING WITH ME!
NY
LET GO OF MY SHIRT, JAN.

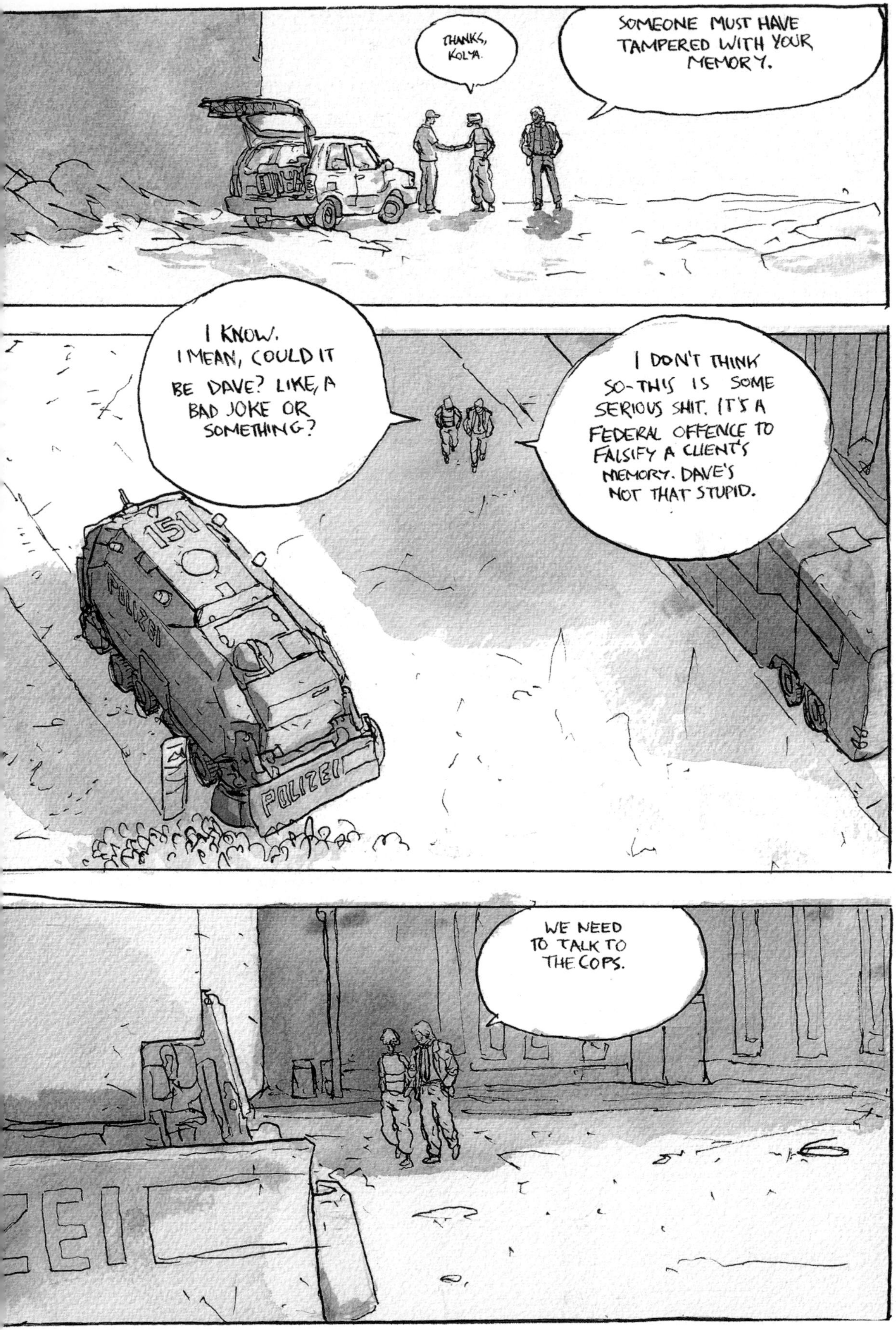
THANKS, KOLYA.
SOMEONE MUST HAVE TAMPERED WITH YOUR MEMORY.
I KNOW. I MEAN, COULD IT BE DAVE? LIKE, A BAD JOKE OR SOMETHING?
I DON'T THINK SO-THIS IS SOME SERIOUS SHIT. IT'S A FEDERAL OFFENCE TO FALSIFY A CLIENT'S MEMORY. DAVE'S NOT THAT STUPID.
151
POLIZEI
POLIZEI
WE NEED TO TALK TO THE COPS.
ZEI

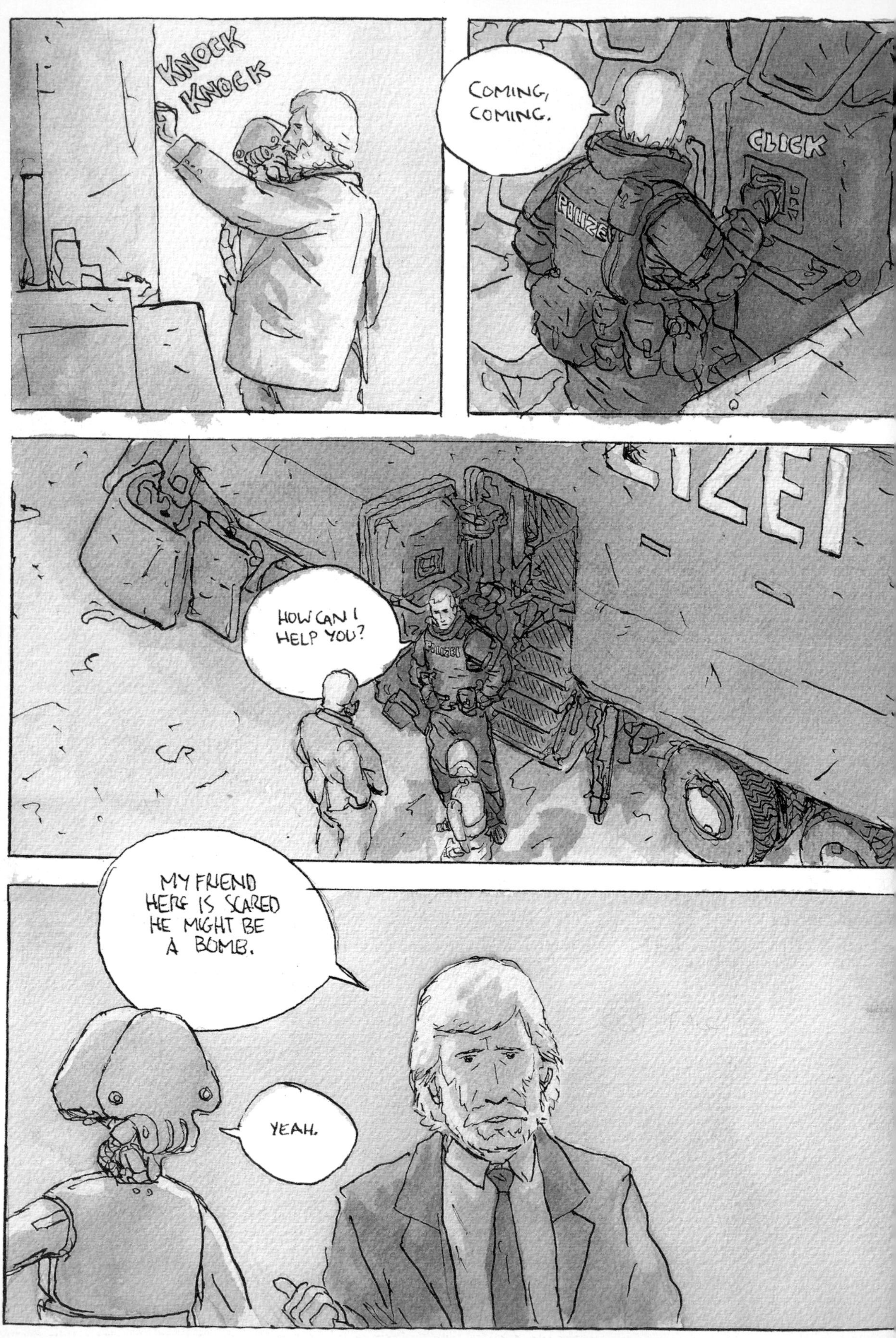
KNOCK KNOCK
COMING, COMING.
CLICK
POLIZEI
LIZEI
HOW CAN I HELP YOU?
POLIZEI
MY FRIEND HERE IS SCARED HE MIGHT BE A BOMB.
YEAH.

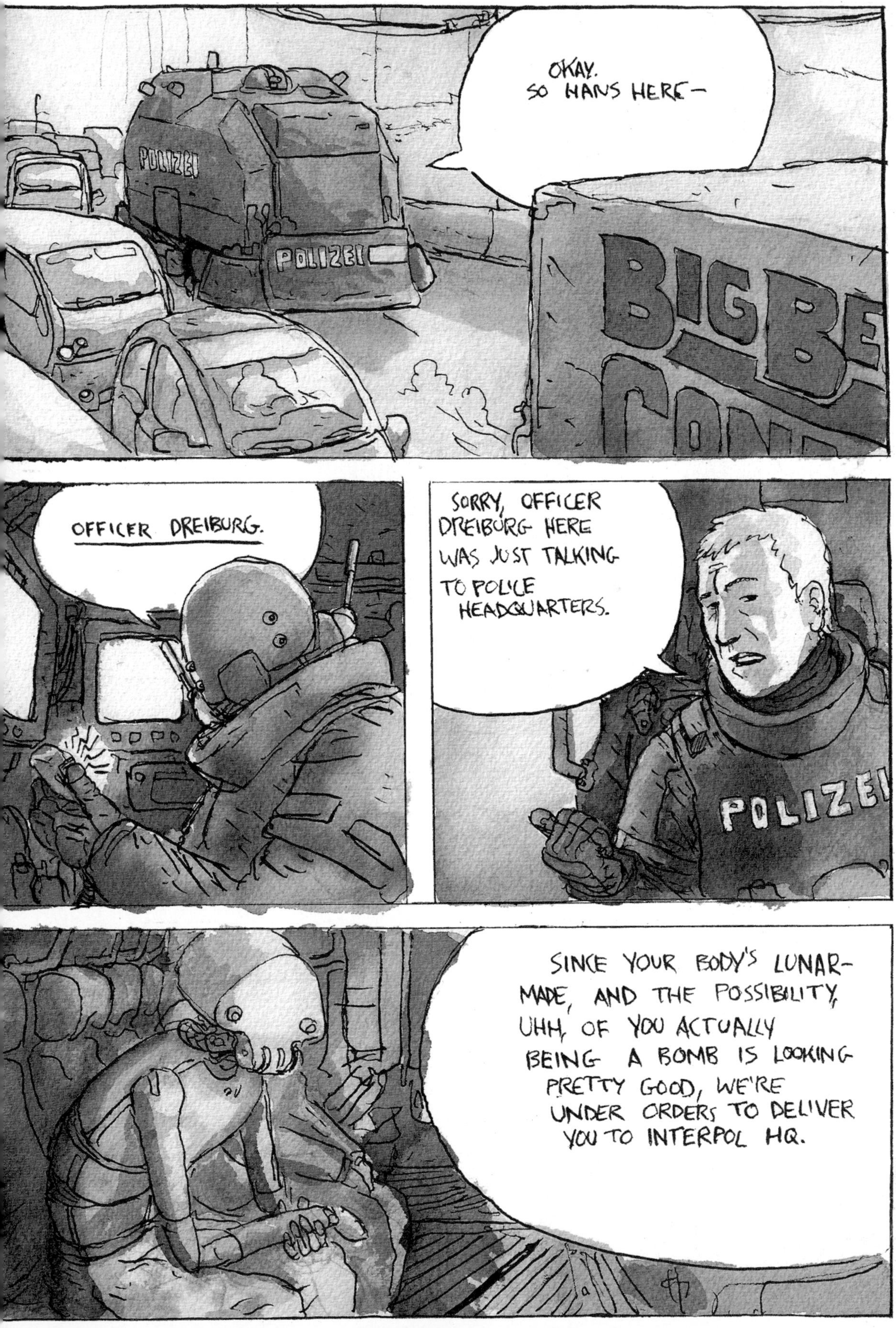
OKAY. SO HANS HERE—
POLIZEI
POLIZEI
OFFICER DREIBURG.
SORRY, OFFICER DREIBURG HERE WAS JUST TALKING TO POLICE HEADQUARTERS.
SINCE YOUR BODY'S LUNAR-MADE, AND THE POSSIBILITY, UHH, OF YOU ACTUALLY BEING A BOMB IS LOOKING PRETTY GOOD, WE'RE UNDER ORDERS TO DELIVER YOU TO INTERPOL HQ.

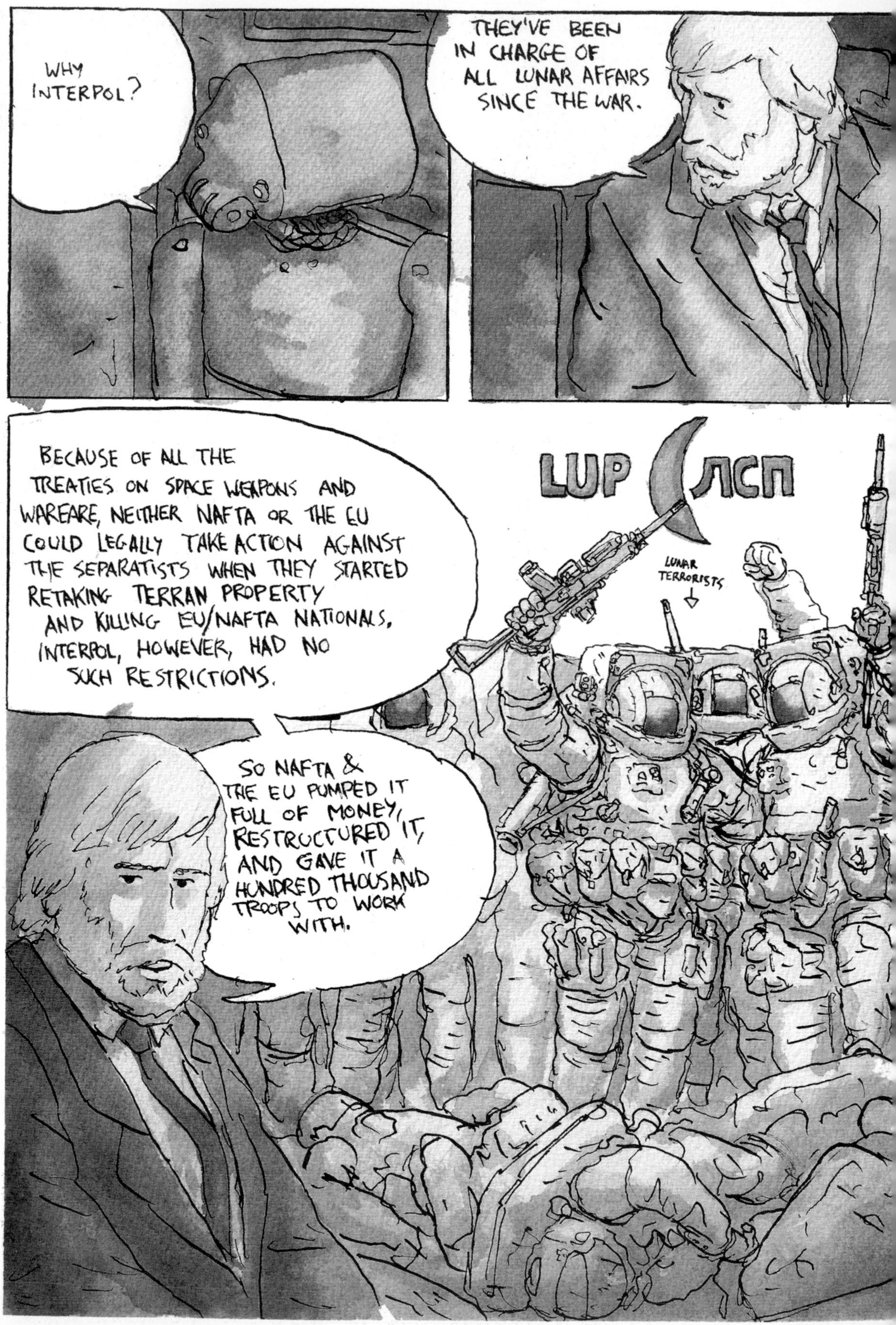
WHY INTERPOL?
THEY'VE BEEN IN CHARGE OF ALL LUNAR AFFAIRS SINCE THE WAR.
BECAUSE OF ALL THE TREATIES ON SPACE WEAPONS AND WARFARE, NEITHER NAFTA OR THE EU COULD LEGALLY TAKE ACTION AGAINST THE SEPARATISTS WHEN THEY STARTED RETAKING TERRAN PROPERTY AND KILLING EU/NAFTA NATIONALS. INTERPOL, HOWEVER, HAD NO SUCH RESTRICTIONS.
LUP ЛСП
LUNAR TERRORISTS
SO NAFTA & THE EU PUMPED IT FULL OF MONEY, RESTRUCTURED IT, AND GAVE IT A HUNDRED THOUSAND TROOPS TO WORK WITH.

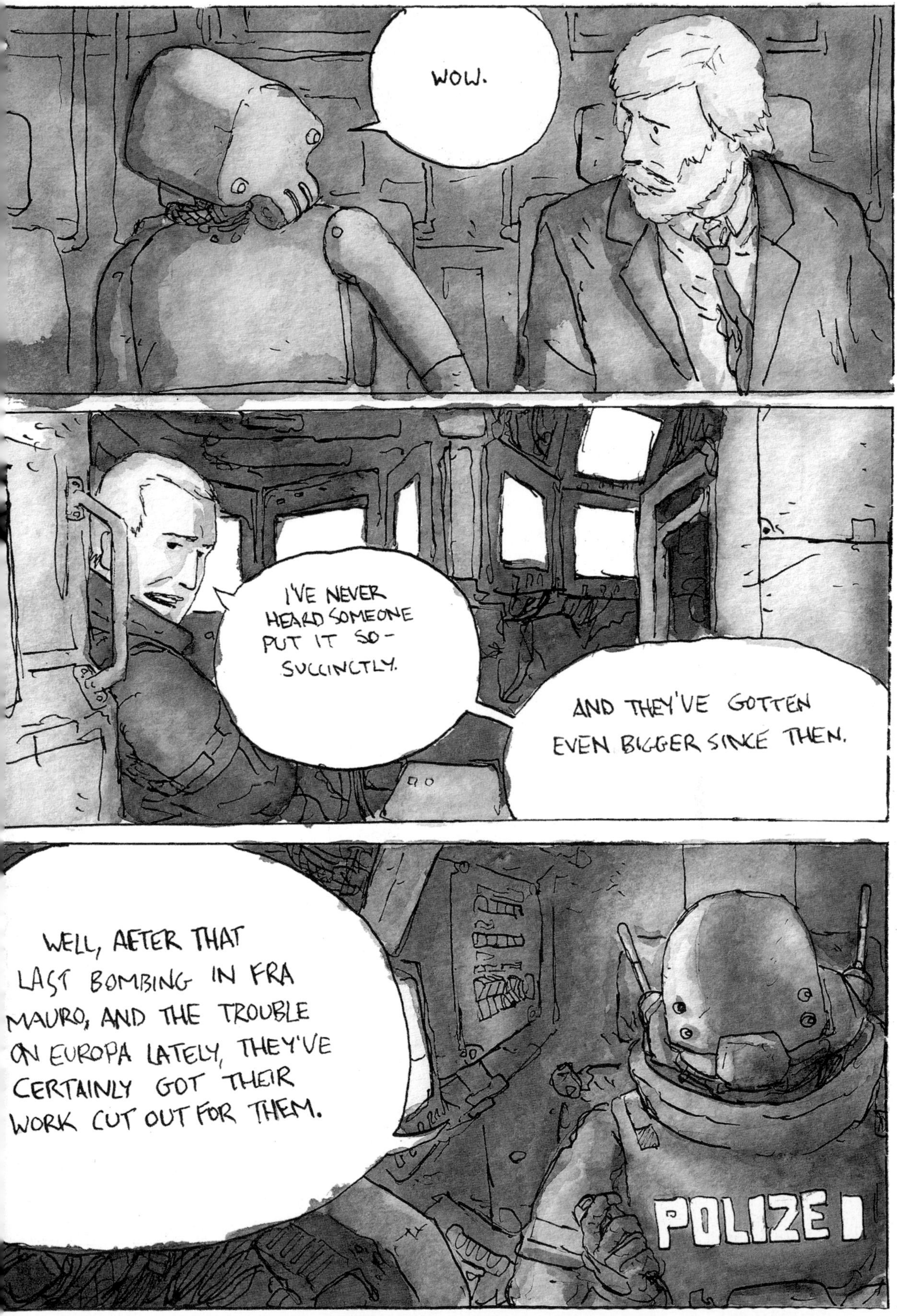
WOW.
I'VE NEVER HEARD SOMEONE PUT IT SO- SUCCINCTLY.
AND THEY'VE GOTTEN EVEN BIGGER SINCE THEN.
WELL, AFTER THAT LAST BOMBING IN FRA MAURO, AND THE TROUBLE ON EUROPA LATELY, THEY'VE CERTAINLY GOT THEIR WORK CUT OUT FOR THEM.
POLIZEI

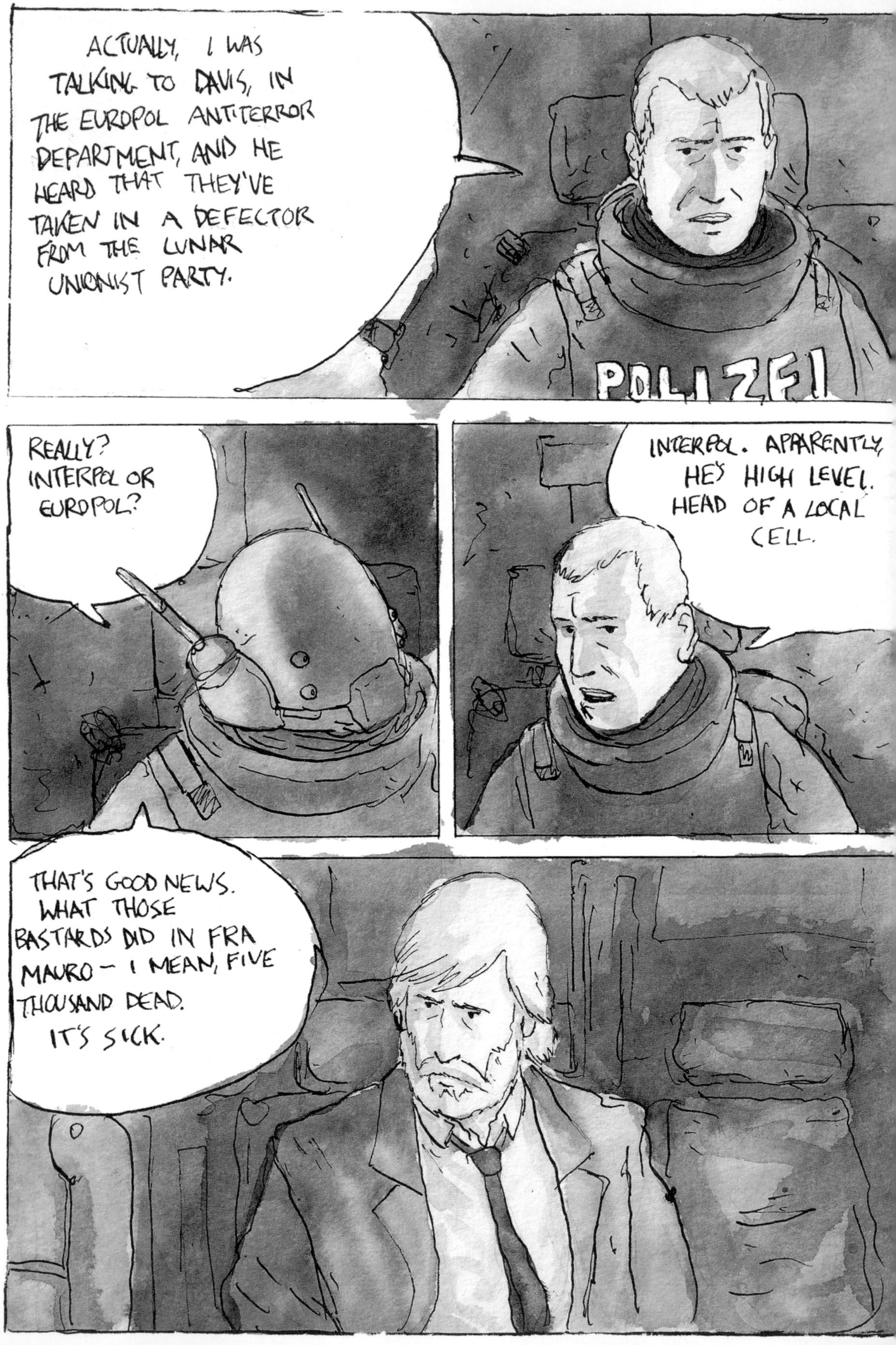
ACTUALLY, I WAS TALKING TO DAVIS, IN THE EUROPOL ANTITERROR DEPARTMENT, AND HE HEARD THAT THEY'VE TAKEN IN A DEFECTOR FROM THE LUNAR UNIONIST PARTY.
POLIZEI
REALLY? INTERPOL OR EUROPOL?
INTERPOL. APPARENTLY, HE'S HIGH LEVEL. HEAD OF A LOCAL CELL.
THAT'S GOOD NEWS. WHAT THOSE BASTARDS DID IN FRA MAURO — I MEAN, FIVE THOUSAND DEAD. IT'S SICK.

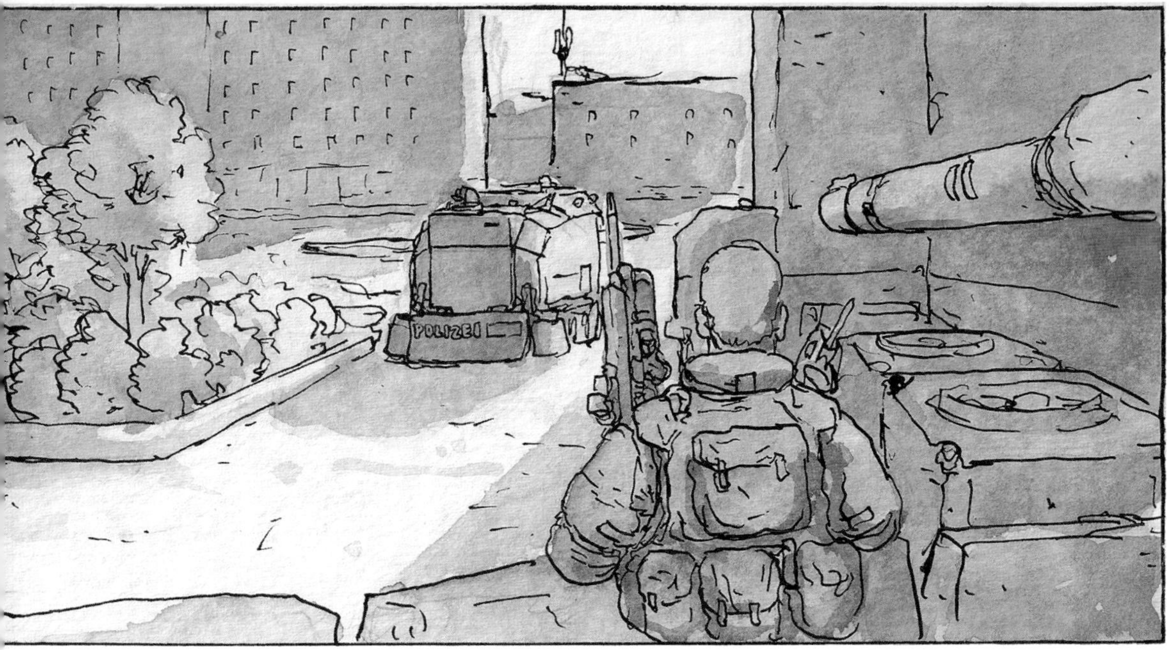
POLIZEI

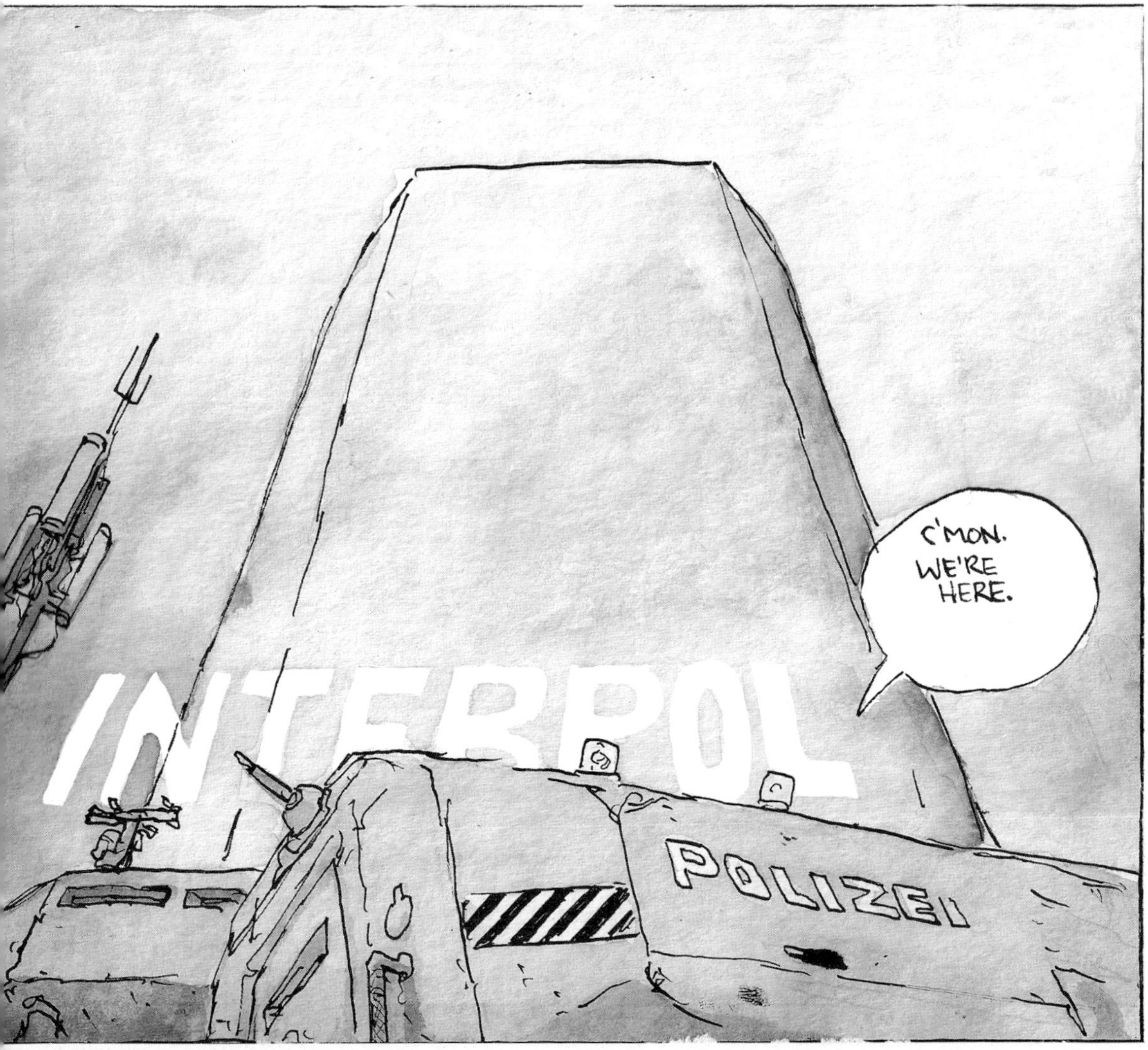
C'MON. WE'RE HERE.
INTERPOL
POLIZEI

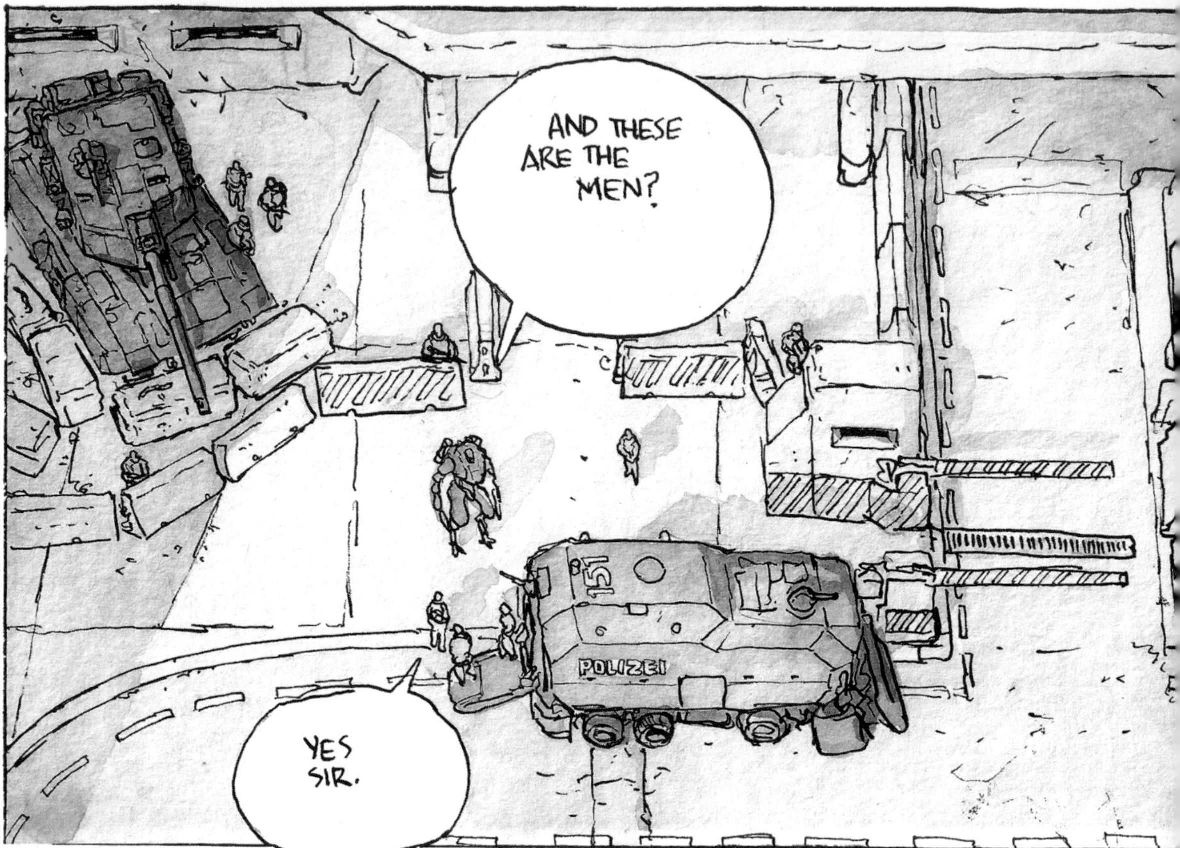
AND THESE ARE THE MEN?
151
POLIZEI
YES SIR.

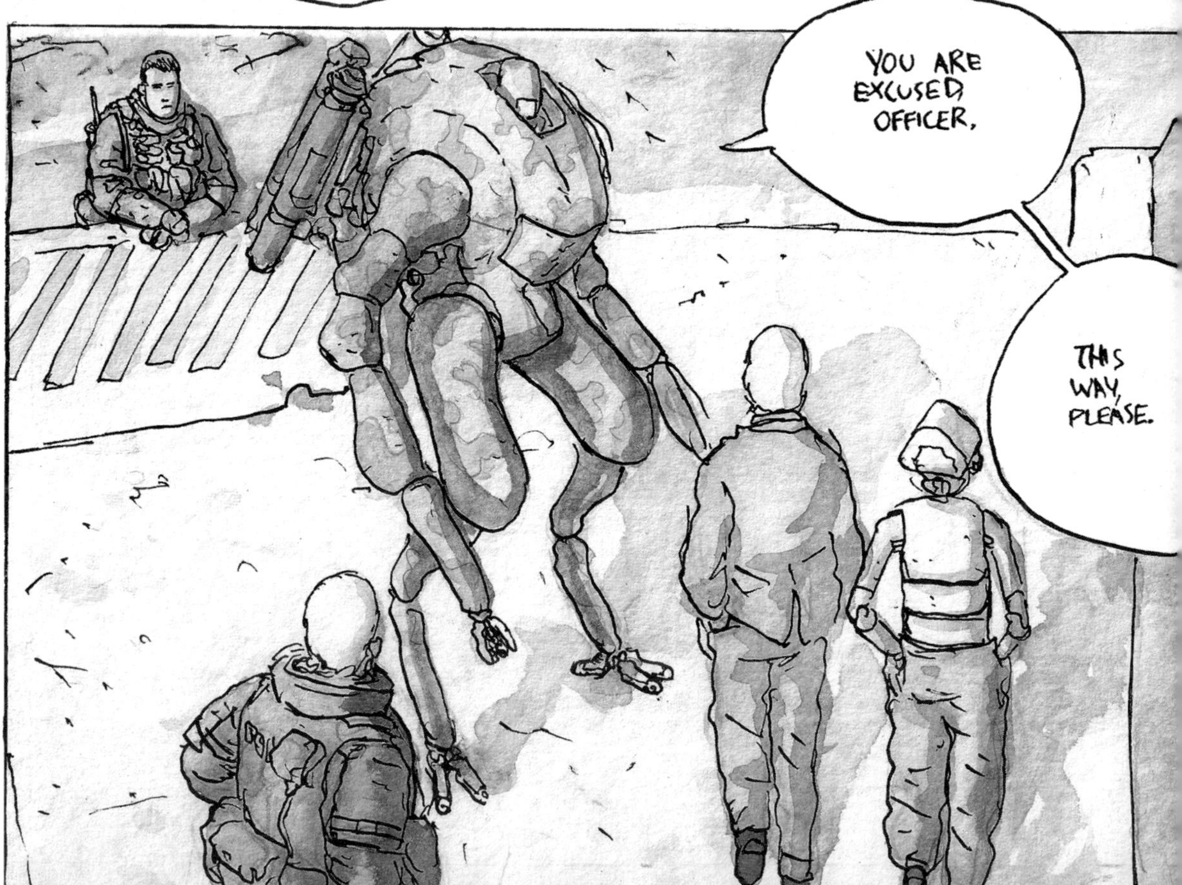
YOU ARE EXCUSED, OFFICER.
THIS WAY, PLEASE.

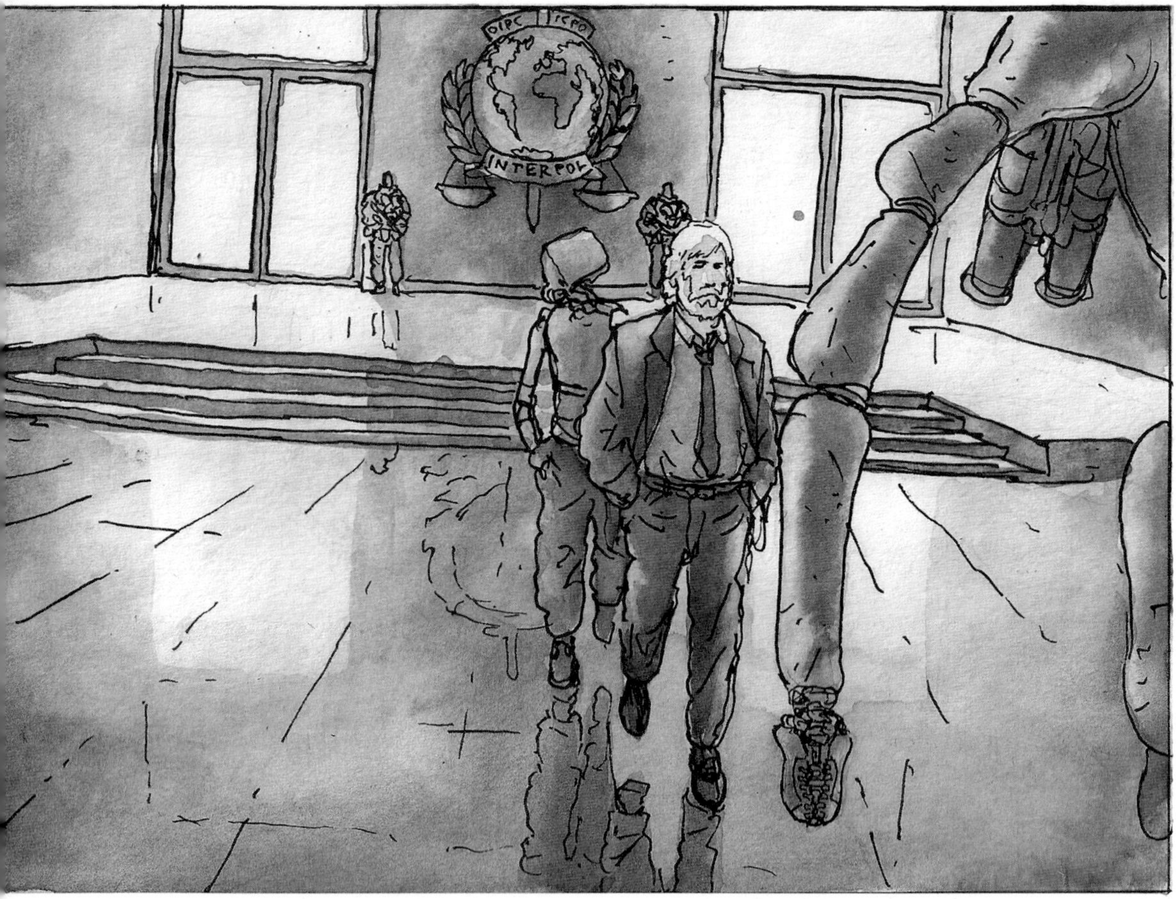
OIPC ICPO
INTERPOL

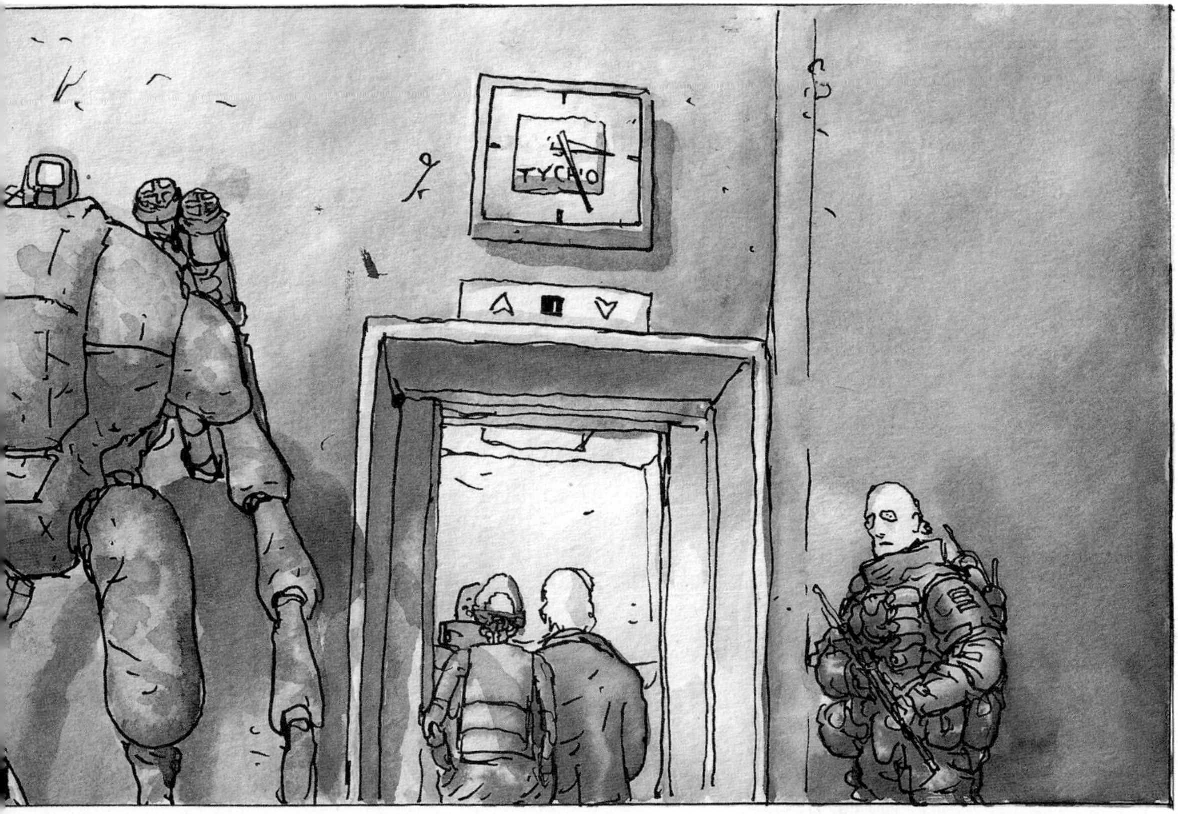
TYCHO

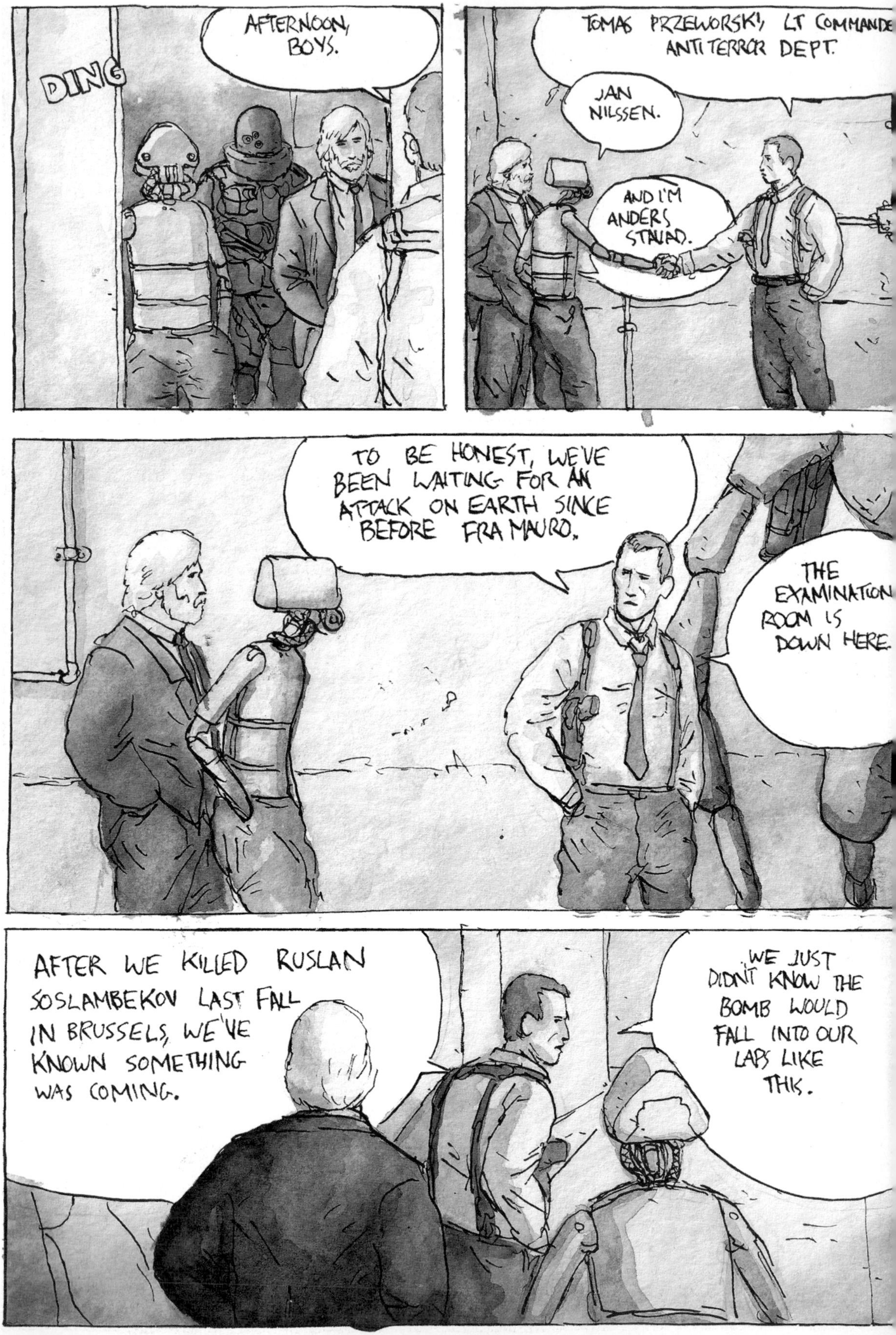
DING
AFTERNOON, BOYS.
TOMAS PRZEWORSKI, LT COMMANDE ANTI TERROR DEPT.
JAN NILSSEN.
AND I'M ANDERS STAVAD.
TO BE HONEST, WE'VE BEEN WAITING FOR AN ATTACK ON EARTH SINCE BEFORE FRA MAURO.
THE EXAMINATION ROOM IS DOWN HERE.
AFTER WE KILLED RUSLAN SOSLAMBEKOV LAST FALL IN BRUSSELS, WE'VE KNOWN SOMETHING WAS COMING.
WE JUST DIDN'T KNOW THE BOMB WOULD FALL INTO OUR LAPS LIKE THIS.

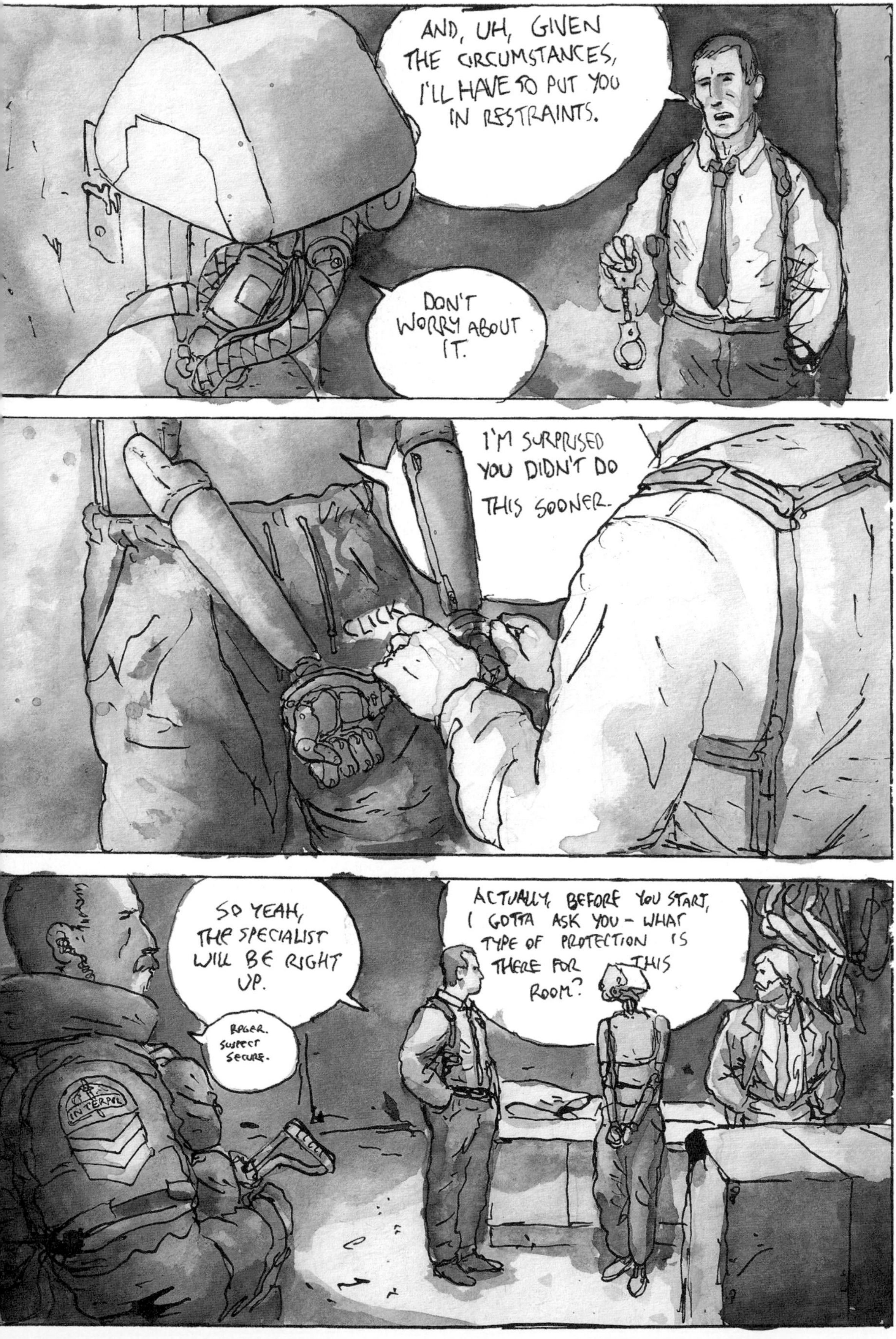
AND, UH, GIVEN THE CIRCUMSTANCES, I'LL HAVE TO PUT YOU IN RESTRAINTS.
DON'T WORRY ABOUT IT.
I'M SURPRISED YOU DIDN'T DO THIS SOONER.
CLICK
SO YEAH, THE SPECIALIST WILL BE RIGHT UP.
ROGER. SUSPECT SECURE.
INTERPOL
ACTUALLY, BEFORE YOU START, I GOTTA ASK YOU - WHAT TYPE OF PROTECTION IS THERE FOR THIS ROOM?

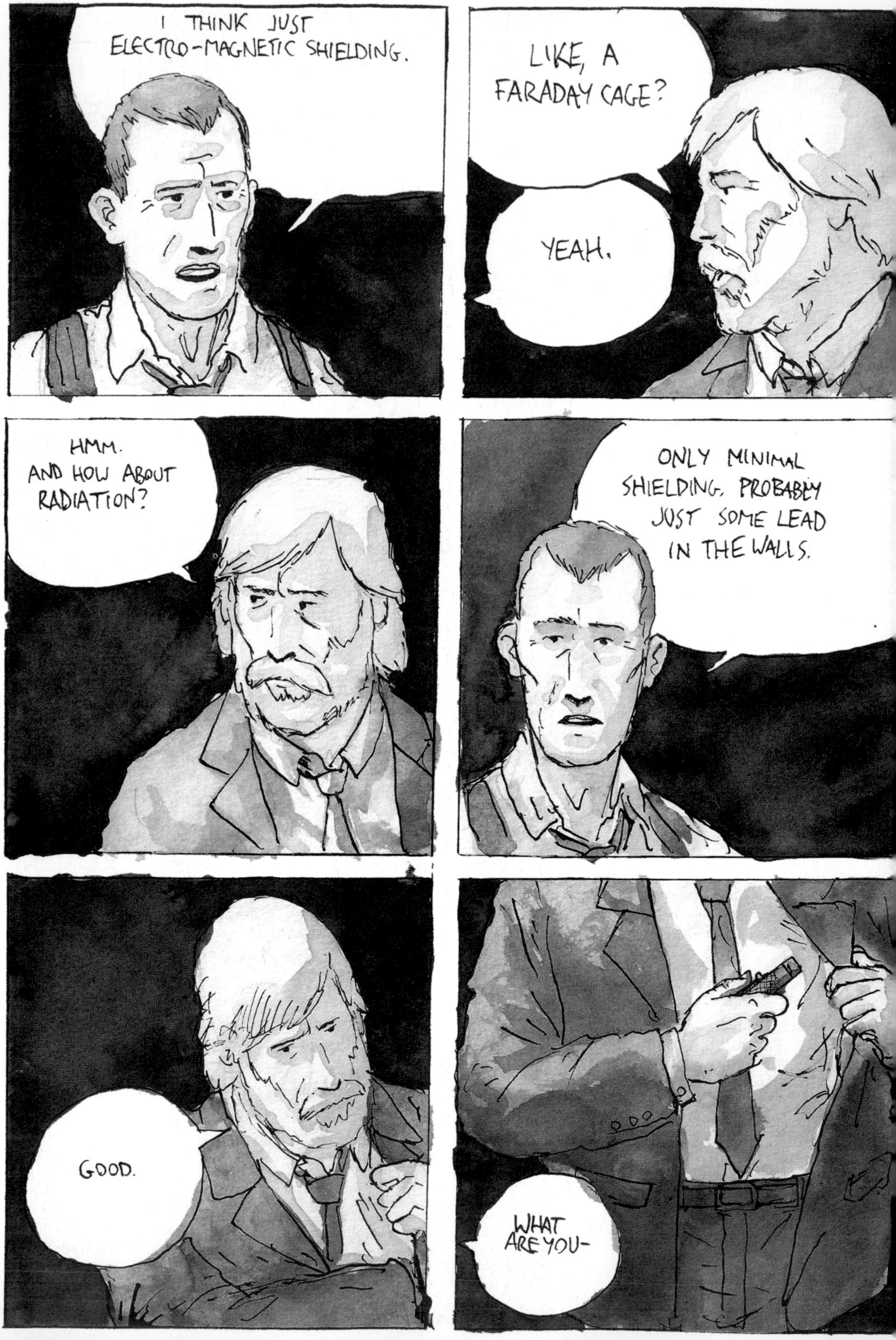
I THINK JUST ELECTRO-MAGNETIC SHIELDING.
LIKE, A FARADAY CAGE?
YEAH.
HMM. AND HOW ABOUT RADIATION?
ONLY MINIMAL SHIELDING. PROBABLY JUST SOME LEAD IN THE WALLS.
GOOD.
WHAT ARE YOU-

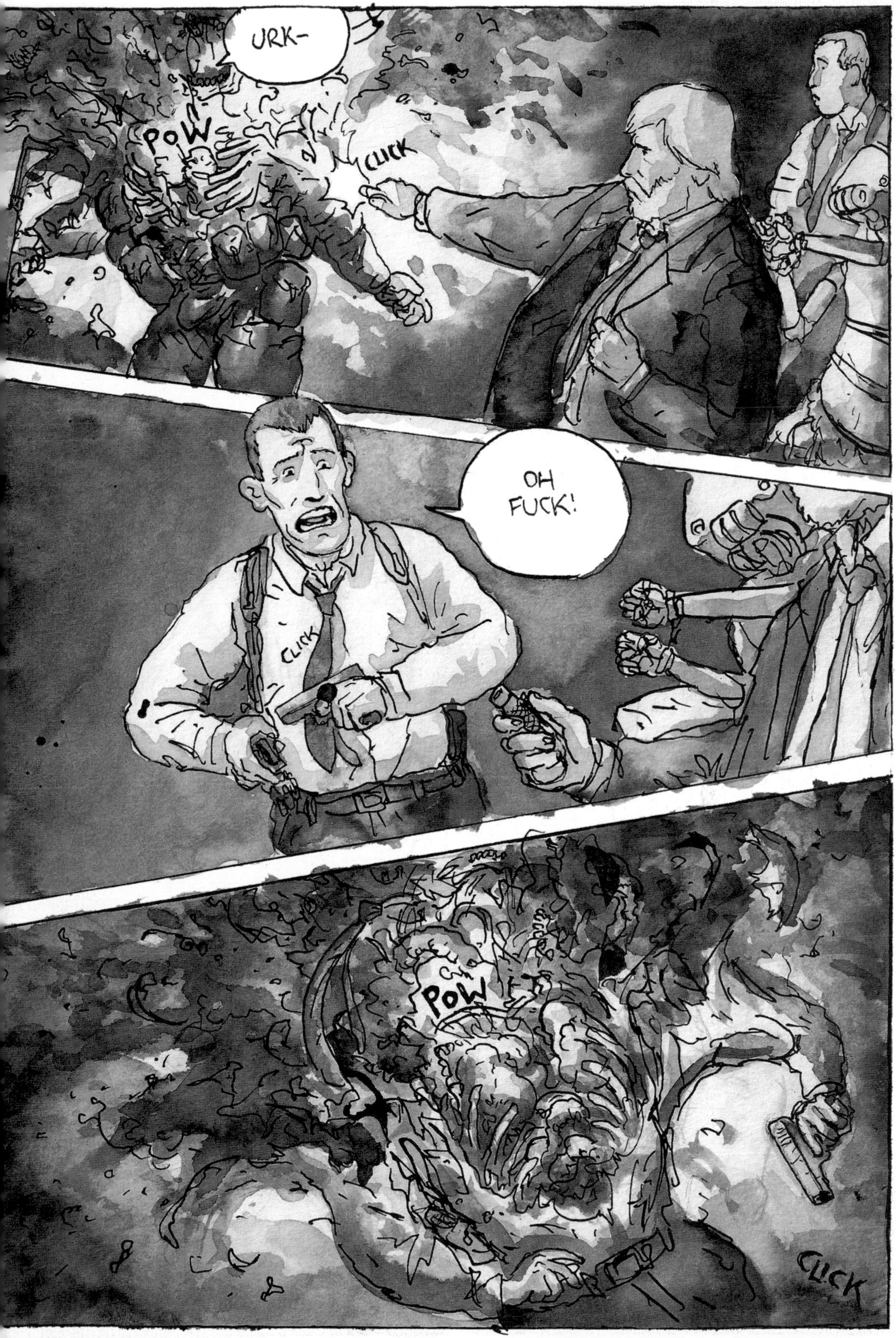
URK-
POW
CLICK
OH FUCK!
CLICK
POW
CLICK

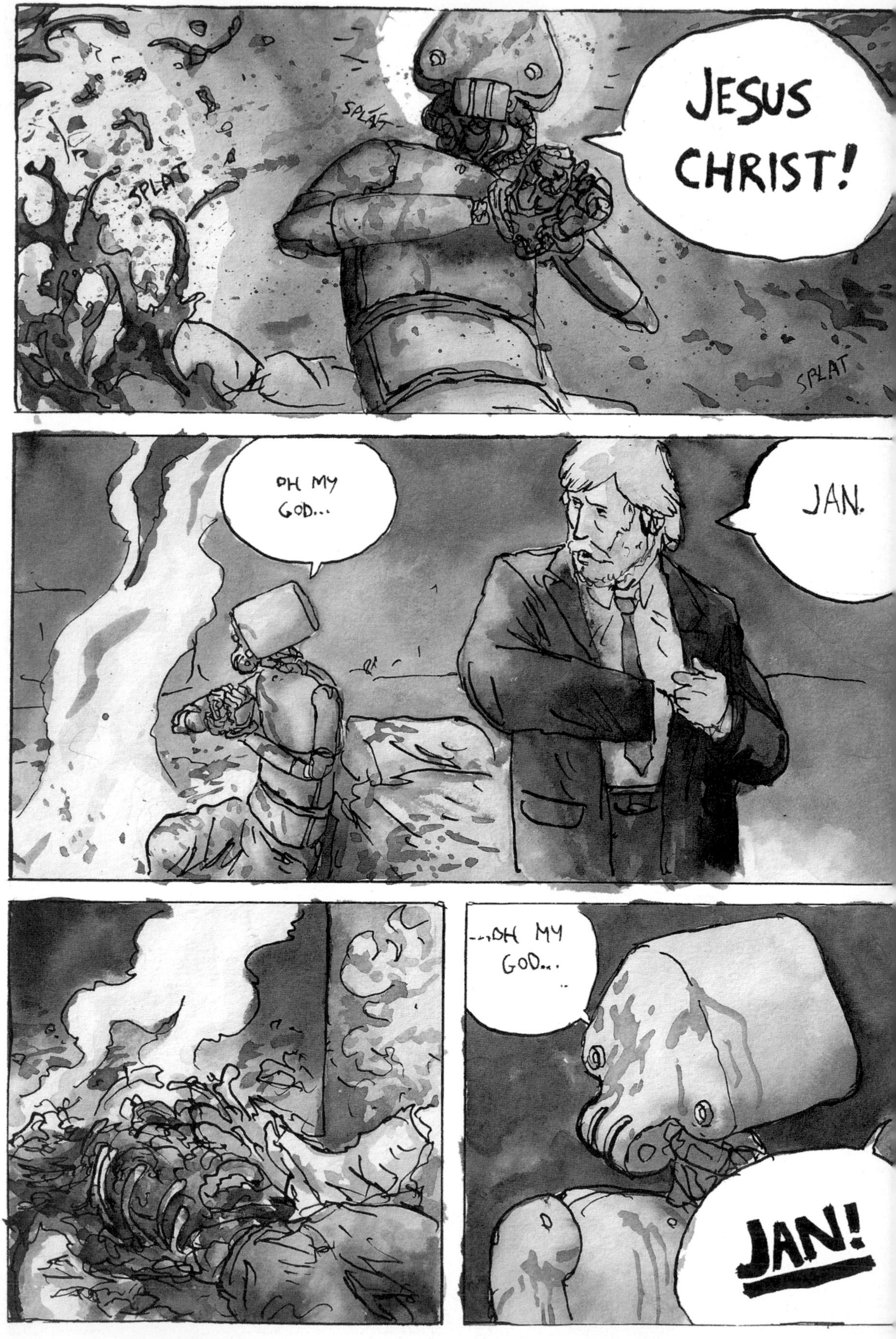
SPLAT
SPLAT
JESUS CHRIST!
SPLAT
OH MY GOD...
JAN.
...OH MY GOD...
JAN!

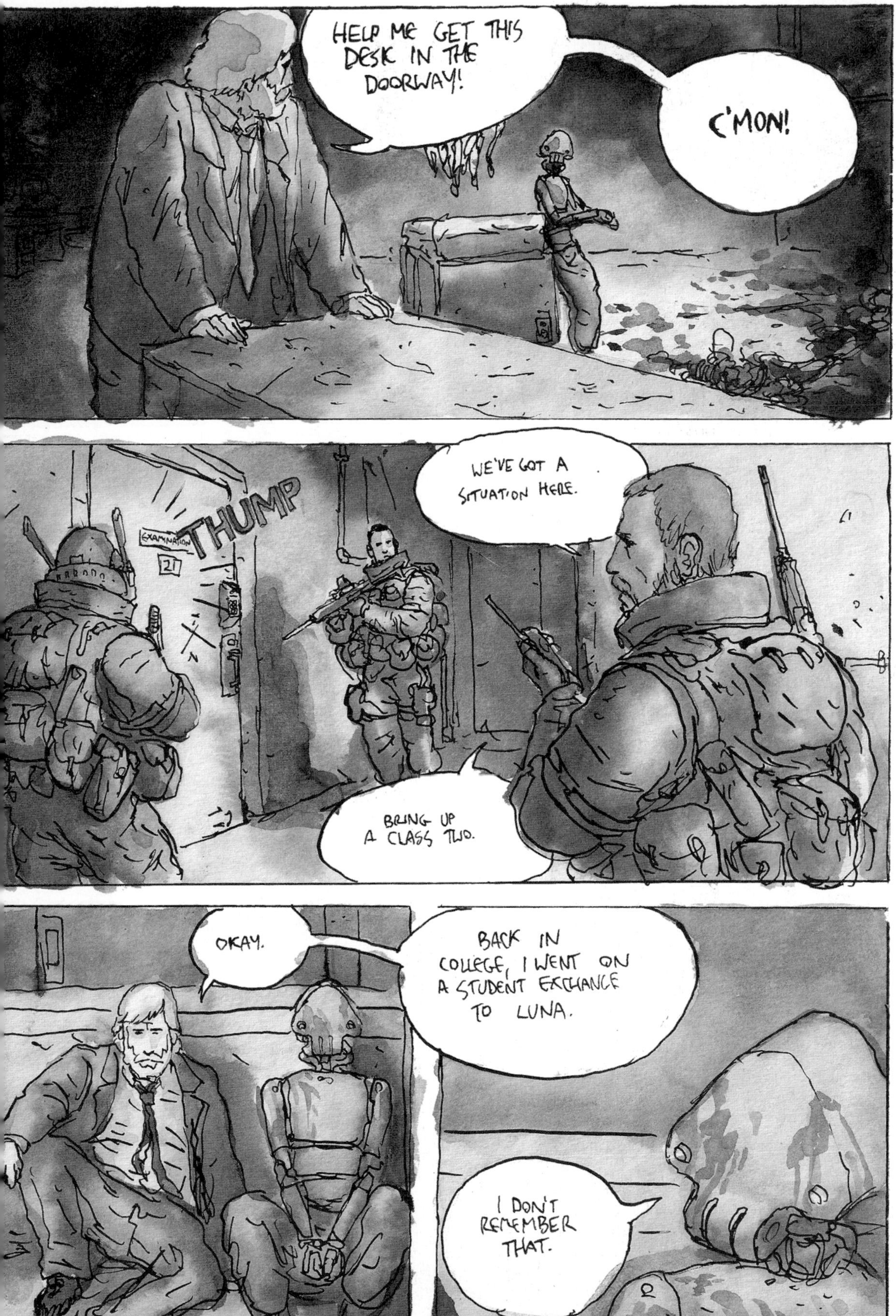
HELP ME GET THIS DESK IN THE DOORWAY!
C'MON!
THUMP
EXAMINATION
21
WE'VE GOT A SITUATION HERE.
BRING UP A CLASS TWO.
OKAY.
BACK IN COLLEGE, I WENT ON A STUDENT EXCHANGE TO LUNA.
I DON'T REMEMBER THAT.

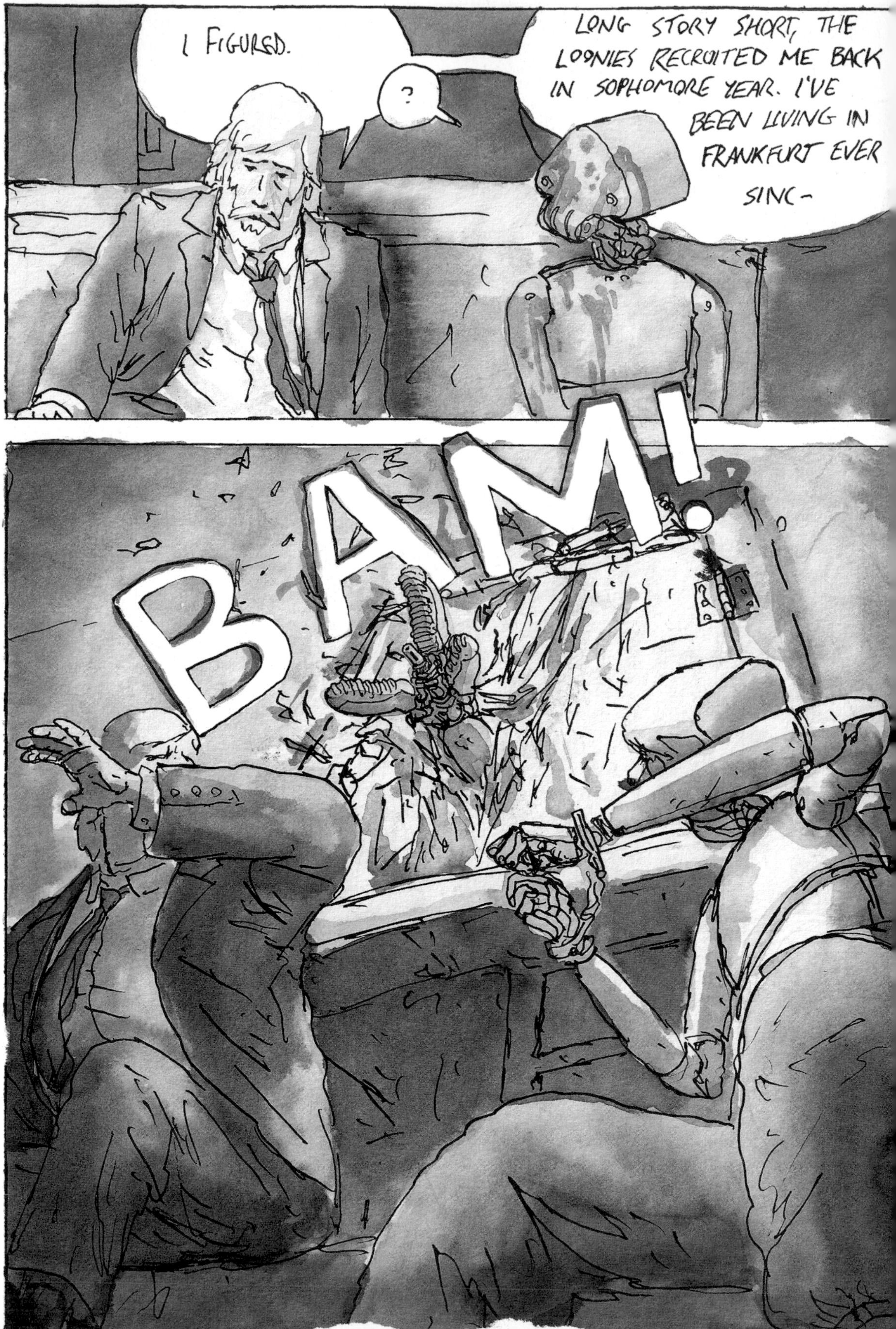
I FIGURED.
?
LONG STORY SHORT, THE LOONIES RECRUITED ME BACK IN SOPHOMORE YEAR. I'VE BEEN LIVING IN FRANKFURT EVER SINC-
BAM!

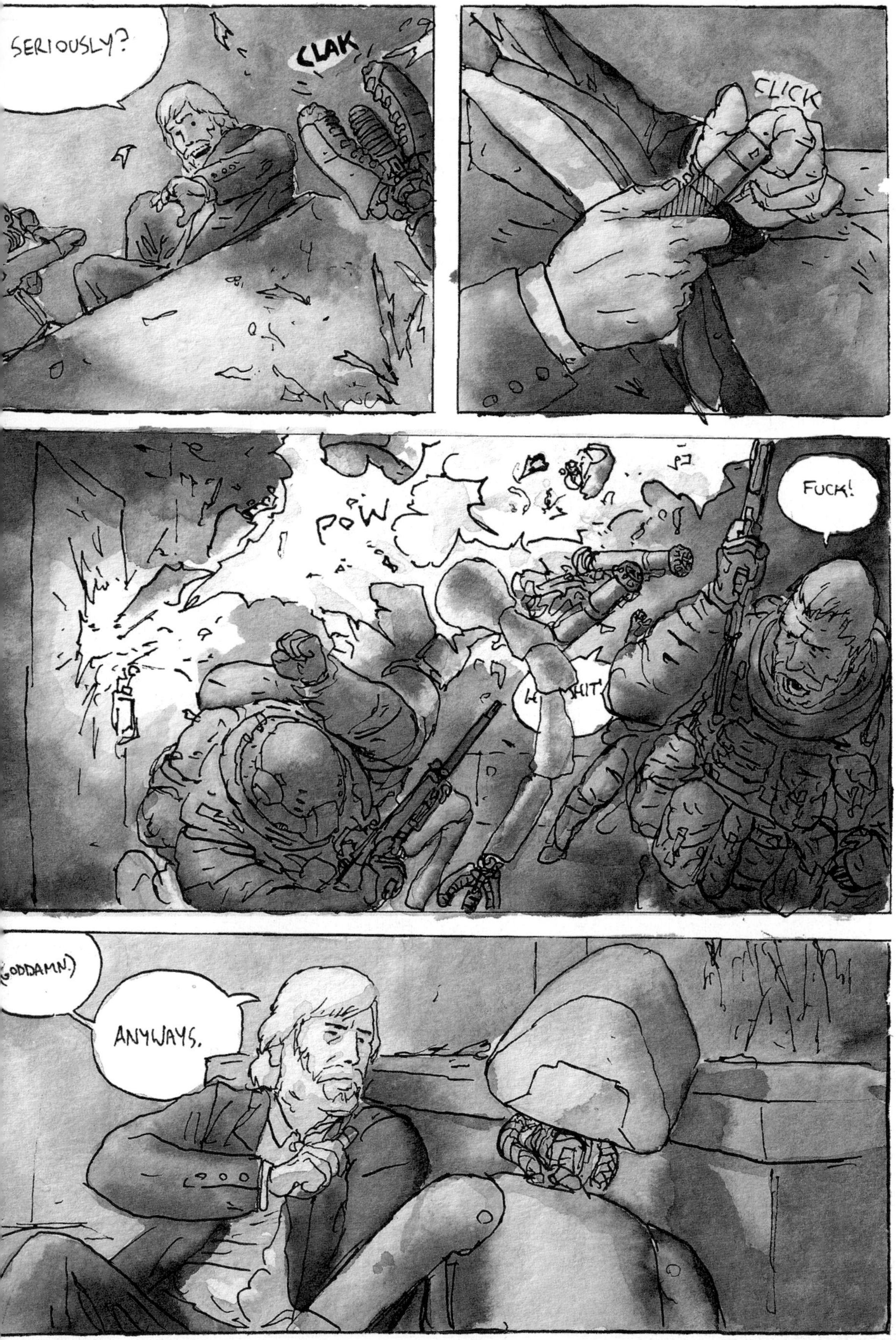
SERIOUSLY?
CLAK
CLICK
POW
FUCK!
HIT!
(GODDAMN.)
ANYWAYS.

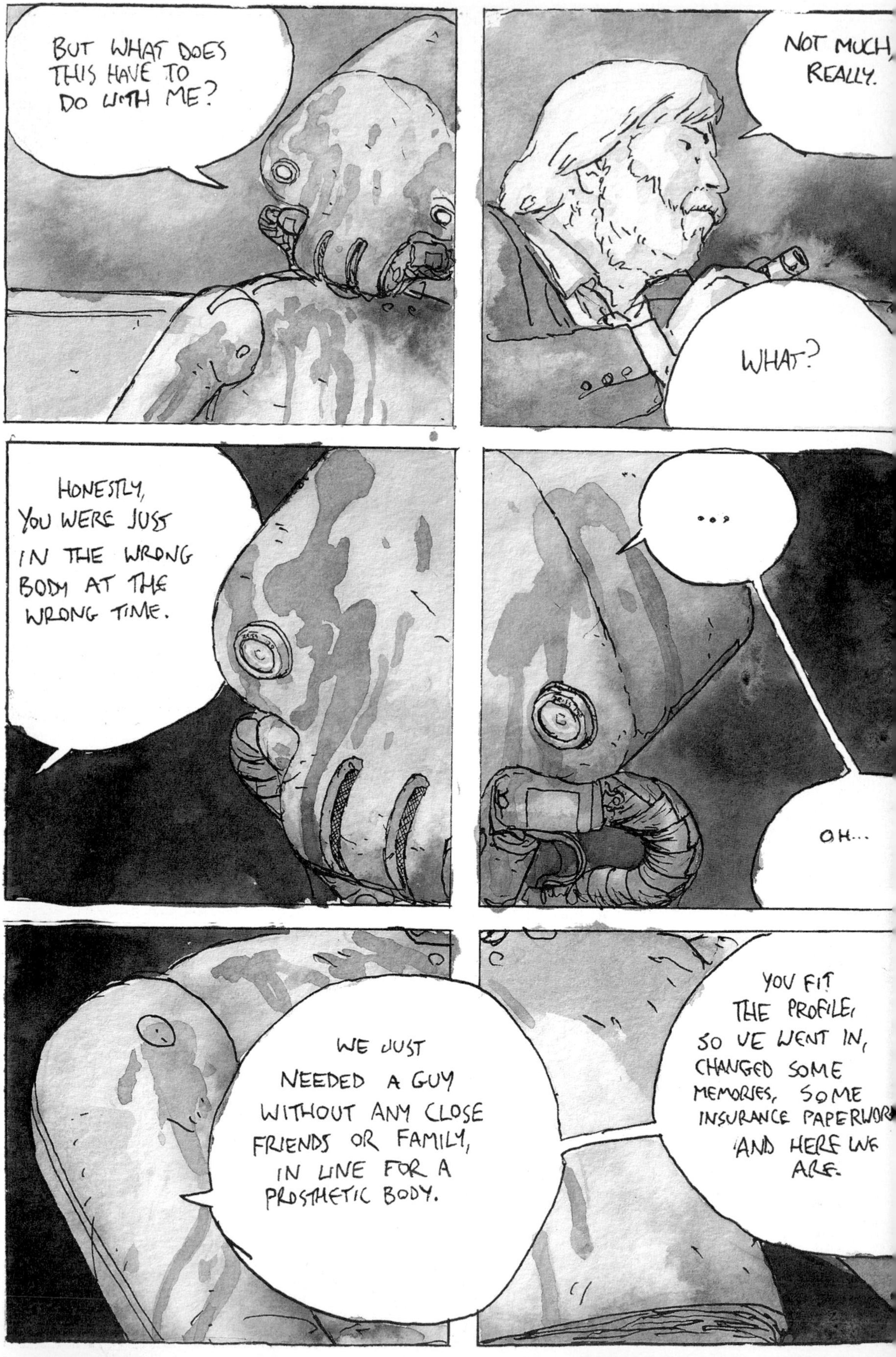

BUT WHAT DOES THIS HAVE TO DO WITH ME?
NOT MUCH, REALLY.
WHAT?
HONESTLY, YOU WERE JUST IN THE WRONG BODY AT THE WRONG TIME.
...
OH...
WE JUST NEEDED A GUY WITHOUT ANY CLOSE FRIENDS OR FAMILY, IN LINE FOR A PROSTHETIC BODY.
YOU FIT THE PROFILE, SO WE WENT IN, CHANGED SOME MEMORIES, SOME INSURANCE PAPERWOR AND HERE WE ARE.

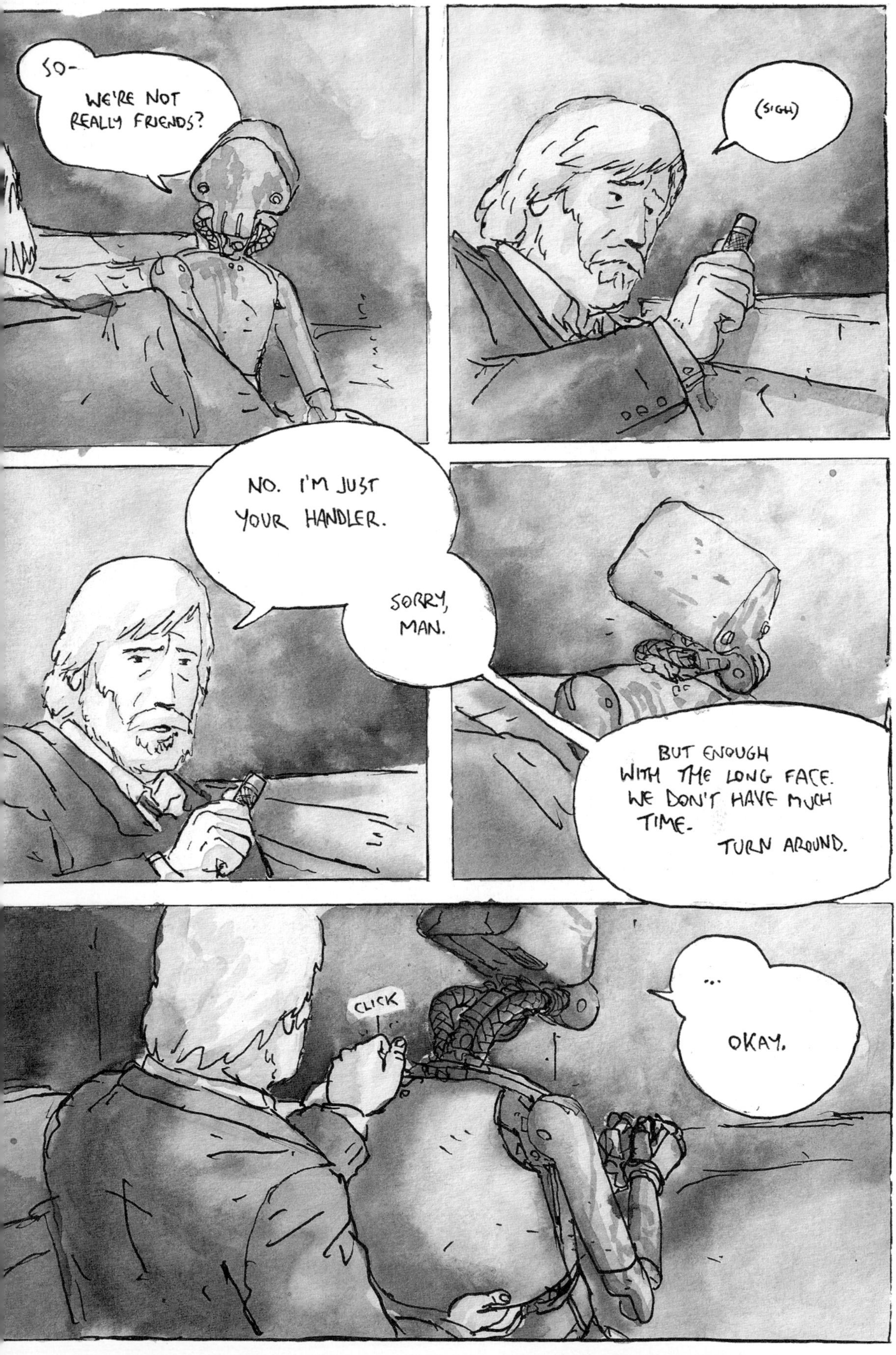

SO-
WE'RE NOT REALLY FRIENDS?
(SIGH)
NO. I'M JUST YOUR HANDLER.
SORRY, MAN.
BUT ENOUGH WITH THE LONG FACE. WE DON'T HAVE MUCH TIME.
TURN AROUND.
CLICK
...
OKAY.

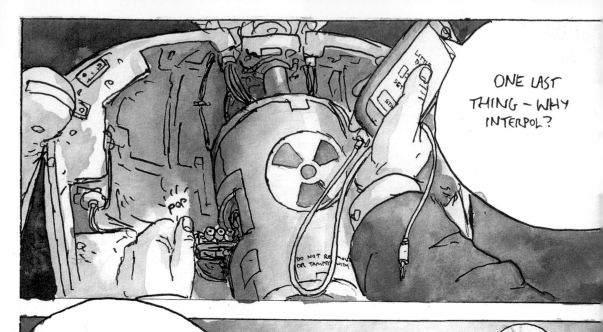

ONE LAST THING — WHY INTERPOL?

POP

DO NOT RE MOVE
OR TAMPER WITH

WELL, YOU WERE SET TO BLOW UP THE FRANKFURT SKYHOOK, BUT ONE OF OUR BOYS DEFECTED, SO PLANS CHANGED. TYING UP LOOSE ENDS AND ALL THAT.

TEAM TWO IN POSITION

BUT INTERPOL IS AT LEAST AS POTENT A TARGET FOR US. NOT QUITE AS GOOD SYMBOLICALLY AS THE SKYHOOK, BUT NOT BAD. IT SENDS A DEFINITE MESSAGE.

CLICK

RUNNING:
LITTLE DOCTOR
(APPLICATION 23 GB)

-1:30:05

MOVE
R WITH

AUSE

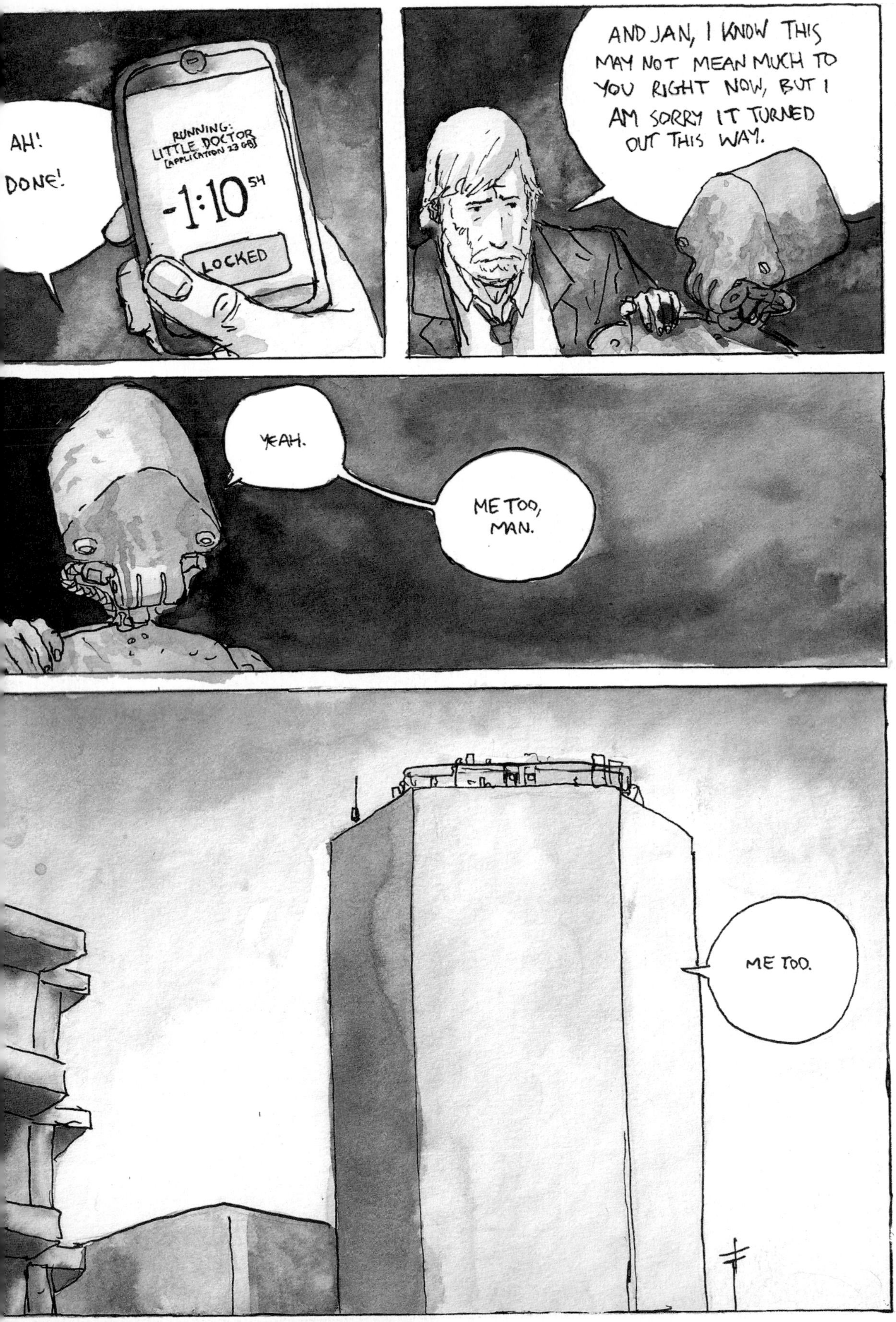
AH! DONE!
RUNNING: LITTLE DOCTOR
[APPLICATION 23 GB]
-1:10 54
LOCKED
AND JAN, I KNOW THIS MAY NOT MEAN MUCH TO YOU RIGHT NOW, BUT I AM SORRY IT TURNED OUT THIS WAY.
YEAH.
ME TOO, MAN.
ME TOO.

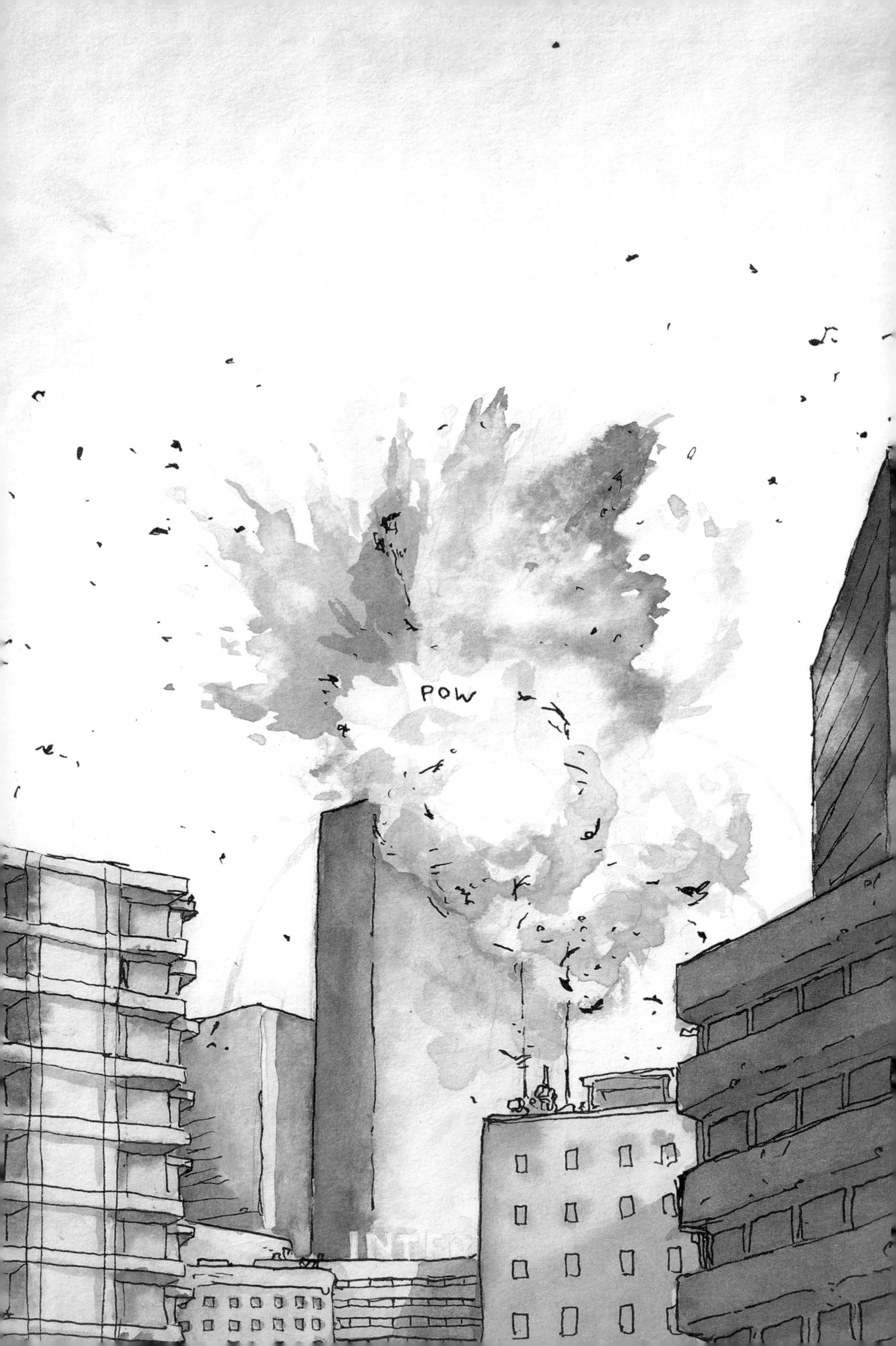
POW

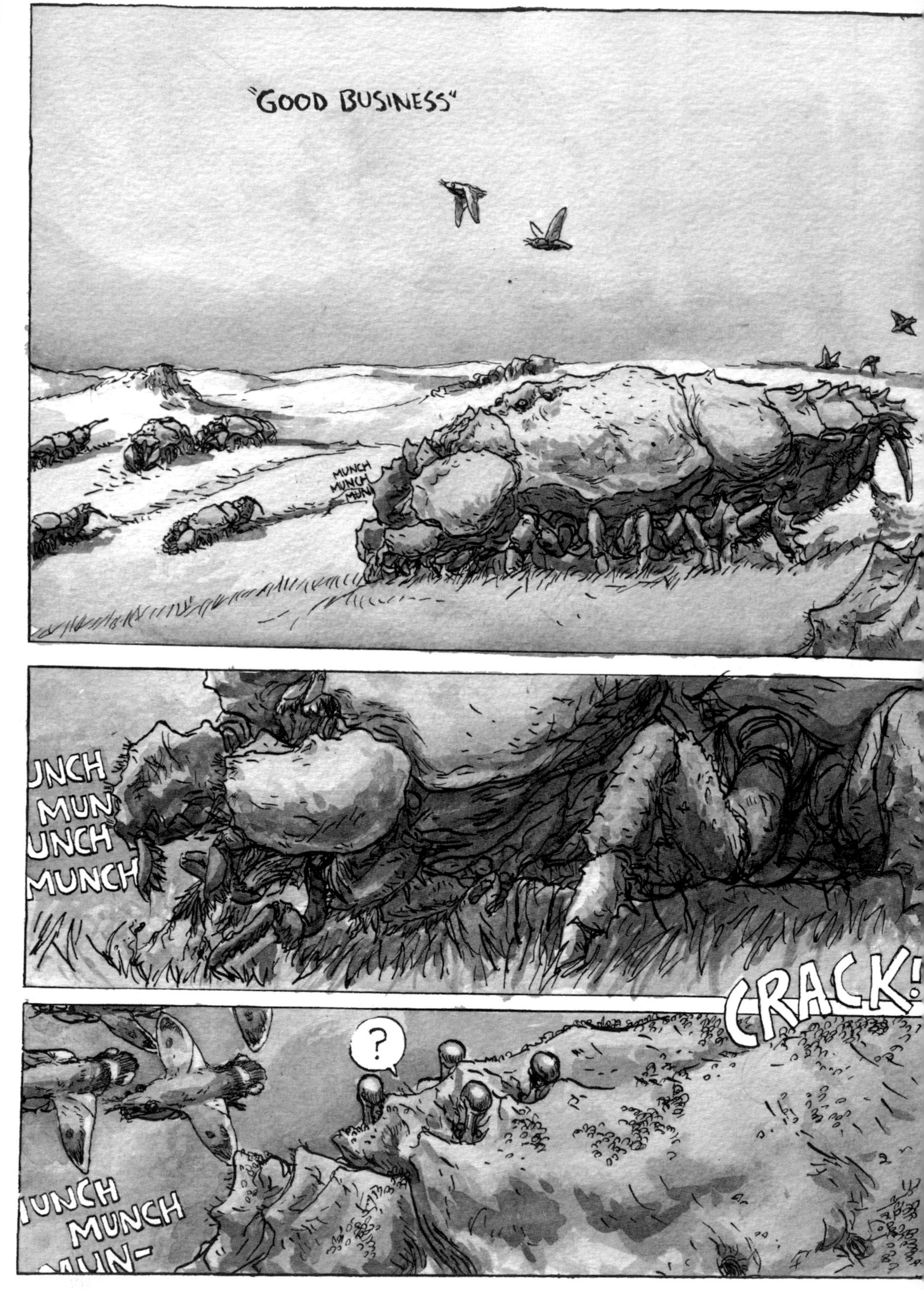
"GOOD BUSINESS"
MUNCH
MUNCH
MUN
UNCH
MUN
UNCH
MUNCH
CRACK!
?
UNCH
MUNCH
MUN-

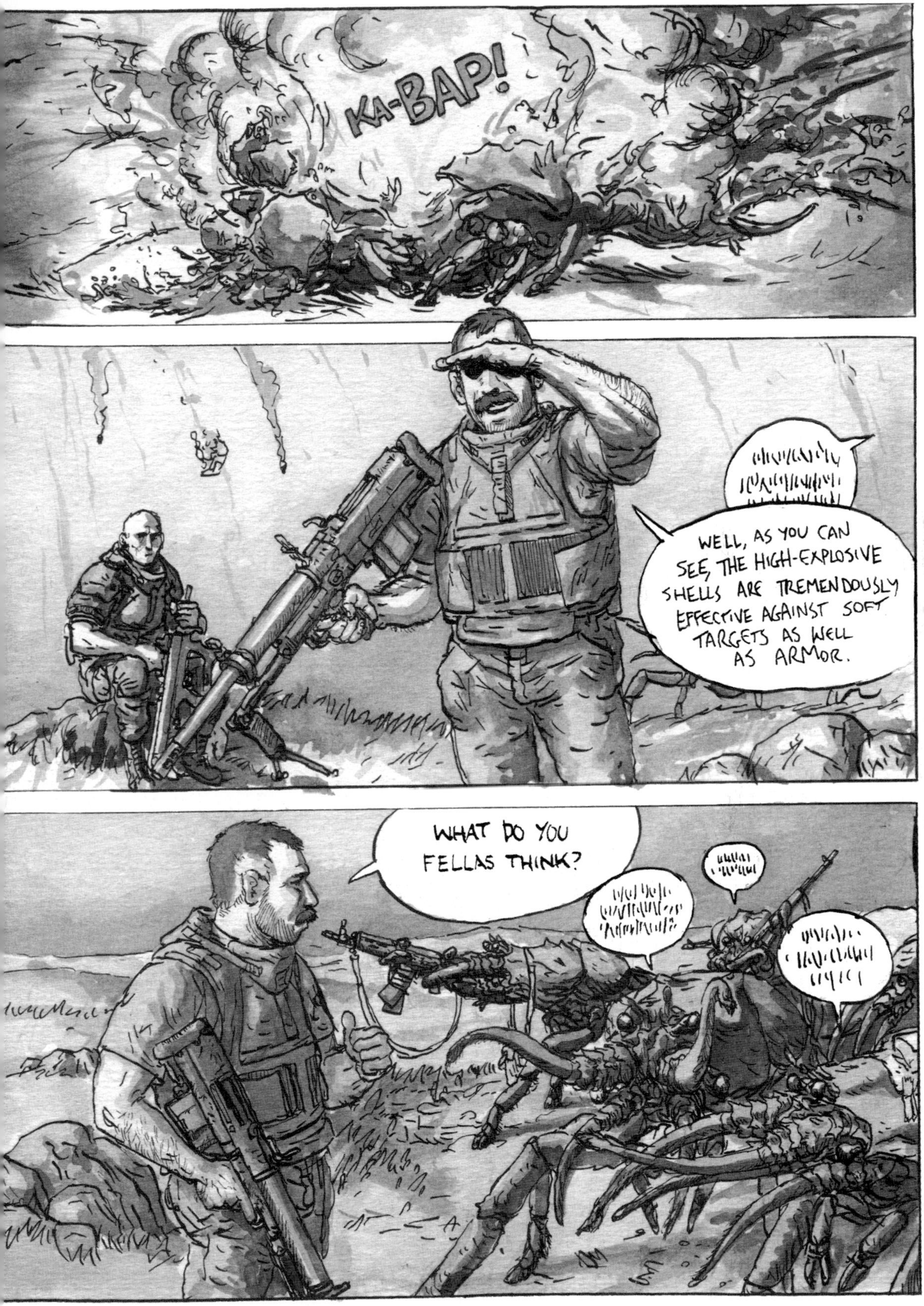
KA-BAP!
WELL, AS YOU CAN SEE, THE HIGH-EXPLOSIVE SHELLS ARE TREMENDOUSLY EFFECTIVE AGAINST SOFT TARGETS AS WELL AS ARMOR.
WHAT DO YOU FELLAS THINK?

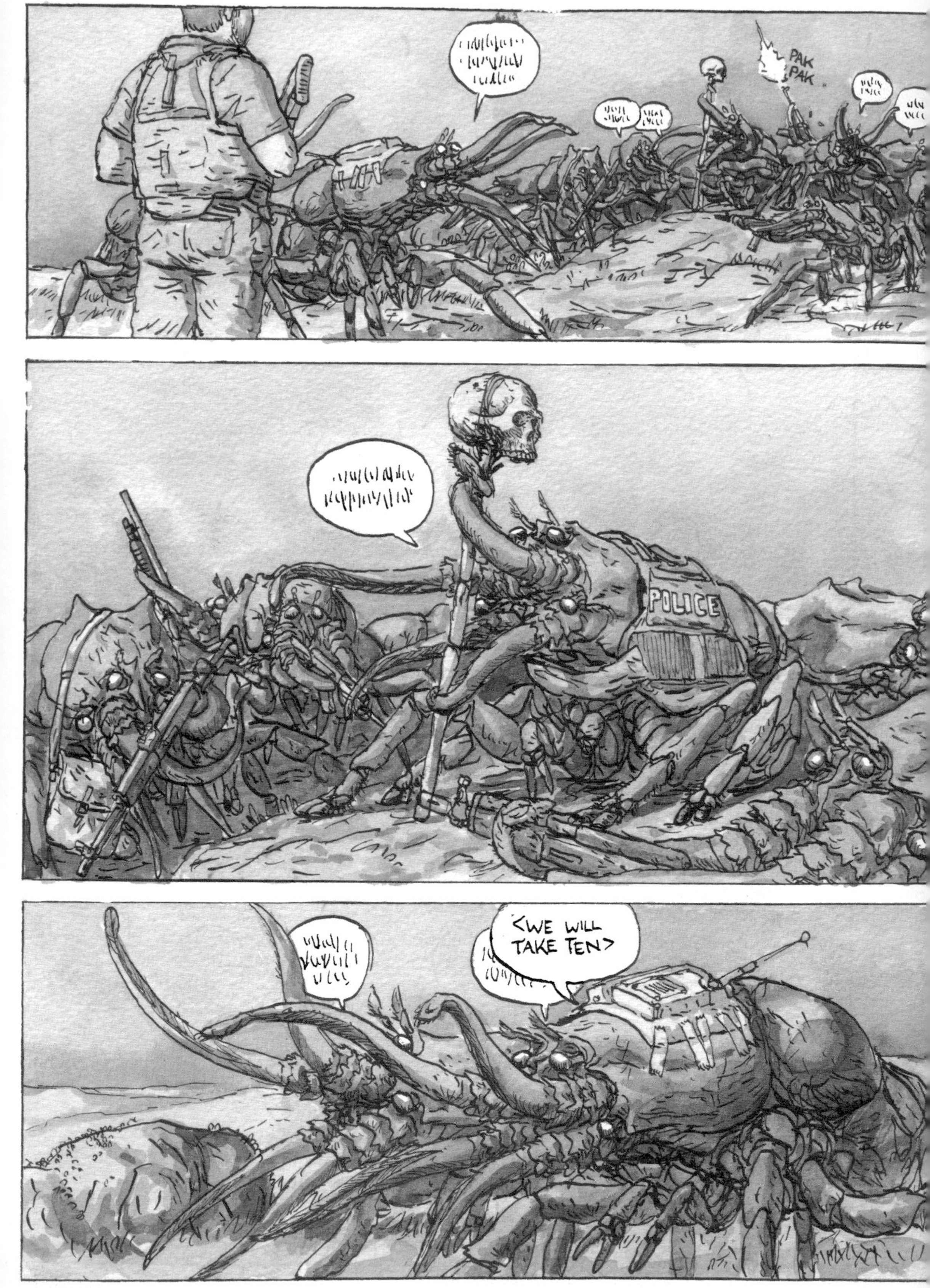
PAK PAK
POLICE
<WE WILL TAKE TEN>

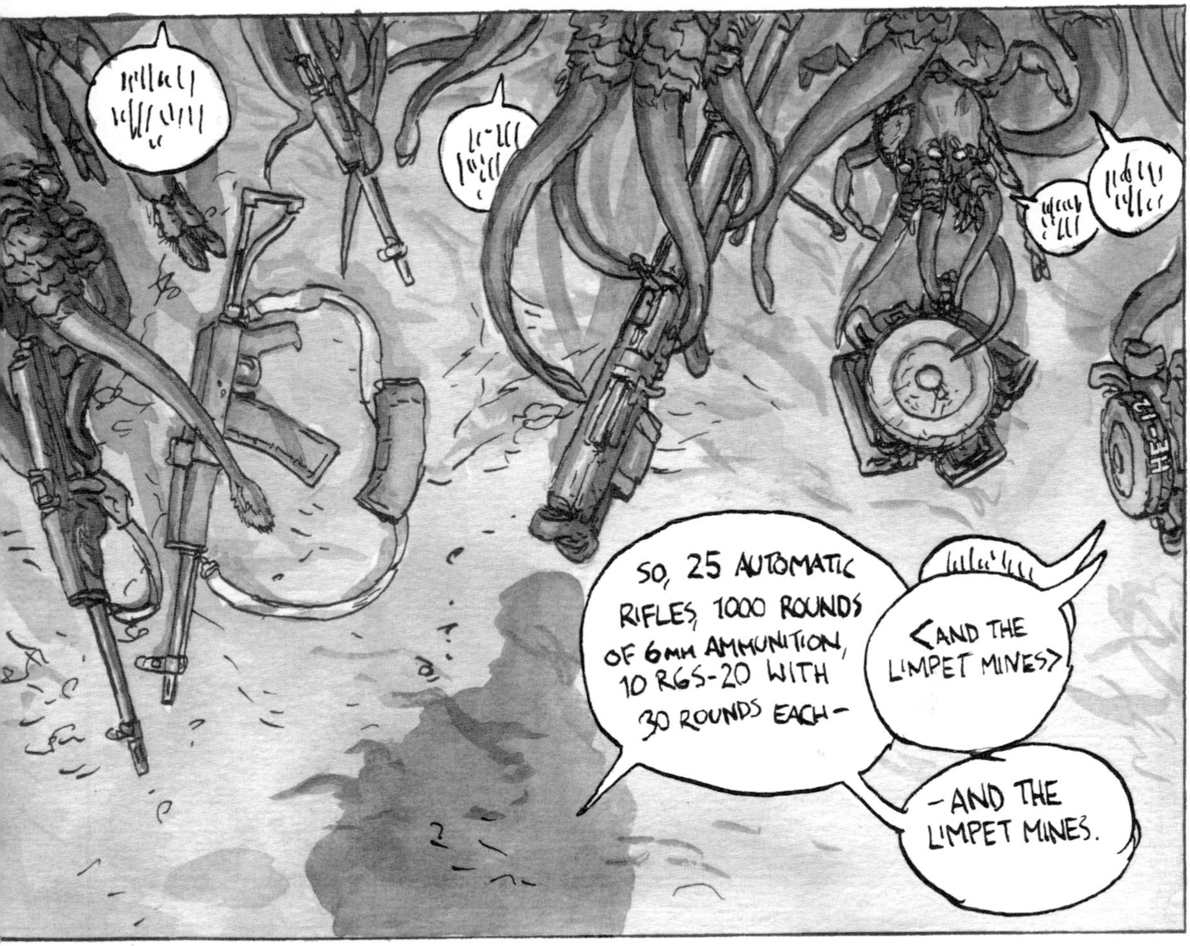
SO, 25 AUTOMATIC RIFLES, 1000 ROUNDS OF 6MM AMMUNITION, 10 RGS-20 WITH 30 ROUNDS EACH-
<AND THE LIMPET MINES>
-AND THE LIMPET MINES.

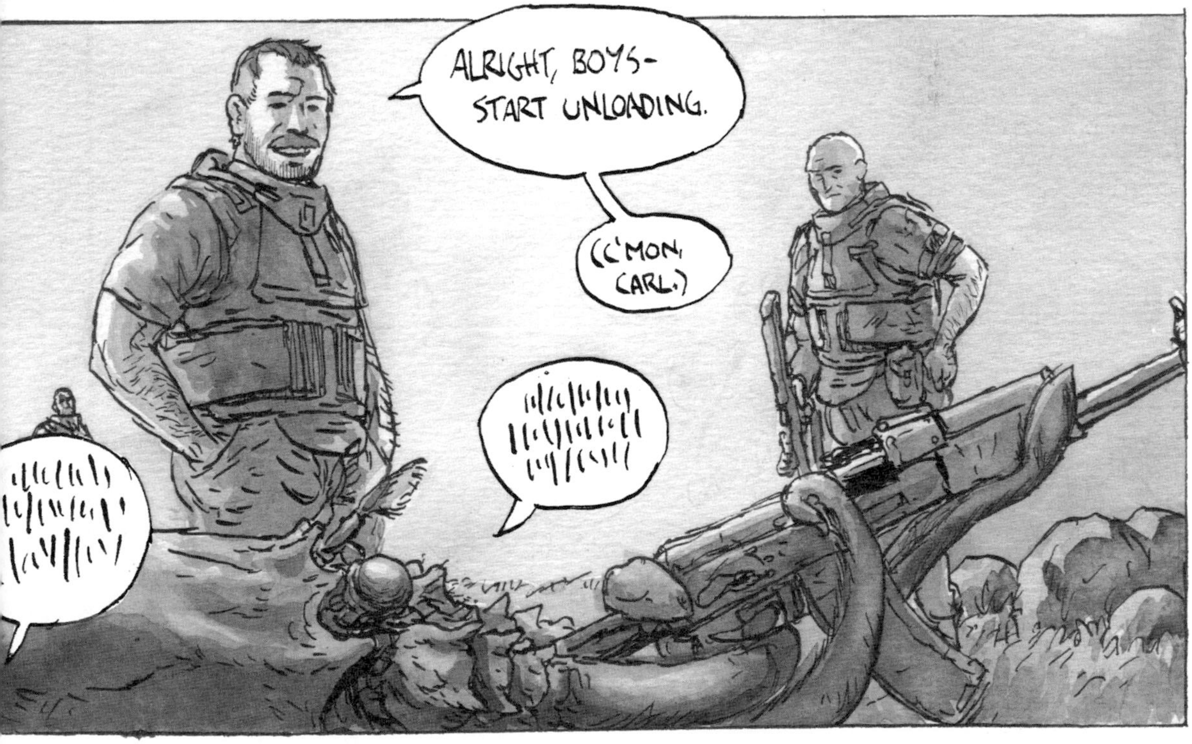
ALRIGHT, BOYS- START UNLOADING.
((C'MON, CARL.))

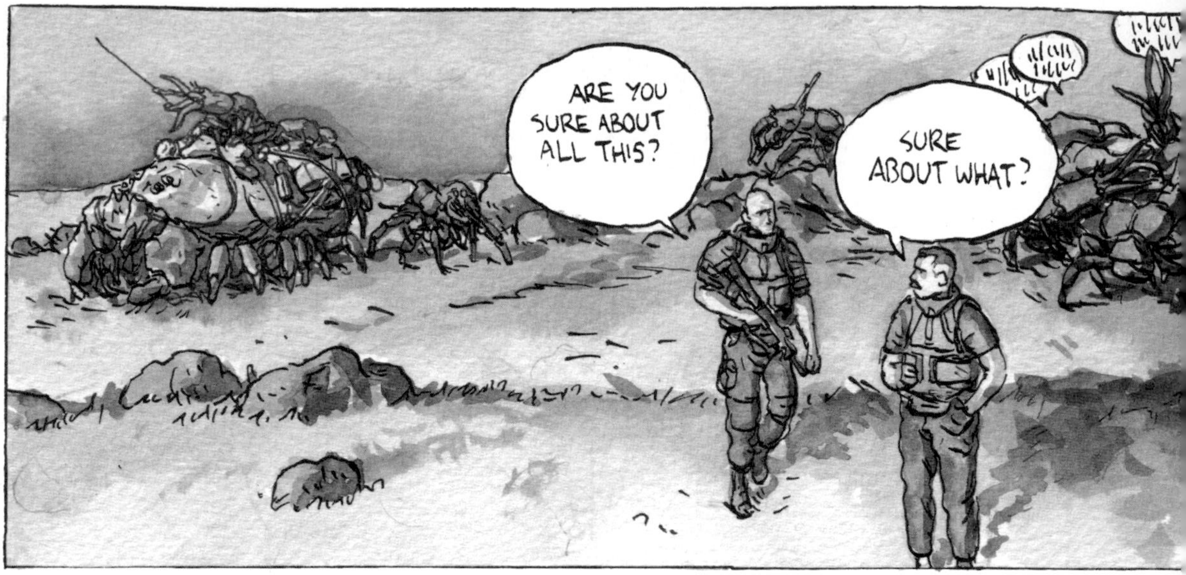
ARE YOU SURE ABOUT ALL THIS?
SURE ABOUT WHAT?

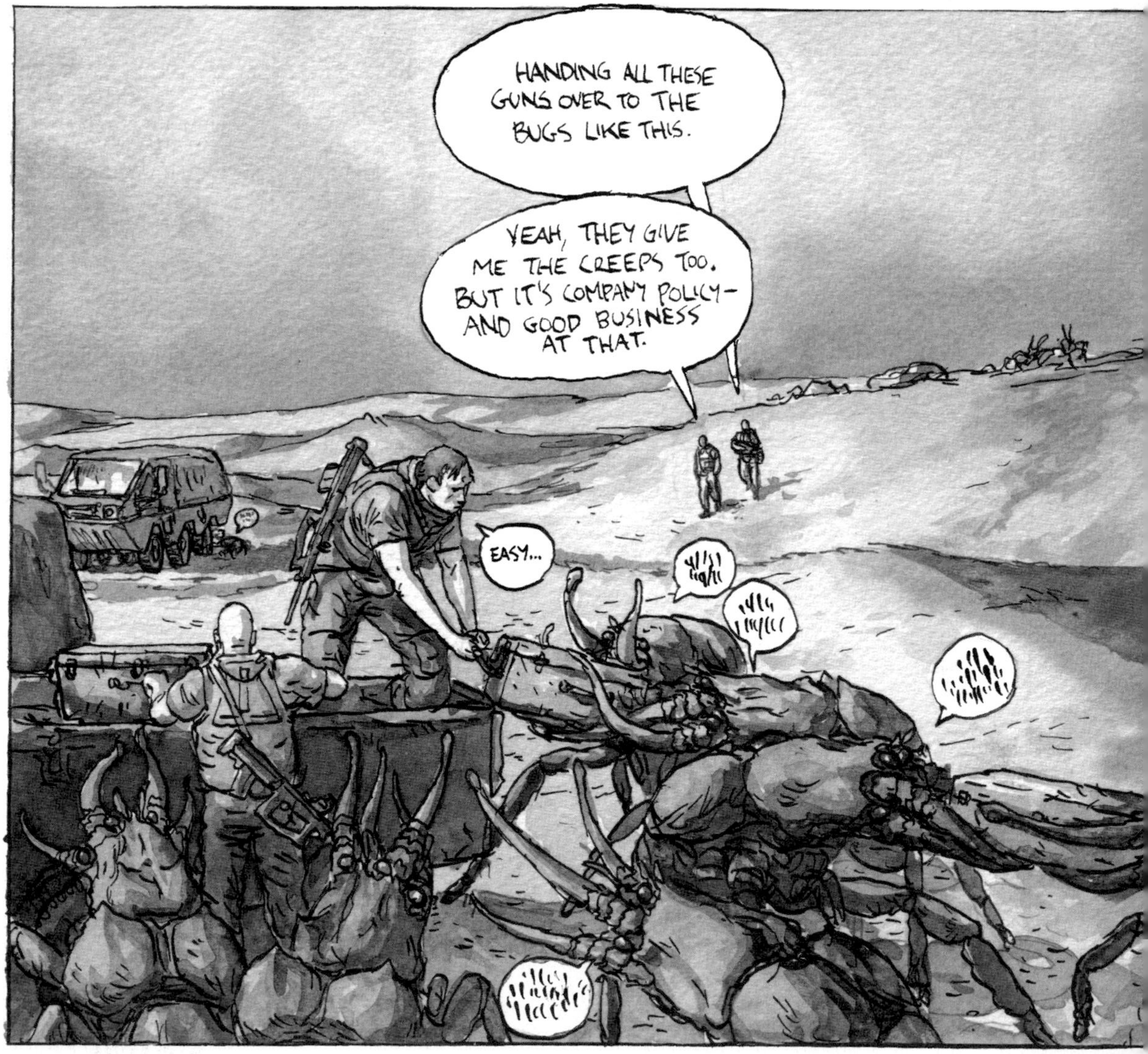
HANDING ALL THESE GUNS OVER TO THE BUGS LIKE THIS.
YEAH, THEY GIVE ME THE CREEPS TOO. BUT IT'S COMPANY POLICY- AND GOOD BUSINESS AT THAT.
EASY...

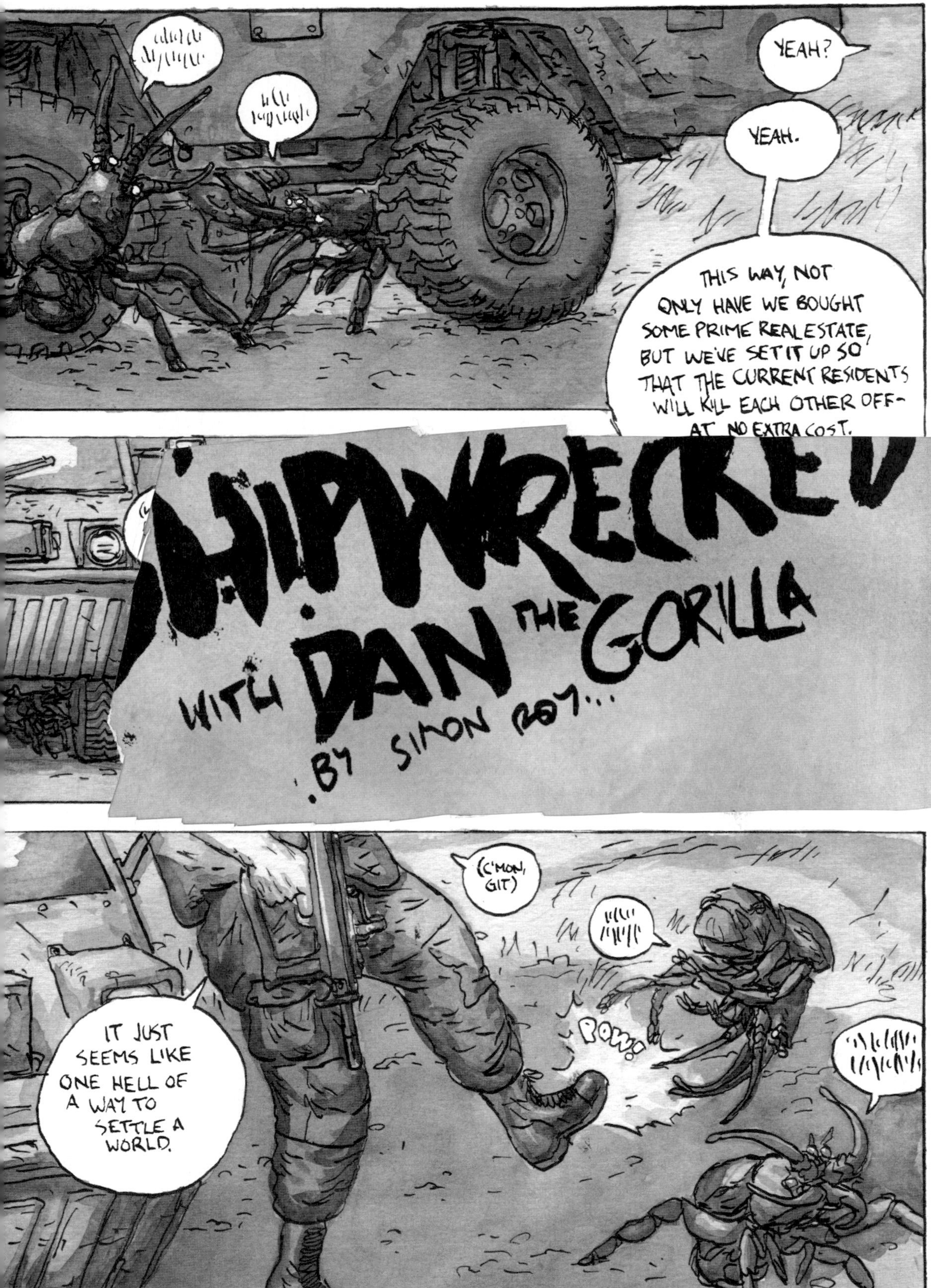
YEAH?
YEAH.
THIS WAY, NOT ONLY HAVE WE BOUGHT SOME PRIME REAL ESTATE, BUT WE'VE SET IT UP SO THAT THE CURRENT RESIDENTS WILL KILL EACH OTHER OFF- AT NO EXTRA COST.
SHIPWRECKED WITH DAN THE GORILLA
.BY SIMON ROY...
(C'MON, GIT)
POW!
IT JUST SEEMS LIKE ONE HELL OF A WAY TO SETTLE A WORLD.

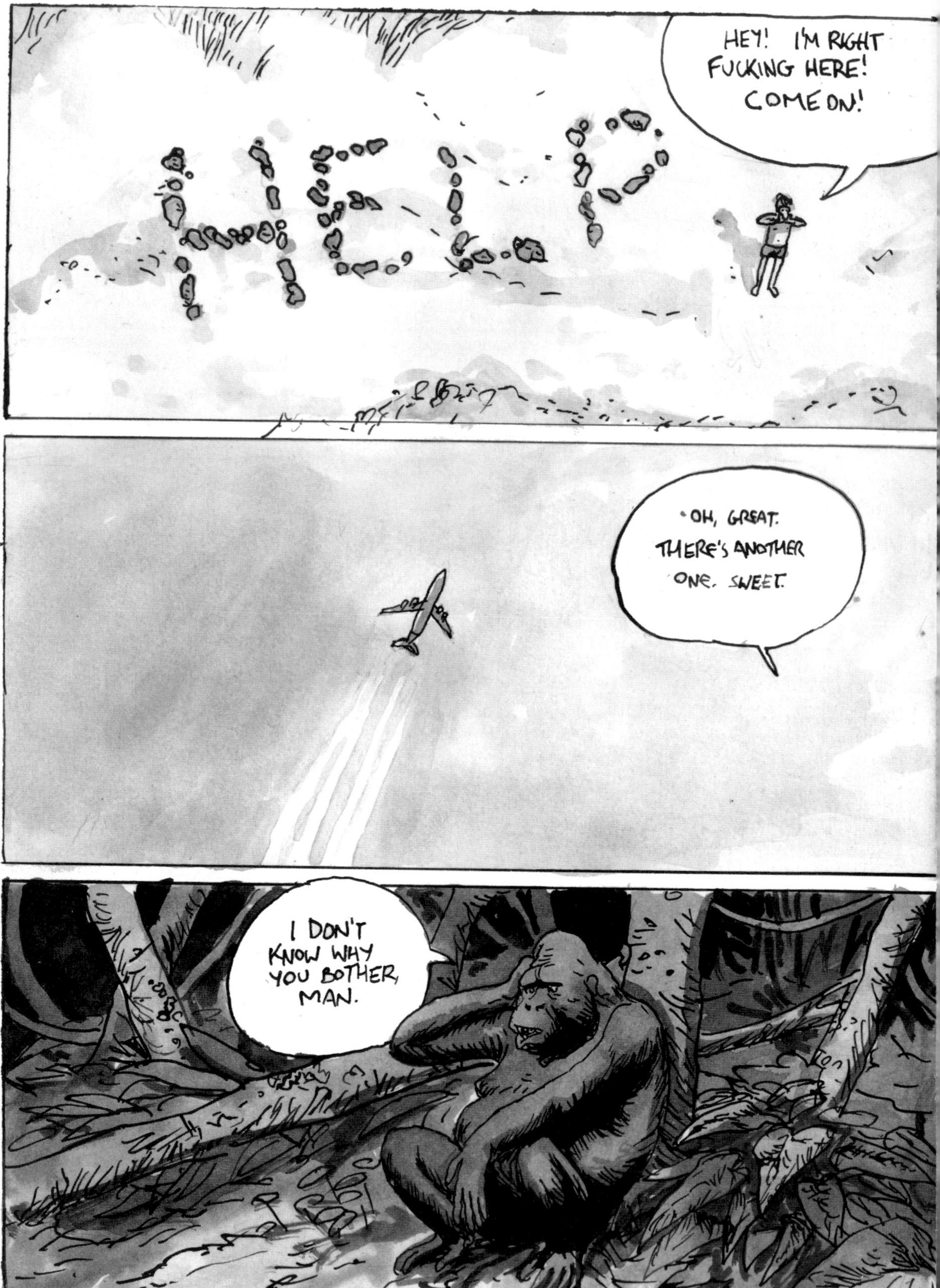
HELP
HEY! I'M RIGHT FUCKING HERE! COME ON!
OH, GREAT. THERE'S ANOTHER ONE. SWEET.
I DON'T KNOW WHY YOU BOTHER, MAN.

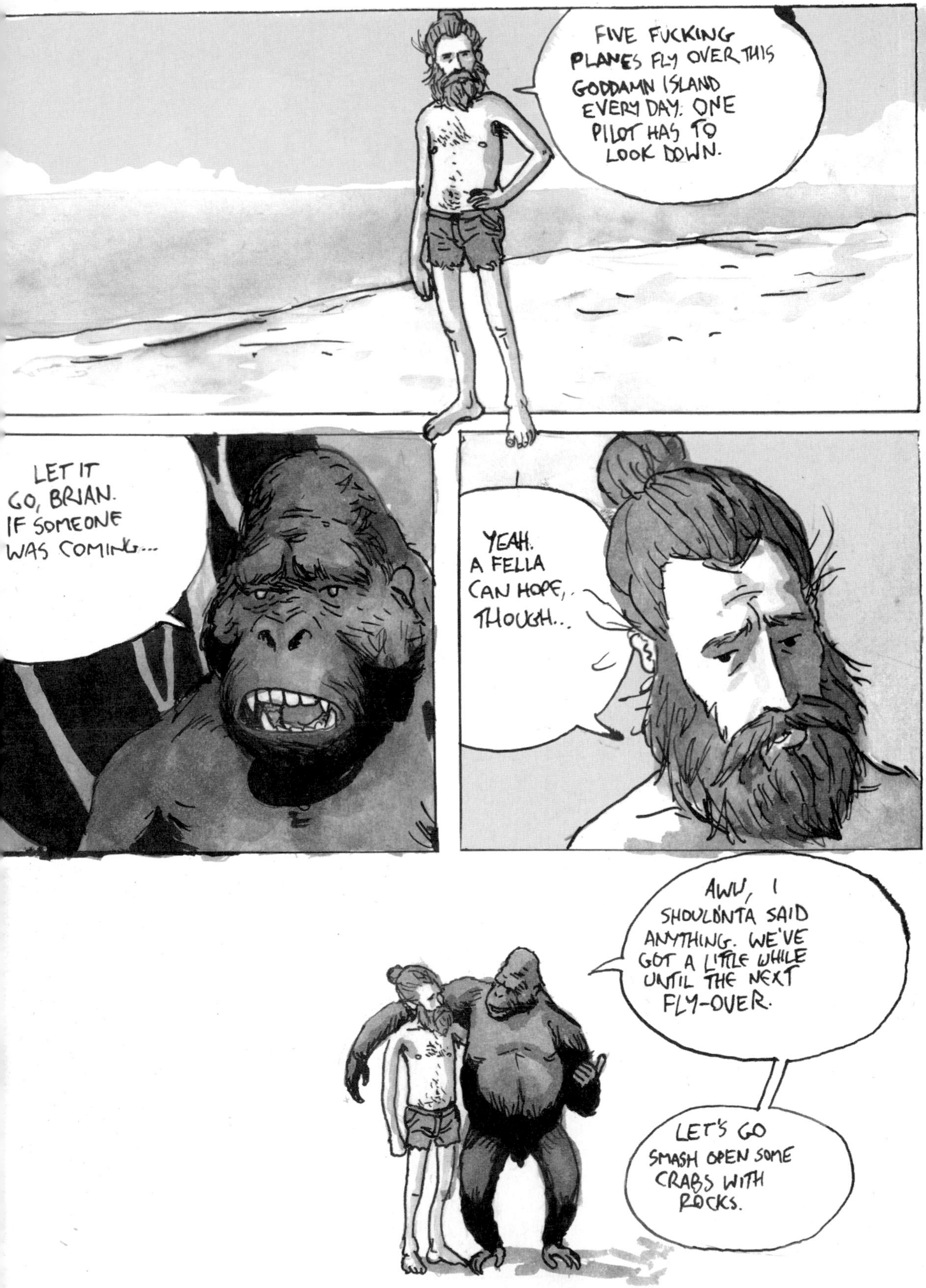
FIVE FUCKING PLANES FLY OVER THIS GODDAMN ISLAND EVERY DAY. ONE PILOT HAS TO LOOK DOWN.
LET IT GO, BRIAN. IF SOMEONE WAS COMING...
YEAH. A FELLA CAN HOPE, THOUGH...
AWW, I SHOULDN'TA SAID ANYTHING. WE'VE GOT A LITTLE WHILE UNTIL THE NEXT FLY-OVER.
LET'S GO SMASH OPEN SOME CRABS WITH ROCKS.

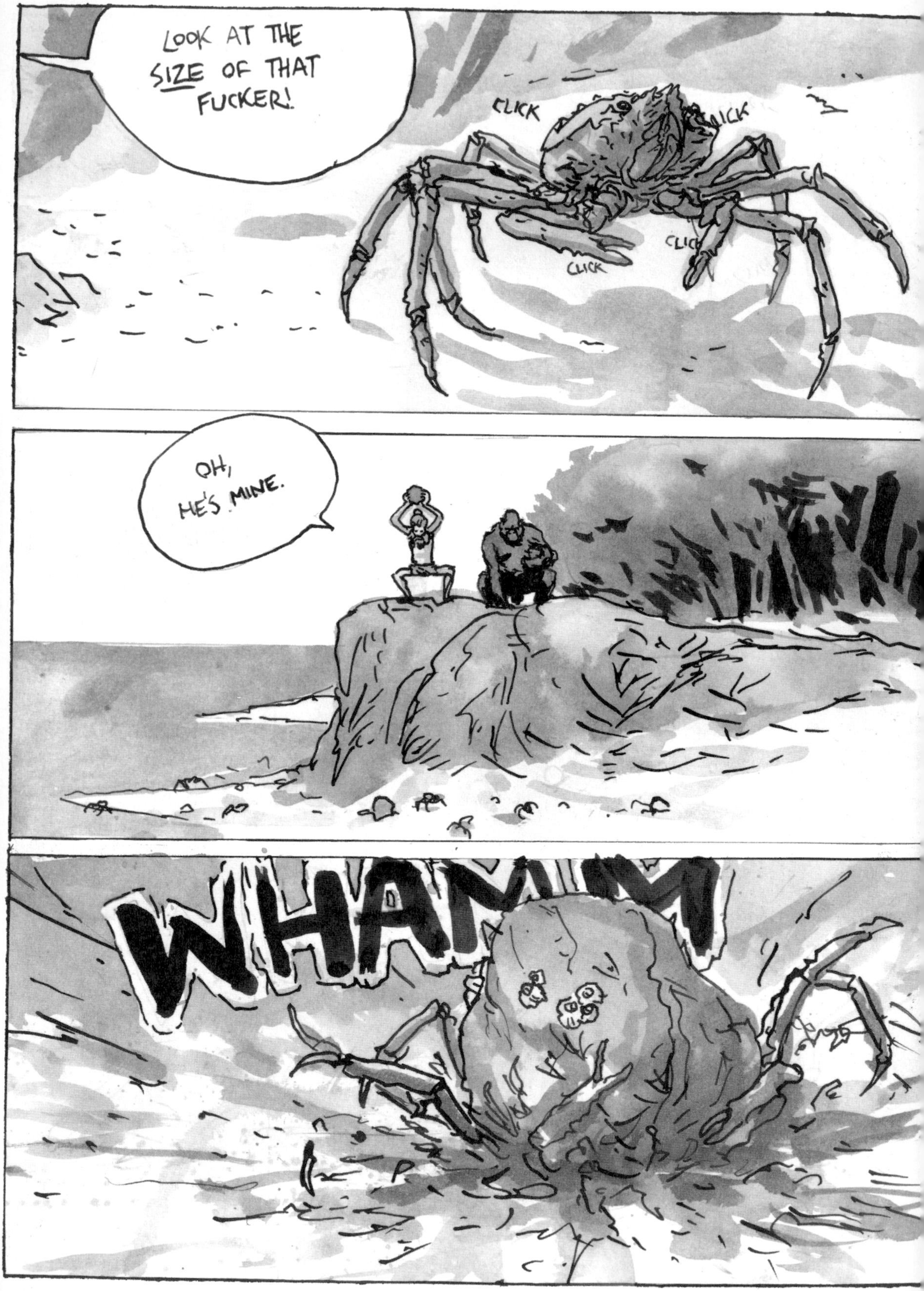
LOOK AT THE SIZE OF THAT FUCKER!
CLICK
CLICK
CLICK
CLICK
OH, HE'S MINE.
WHAMM

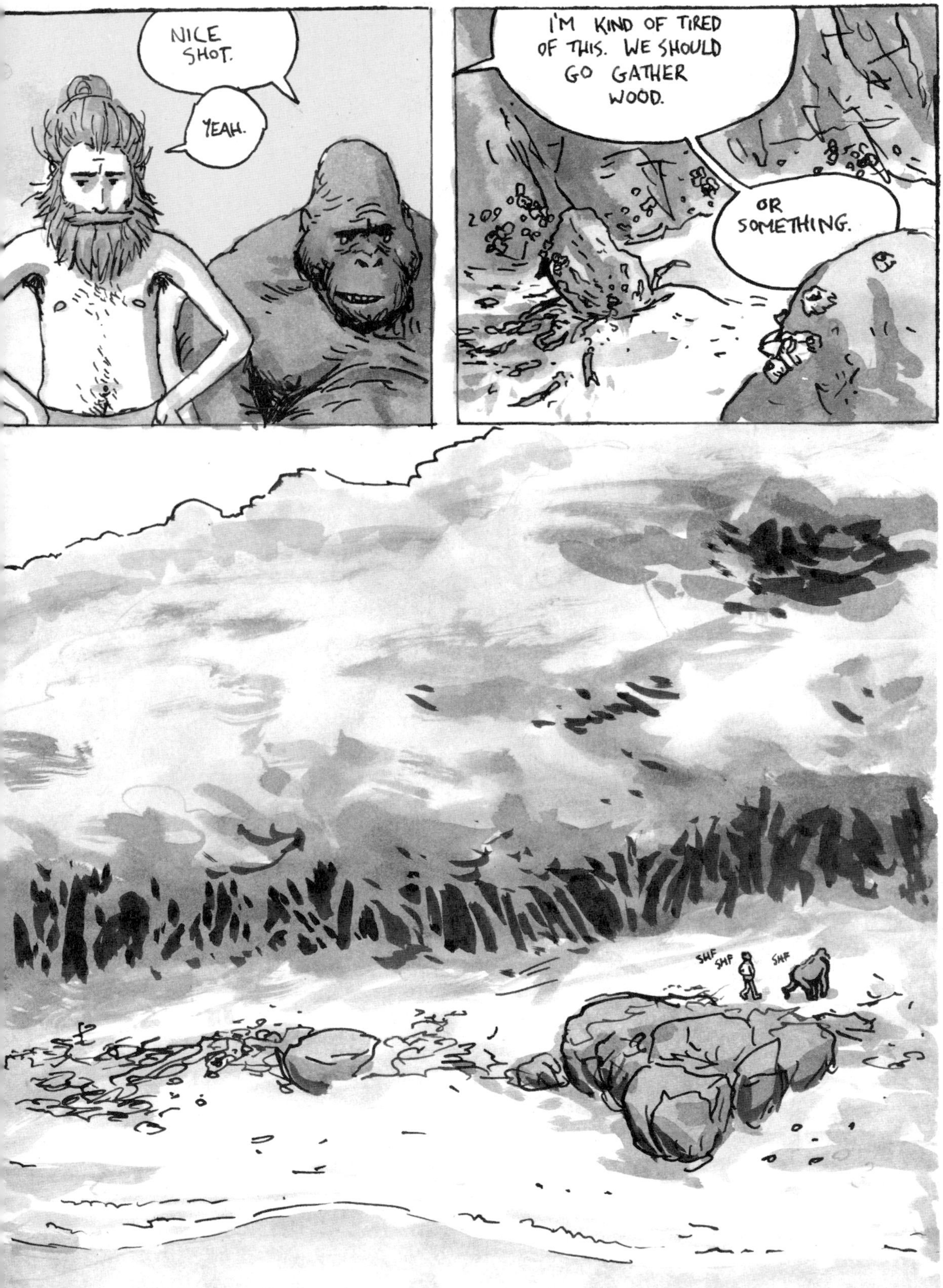
NICE SHOT.
YEAH.
I'M KIND OF TIRED OF THIS. WE SHOULD GO GATHER WOOD.
OR SOMETHING.
SHF
SHF
SHF

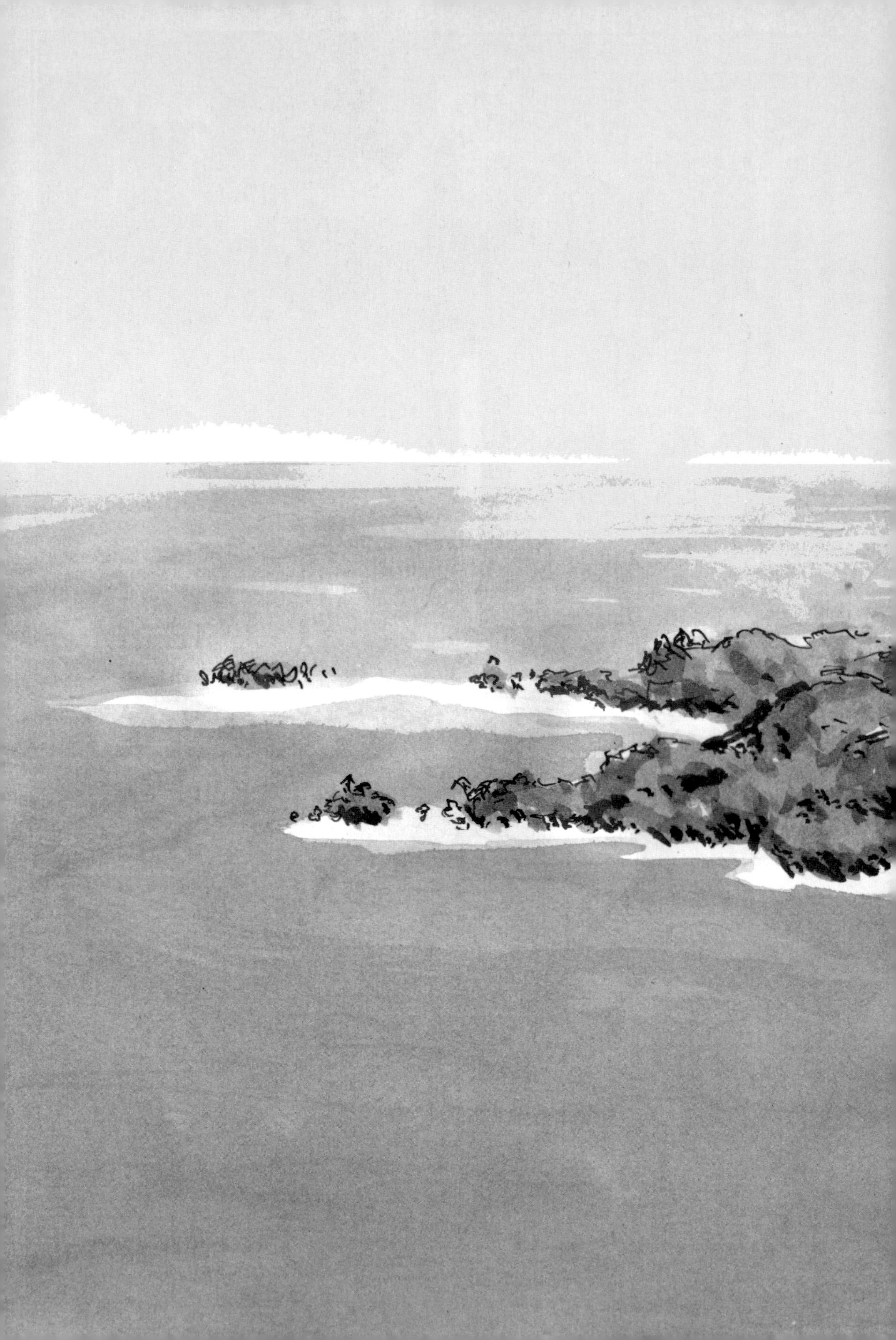

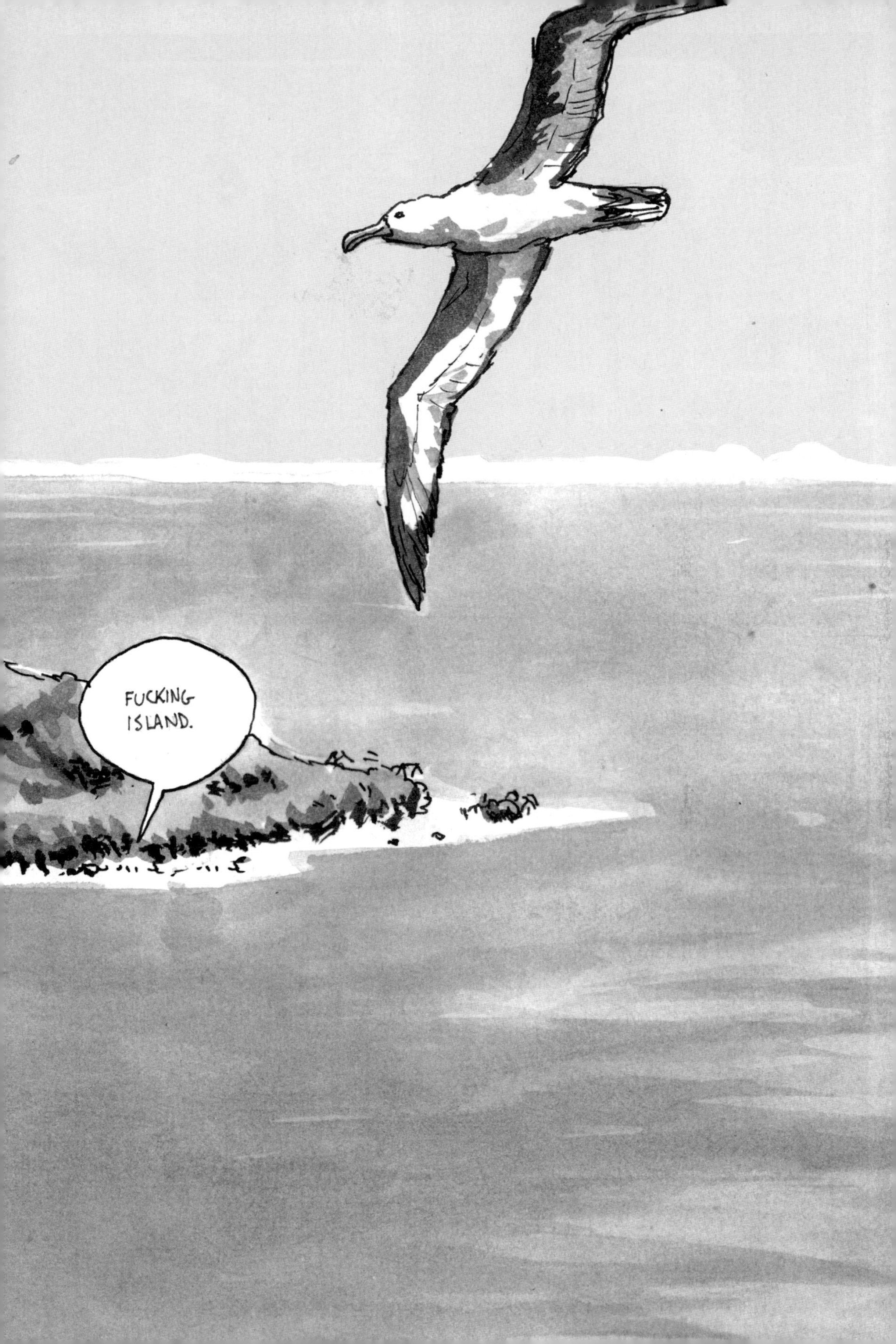
FUCKING ISLAND.

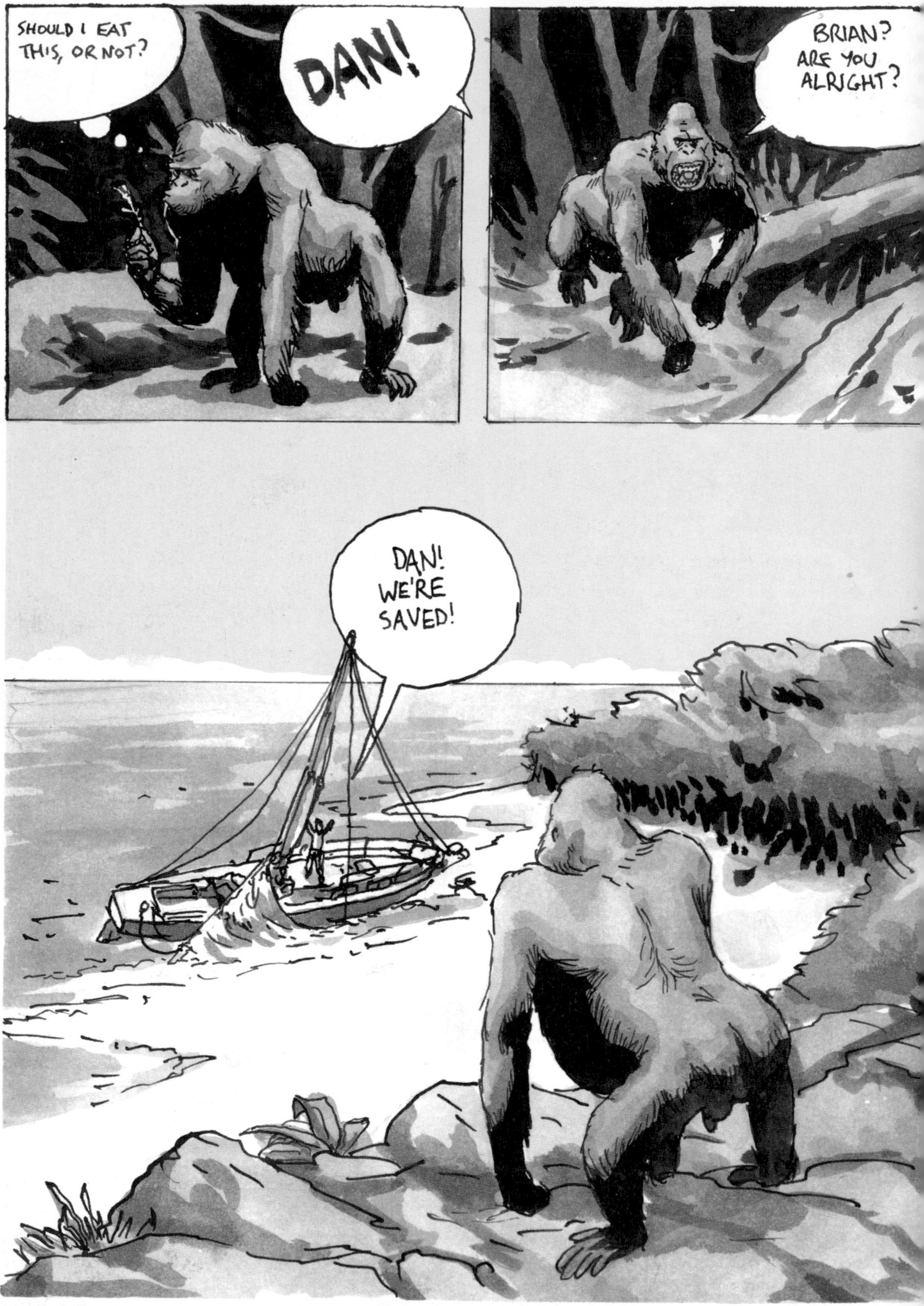
SHOULD I EAT THIS, OR NOT?
DAN!
BRIAN? ARE YOU ALRIGHT?
DAN! WE'RE SAVED!

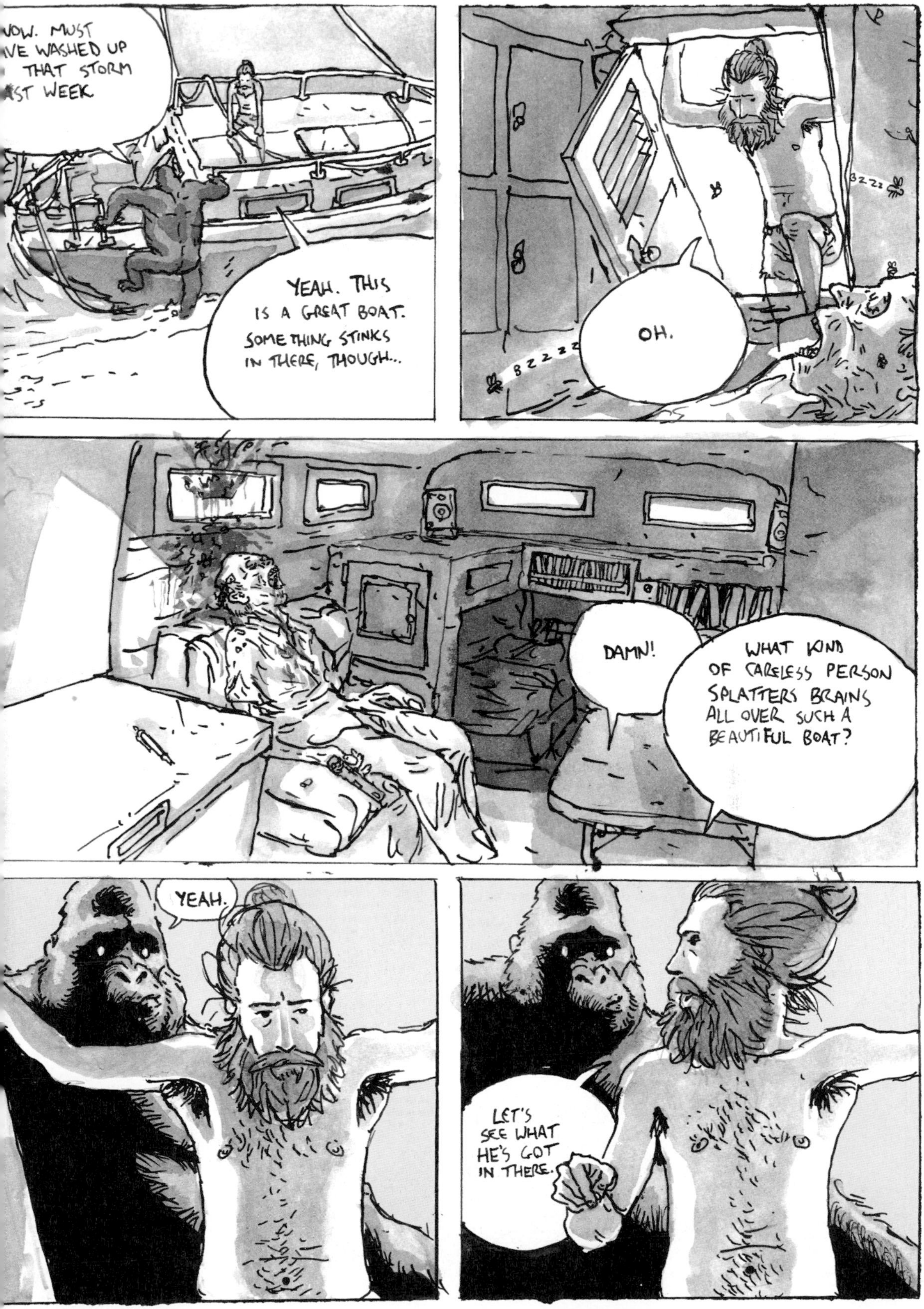
NOW. MUST
VE WASHED UP
THAT STORM
ST WEEK.
YEAH. THIS IS A GREAT BOAT. SOMETHING STINKS IN THERE, THOUGH...
BZZZZ
OH.
BZZZZ
DAMN!
WHAT KIND OF CARELESS PERSON SPLATTERS BRAINS ALL OVER SUCH A BEAUTIFUL BOAT?
YEAH.
LET'S SEE WHAT HE'S GOT IN THERE.

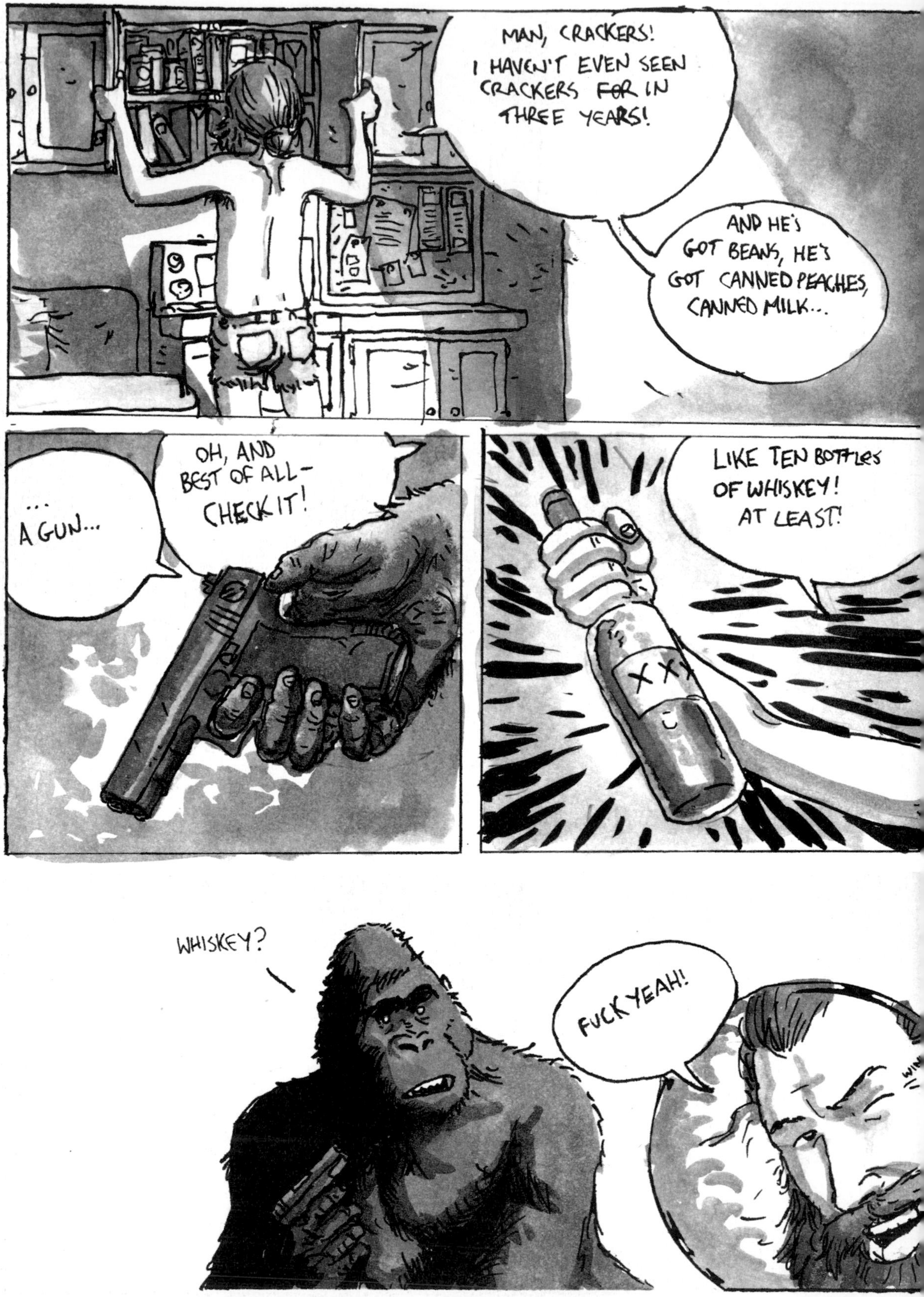
MAN, CRACKERS! I HAVEN'T EVEN SEEN CRACKERS ~~FOR~~ IN THREE YEARS!
AND HE'S GOT BEANS, HE'S GOT CANNED PEACHES, CANNED MILK...
OH, AND BEST OF ALL- CHECK IT!
... A GUN...
LIKE TEN BOTTLES OF WHISKEY! AT LEAST!
WHISKEY?
FUCK YEAH!

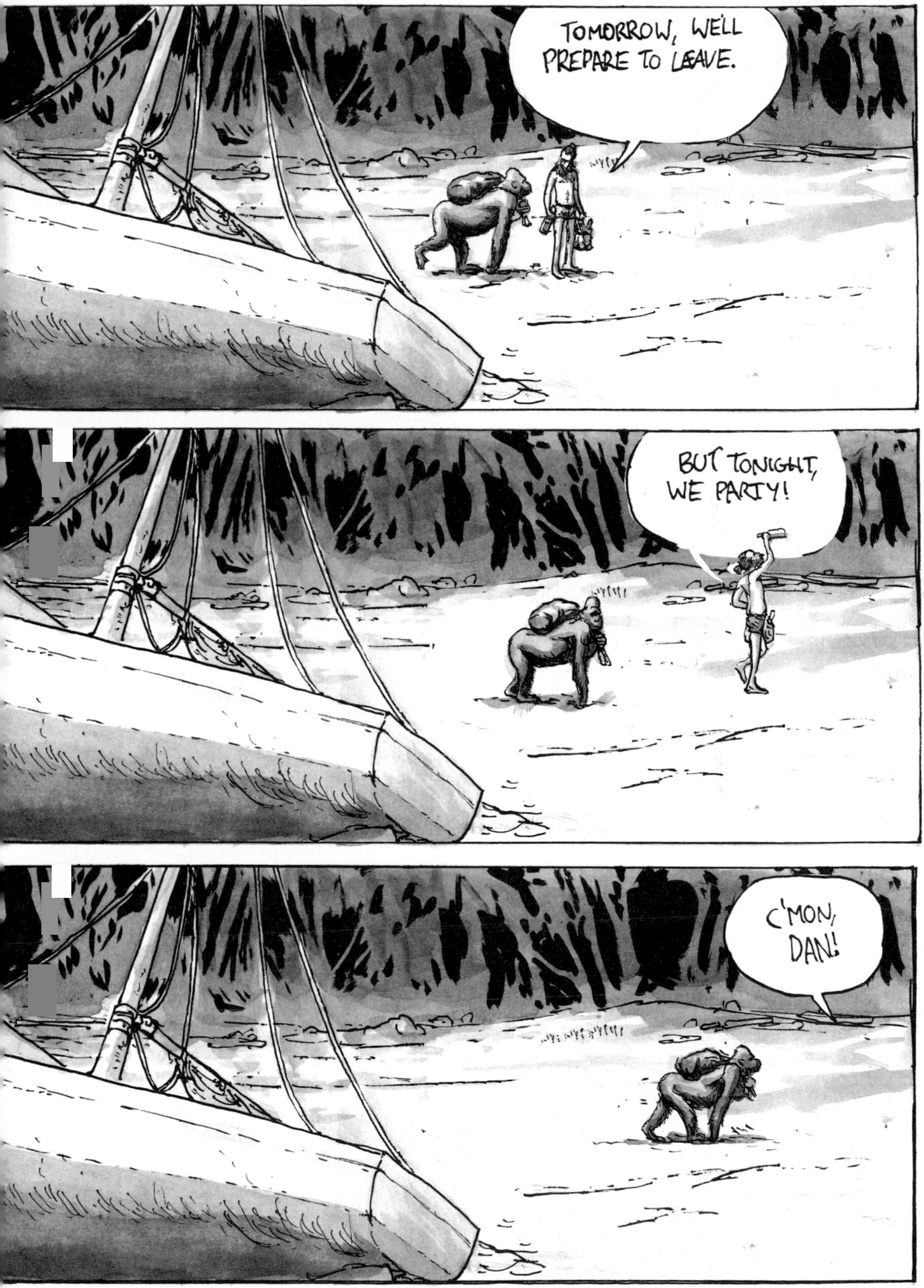
TOMORROW, WE'LL PREPARE TO LEAVE.
BUT TONIGHT, WE PARTY!
C'MON, DAN!

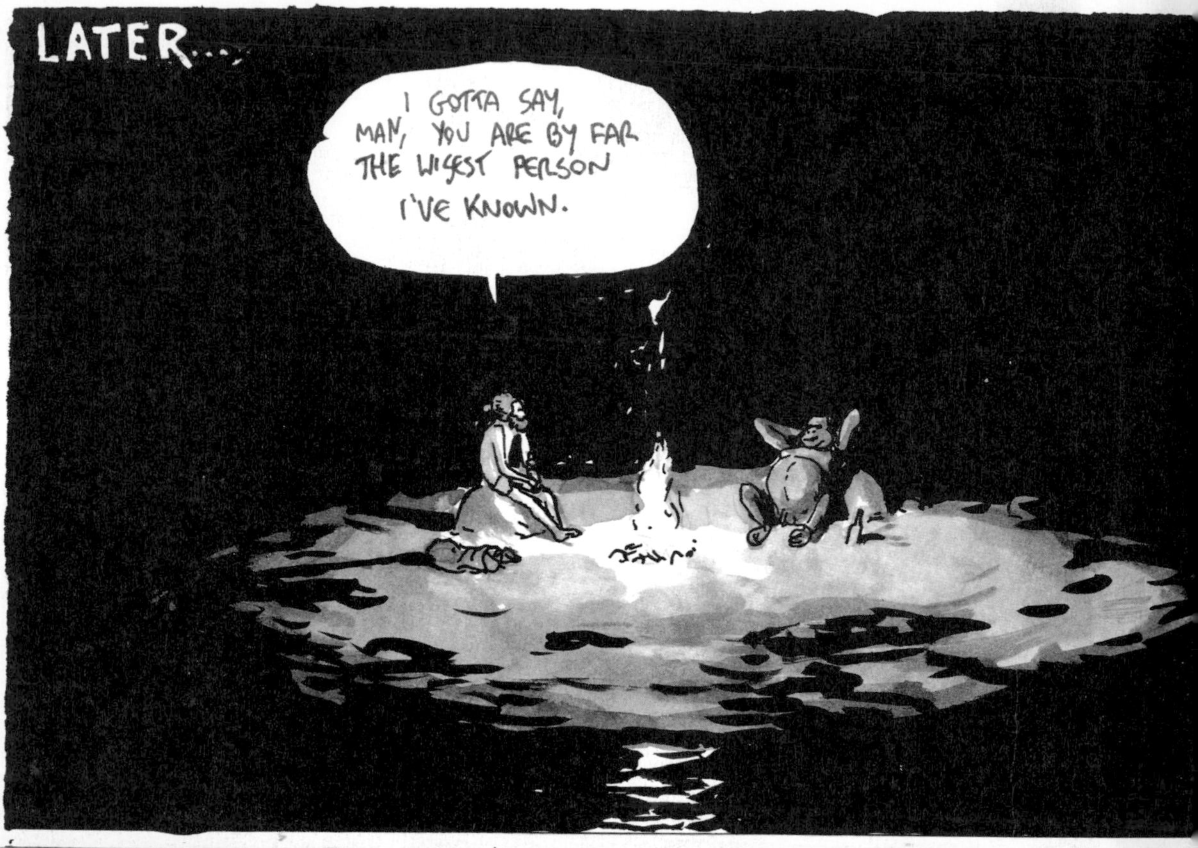
LATER...
I GOTTA SAY, MAN, YOU ARE BY FAR THE WISEST PERSON I'VE KNOWN.

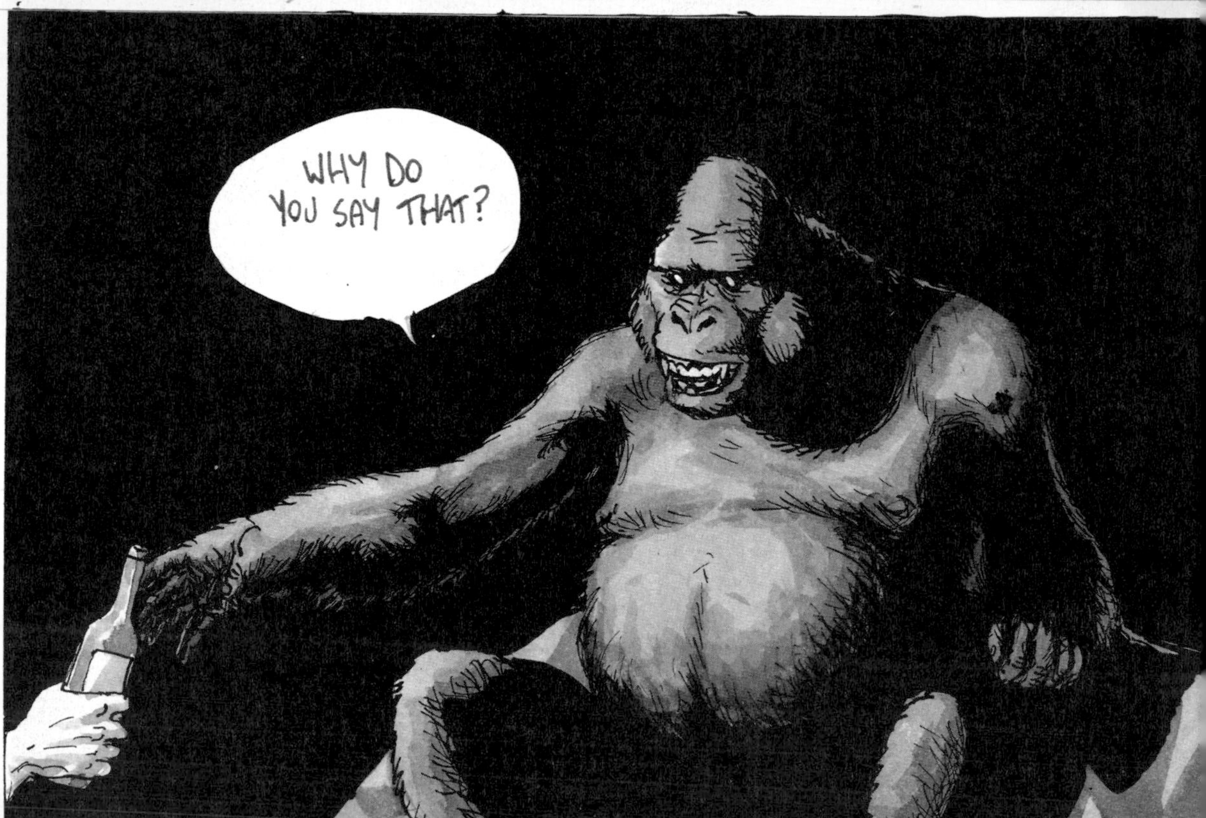
WHY DO YOU SAY THAT?

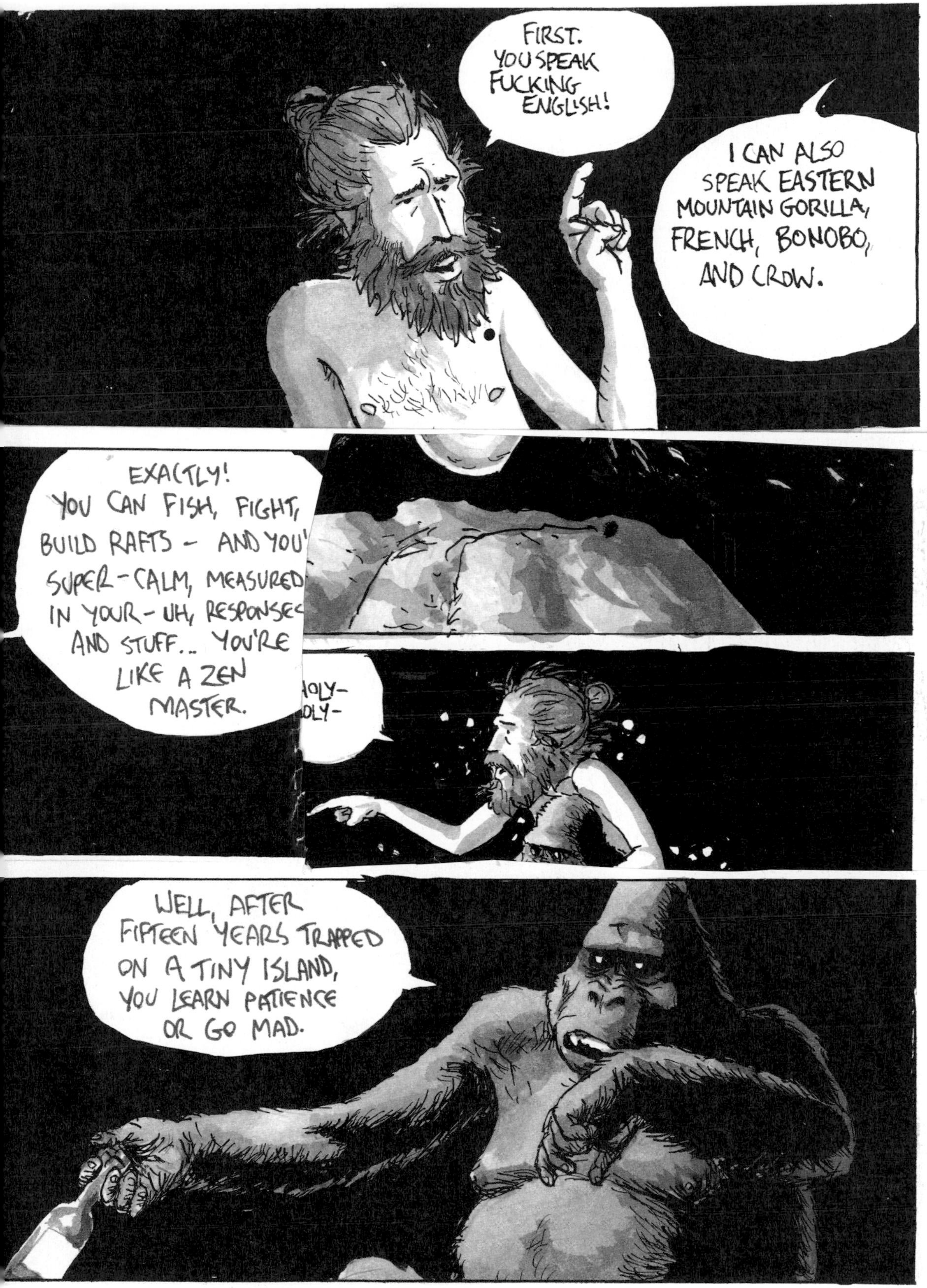
FIRST. YOU SPEAK FUCKING ENGLISH!
I CAN ALSO SPEAK EASTERN MOUNTAIN GORILLA, FRENCH, BONOBO, AND CROW.
EXACTLY! YOU CAN FISH, FIGHT, BUILD RAFTS - AND YOU' SUPER-CALM, MEASURED IN YOUR- UH, RESPONSES AND STUFF... YOU'RE LIKE A ZEN MASTER.
HOLY-
OLY-
WELL, AFTER FIFTEEN YEARS TRAPPED ON A TINY ISLAND, YOU LEARN PATIENCE OR GO MAD.

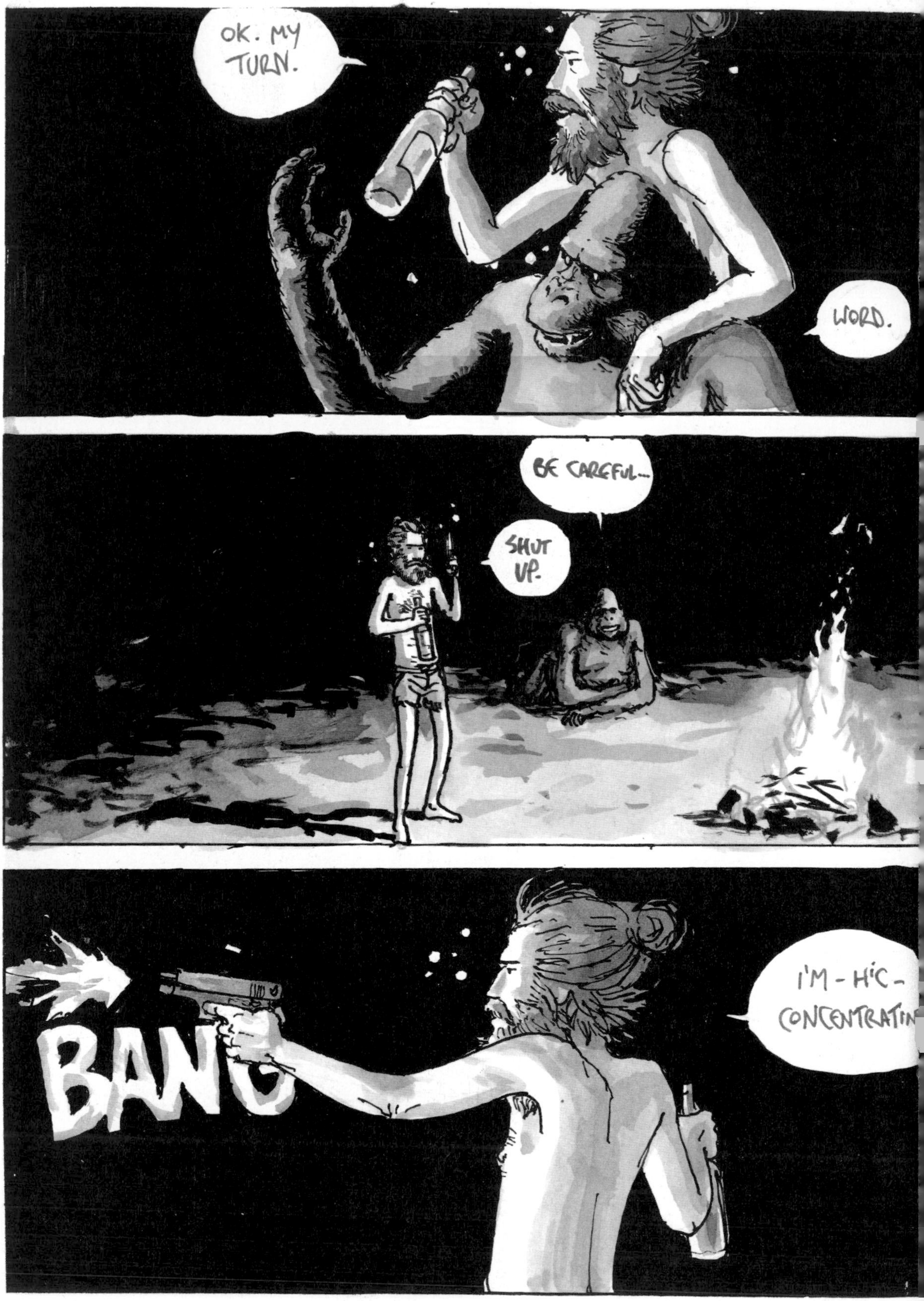

OK. MY TURN.
WORD.
BE CAREFUL...
SHUT UP.
BANG
I'M - H'C - CONCENTRATIN

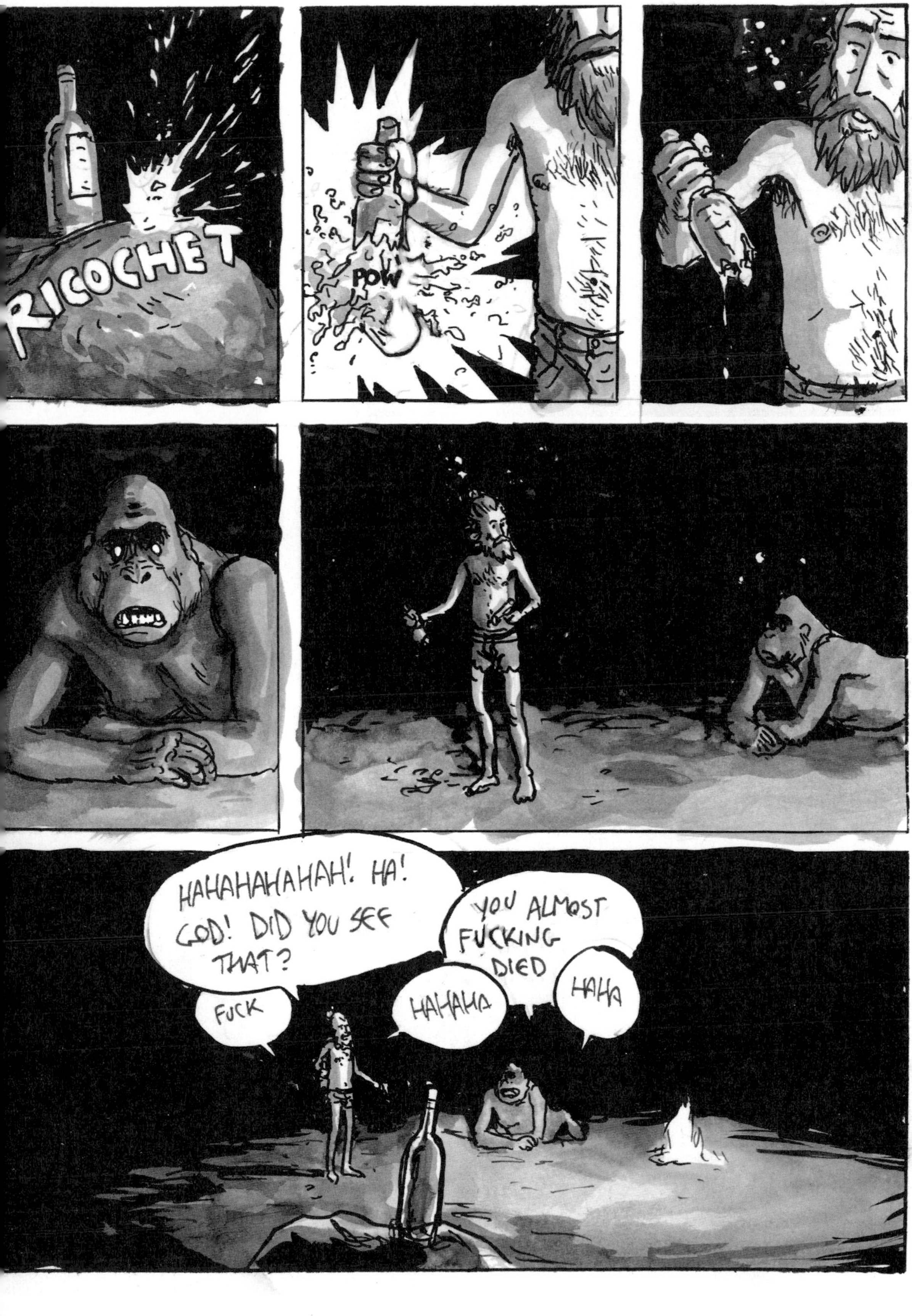
RICOCHET
POW
HAHAHAHAHAH! HA! GOD! DID YOU SEE THAT?
YOU ALMOST FUCKING DIED
FUCK
HAHAHA
HAHA

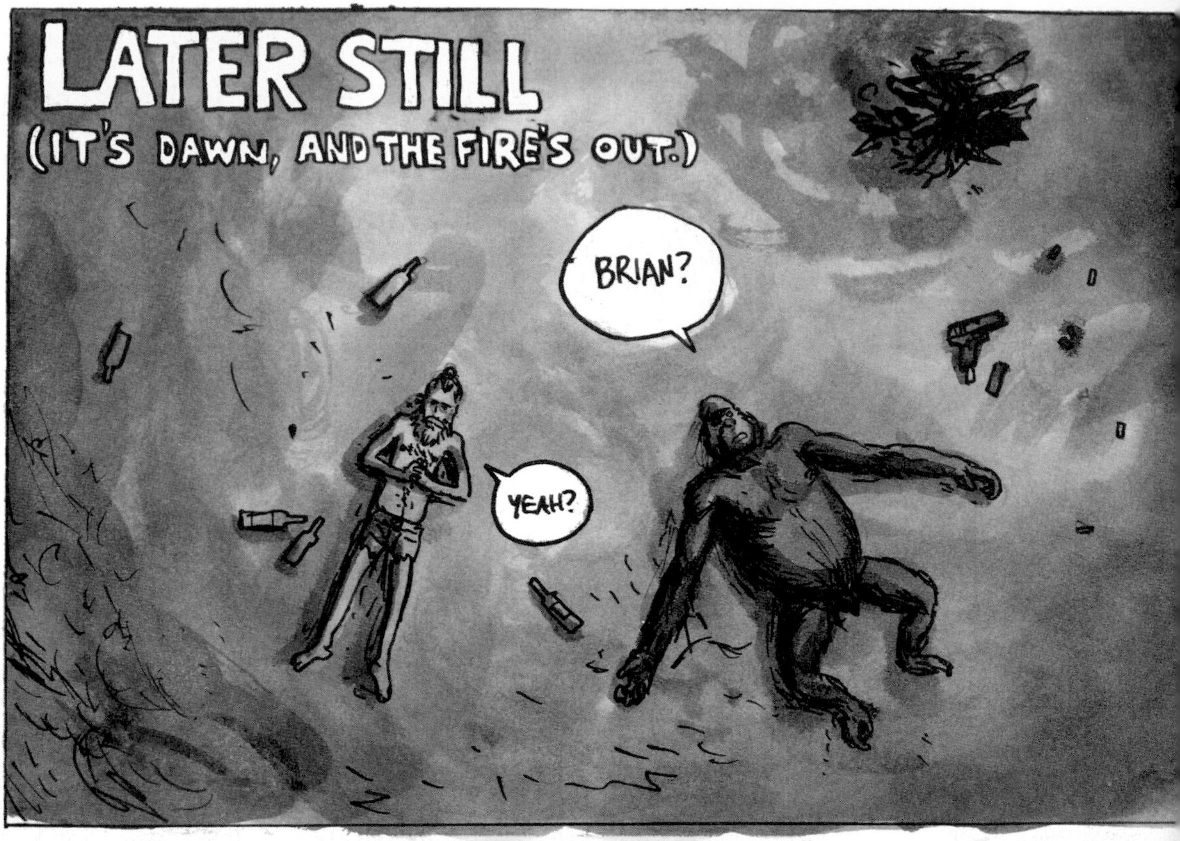
LATER STILL
(IT'S DAWN, AND THE FIRE'S OUT.)
BRIAN?
YEAH?

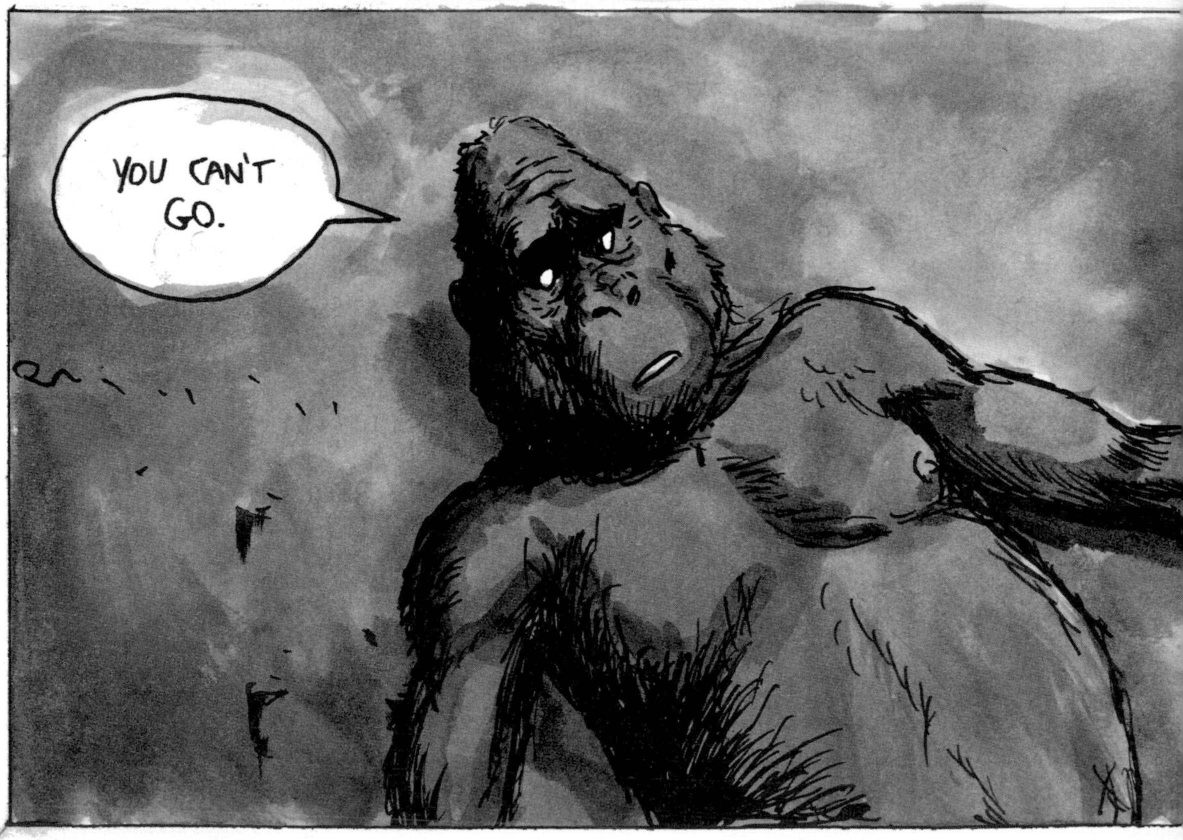
YOU CAN'T GO.

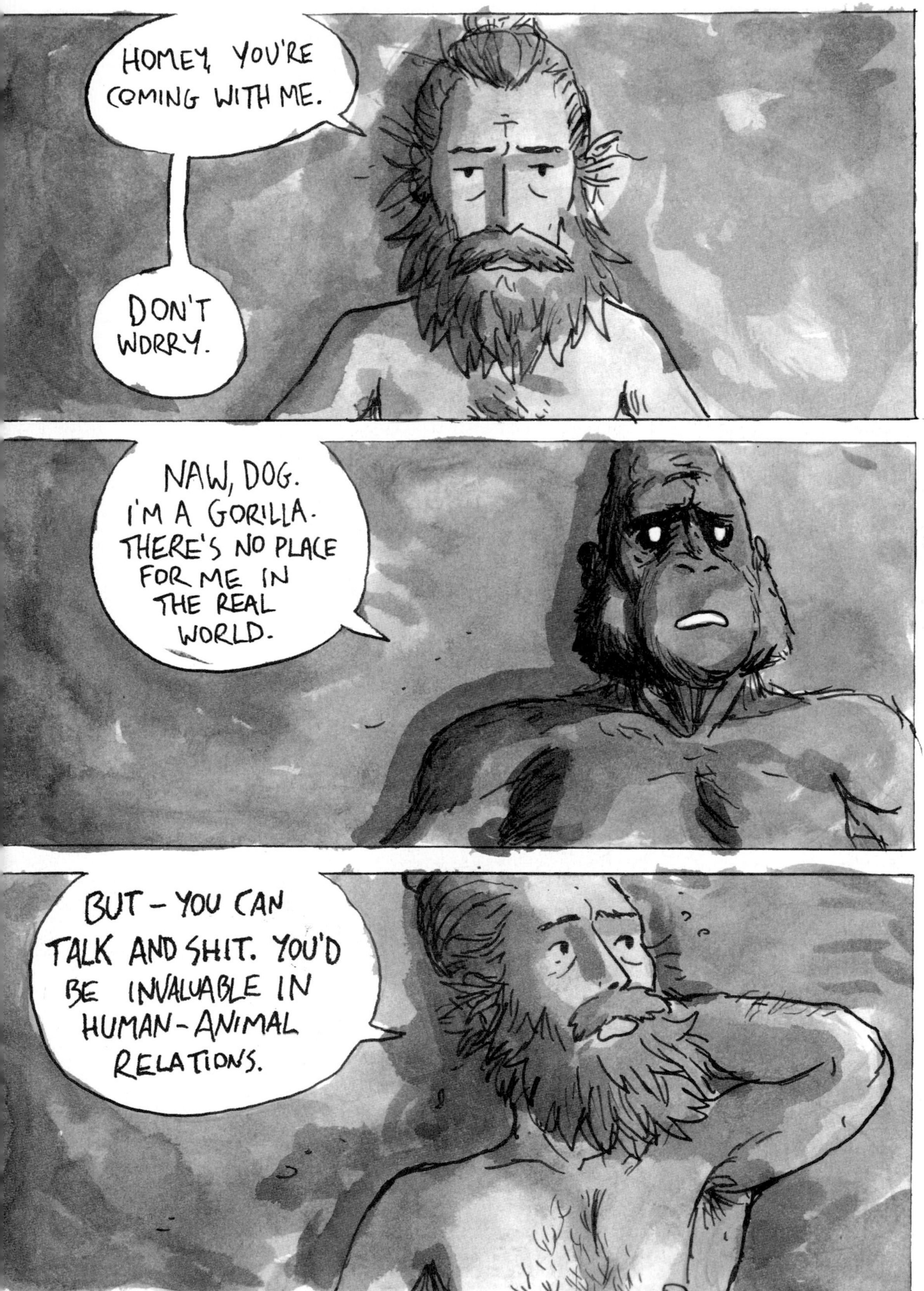
HOMEY, YOU'RE COMING WITH ME.
DON'T WORRY.
NAW, DOG. I'M A GORILLA. THERE'S NO PLACE FOR ME IN THE REAL WORLD.
BUT - YOU CAN TALK AND SHIT. YOU'D BE INVALUABLE IN HUMAN-ANIMAL RELATIONS.

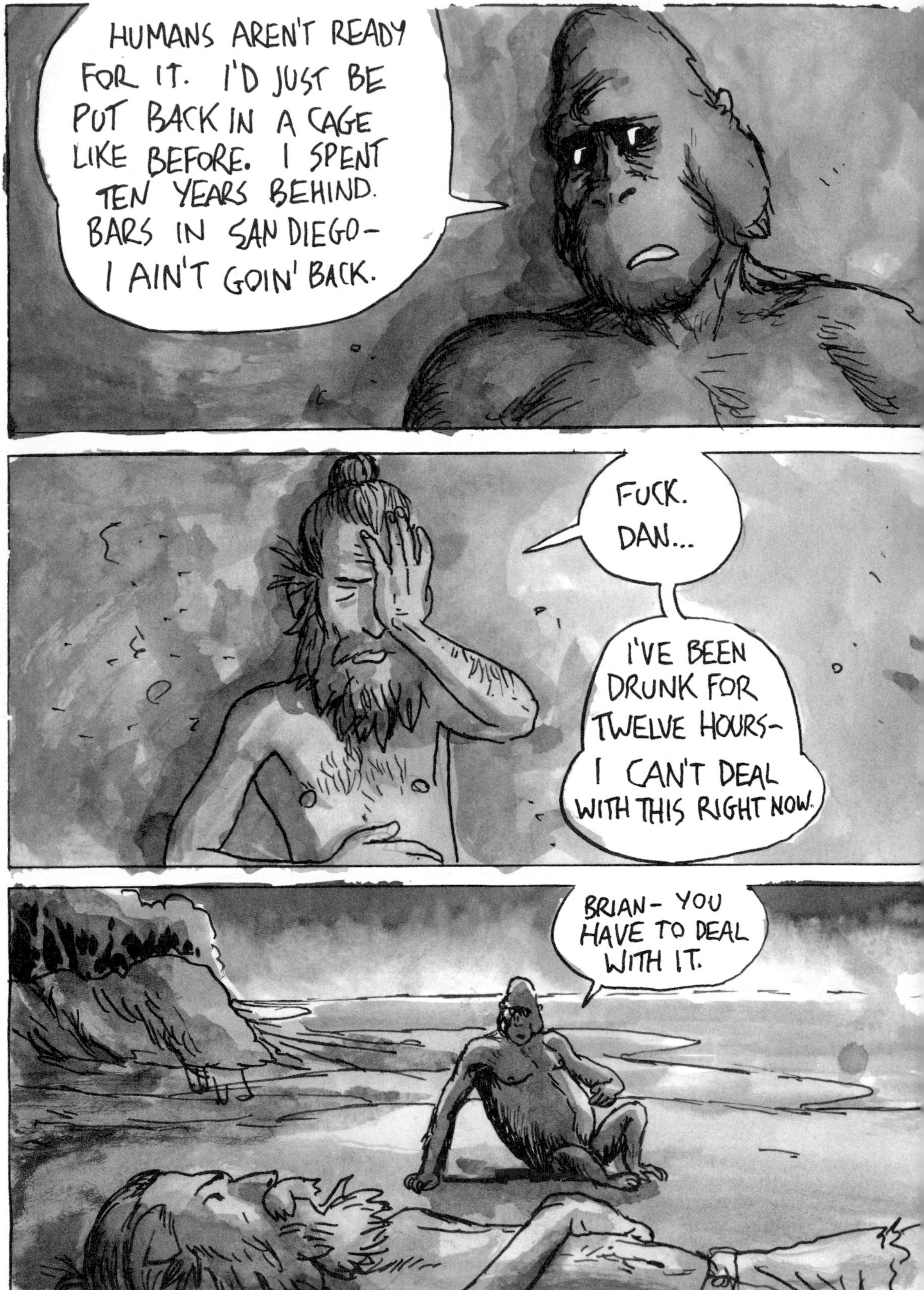
HUMANS AREN'T READY FOR IT. I'D JUST BE PUT BACK IN A CAGE LIKE BEFORE. I SPENT TEN YEARS BEHIND BARS IN SAN DIEGO- I AIN'T GOIN' BACK.
FUCK. DAN...
I'VE BEEN DRUNK FOR TWELVE HOURS- I CAN'T DEAL WITH THIS RIGHT NOW.
BRIAN- YOU HAVE TO DEAL WITH IT.

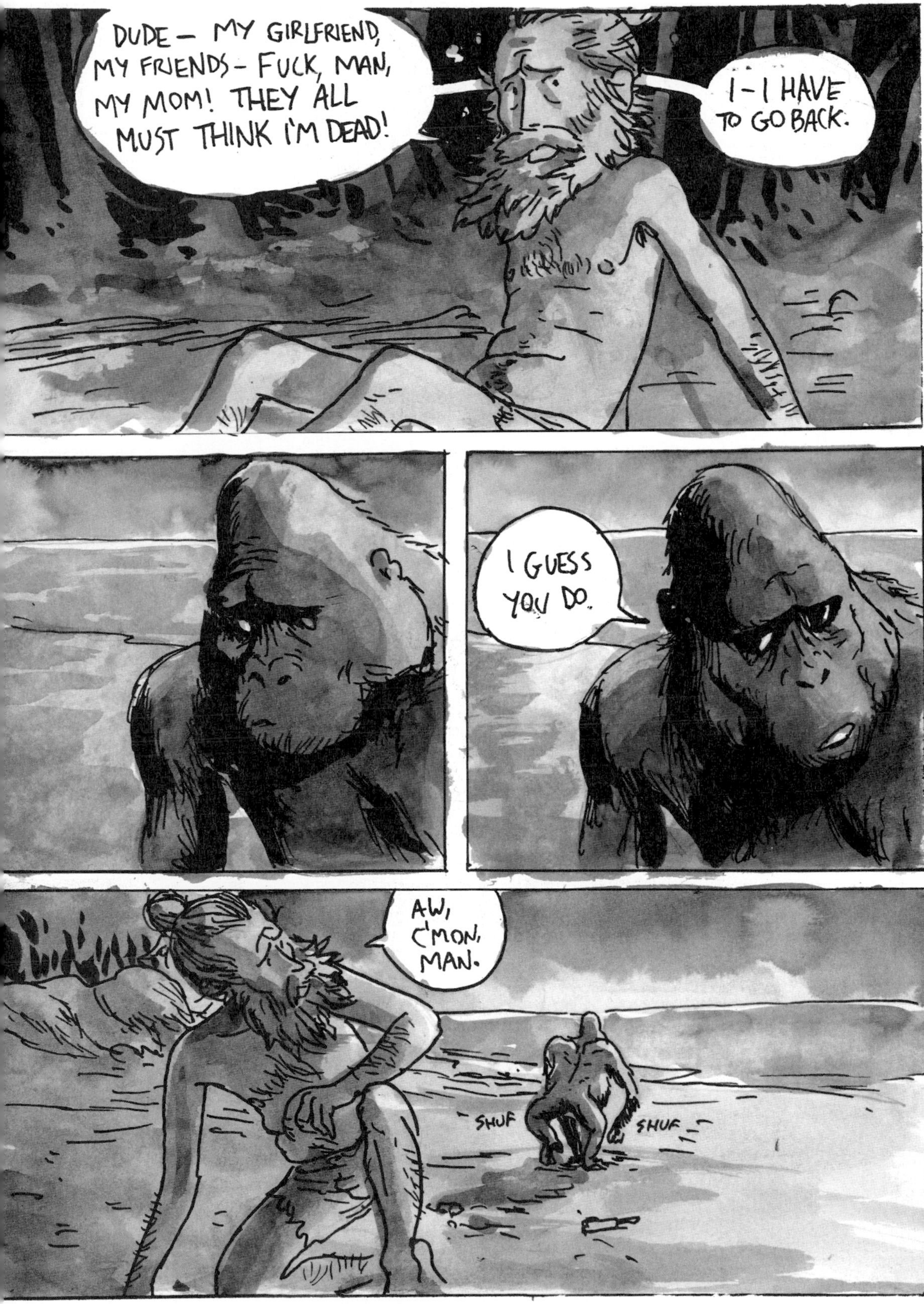
DUDE— MY GIRLFRIEND, MY FRIENDS- FUCK, MAN, MY MOM! THEY ALL MUST THINK I'M DEAD!
I-I HAVE TO GO BACK.
I GUESS YOU DO.
AW, C'MON, MAN.
SHUF
SHUF

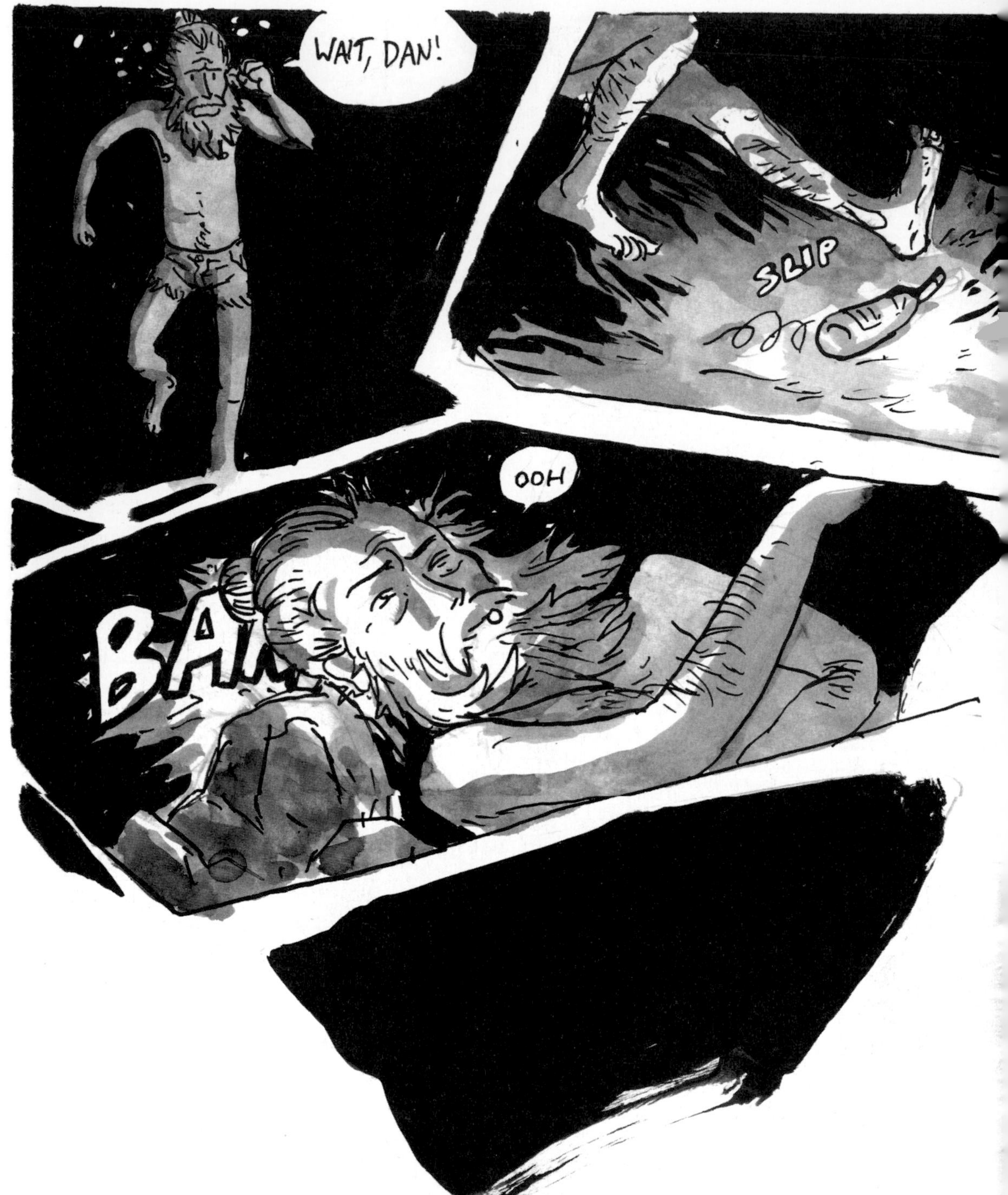
WAIT, DAN!
SLIP
OOH
BA

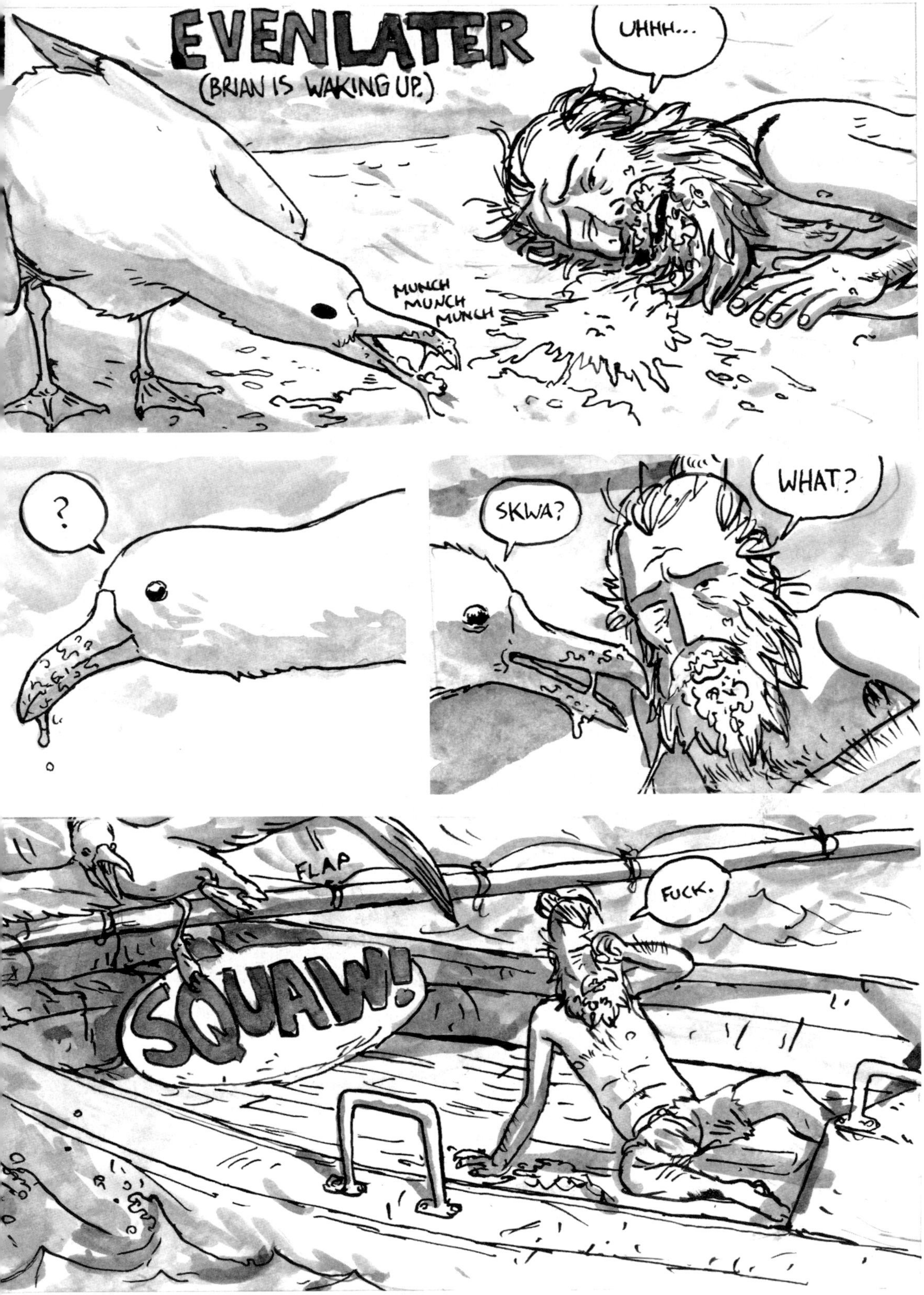
EVENLATER
(BRIAN IS WAKING UP.)
UHHH...
MUNCH MUNCH MUNCH
?
SKWA?
WHAT?
FLAP
FUCK.
SQUAW!

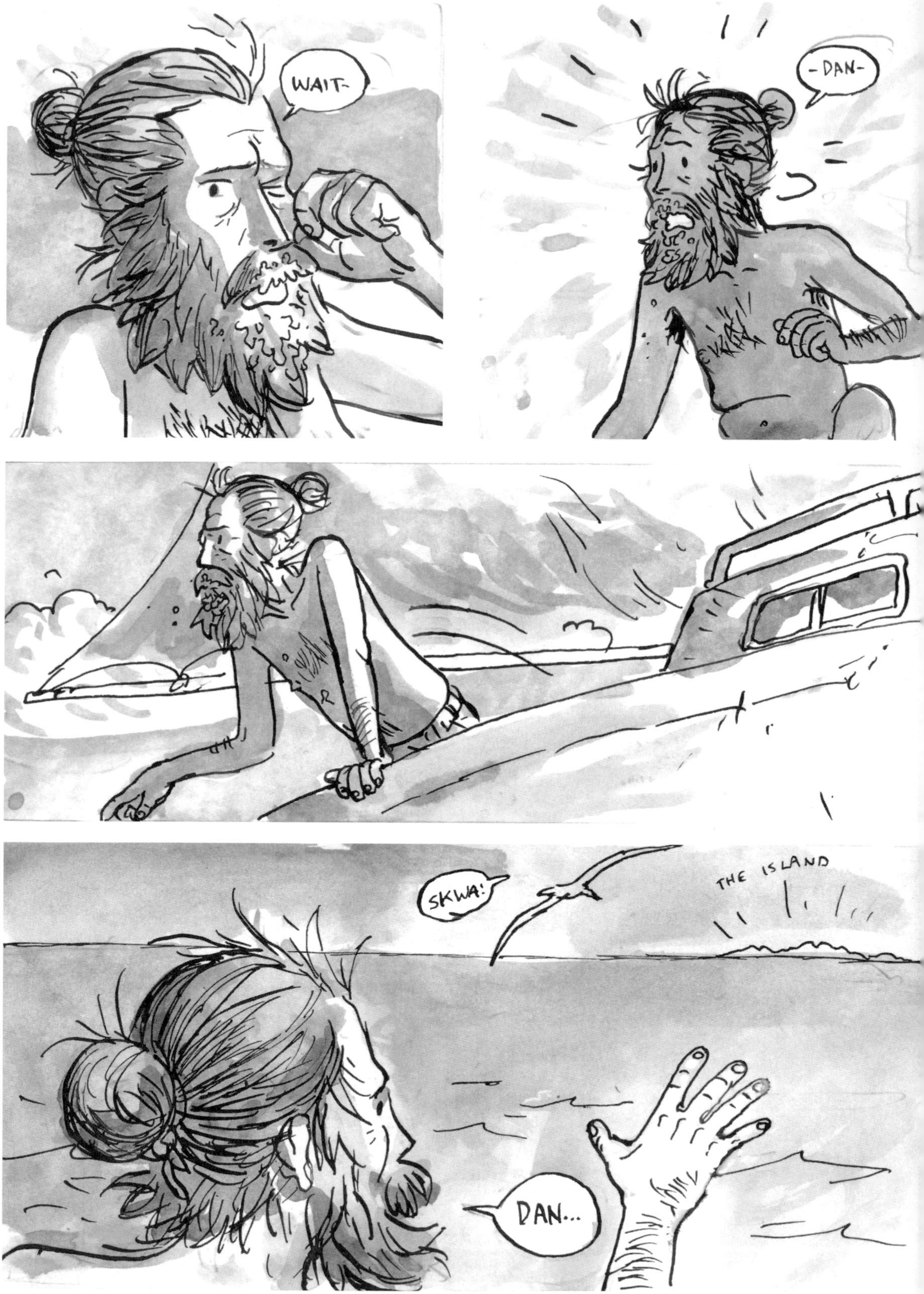
WAIT-
-DAN-
SKWA!
THE ISLAND
DAN...

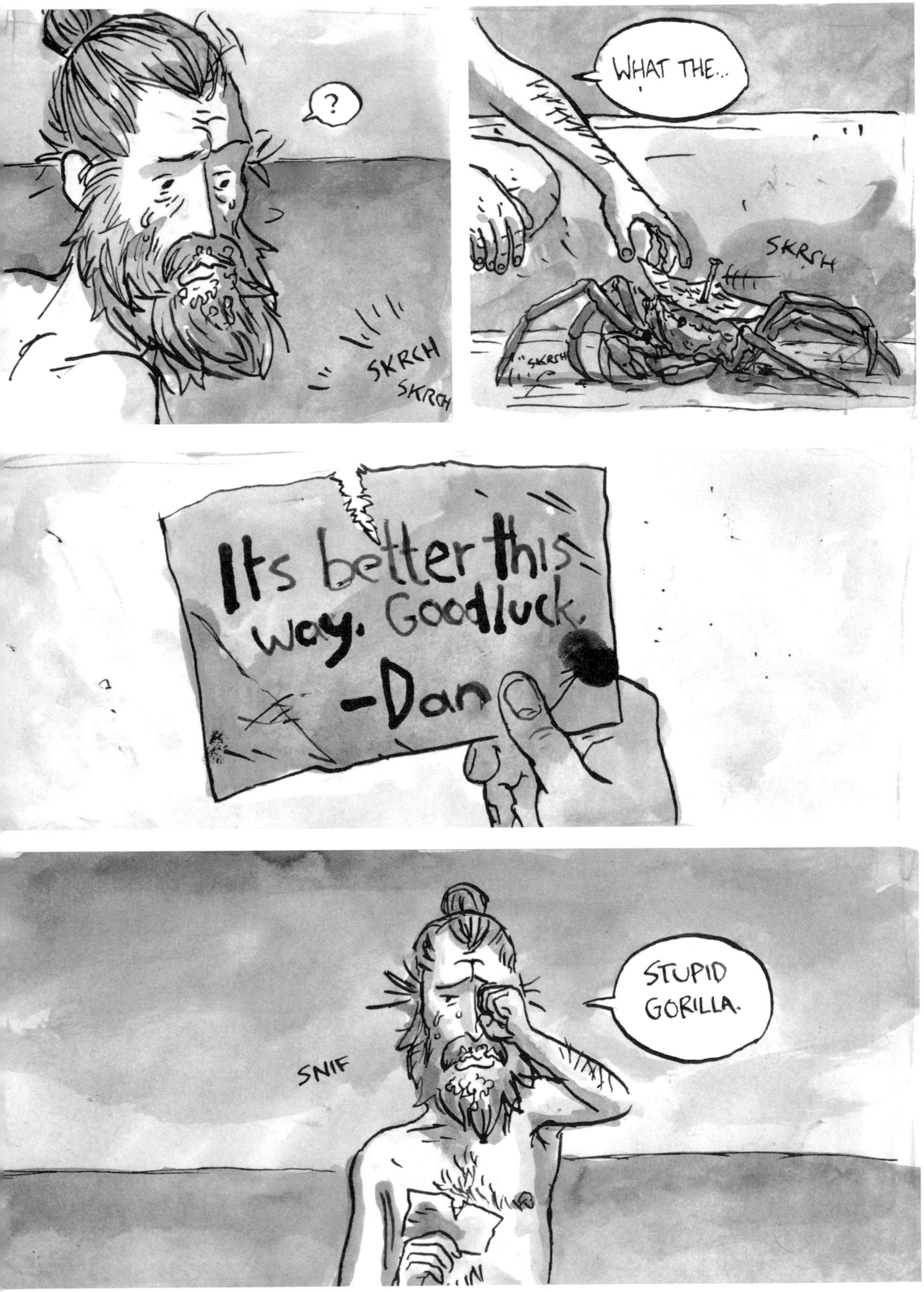
?
SKRCH
SKRCH
WHAT THE...
SKRSH
SKRSH
Its better this way. Goodluck. -Dan
SNIF
STUPID GORILLA.

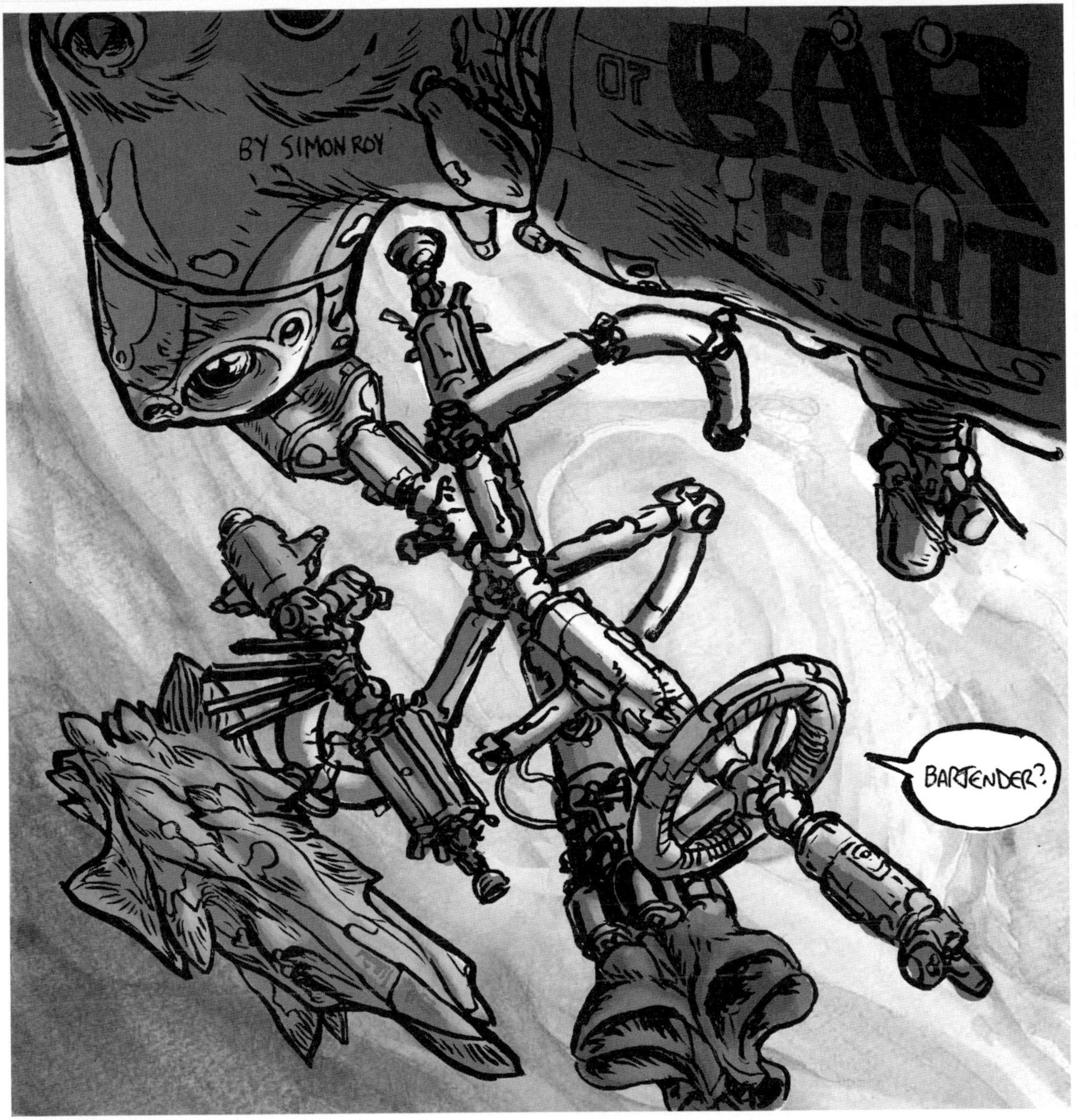
07
BAR FIGHT
BY SIMON ROY
BARTENDER?

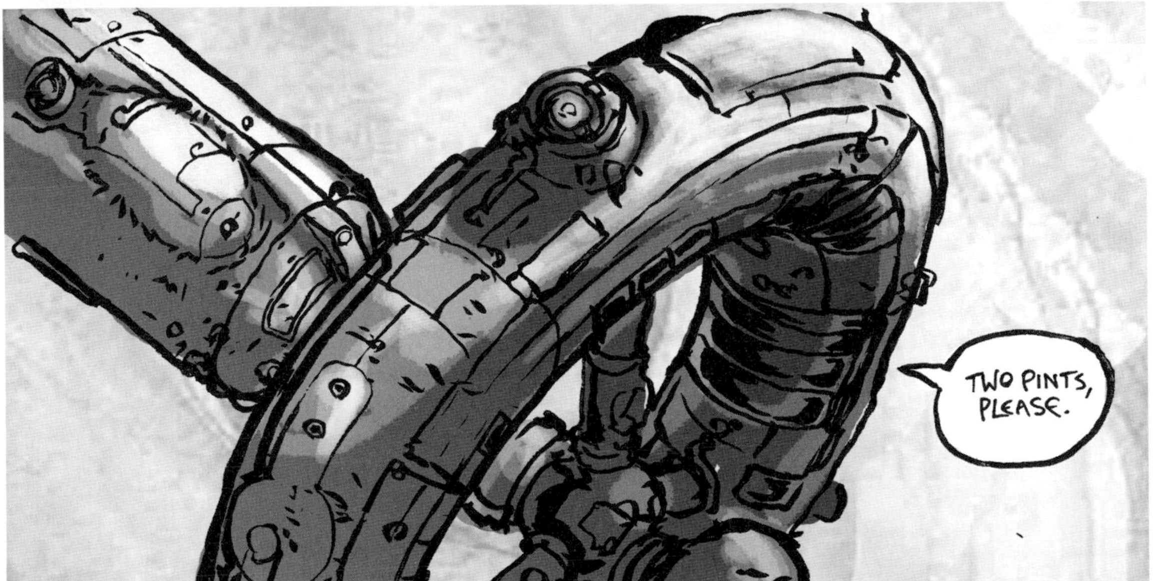
TWO PINTS, PLEASE.

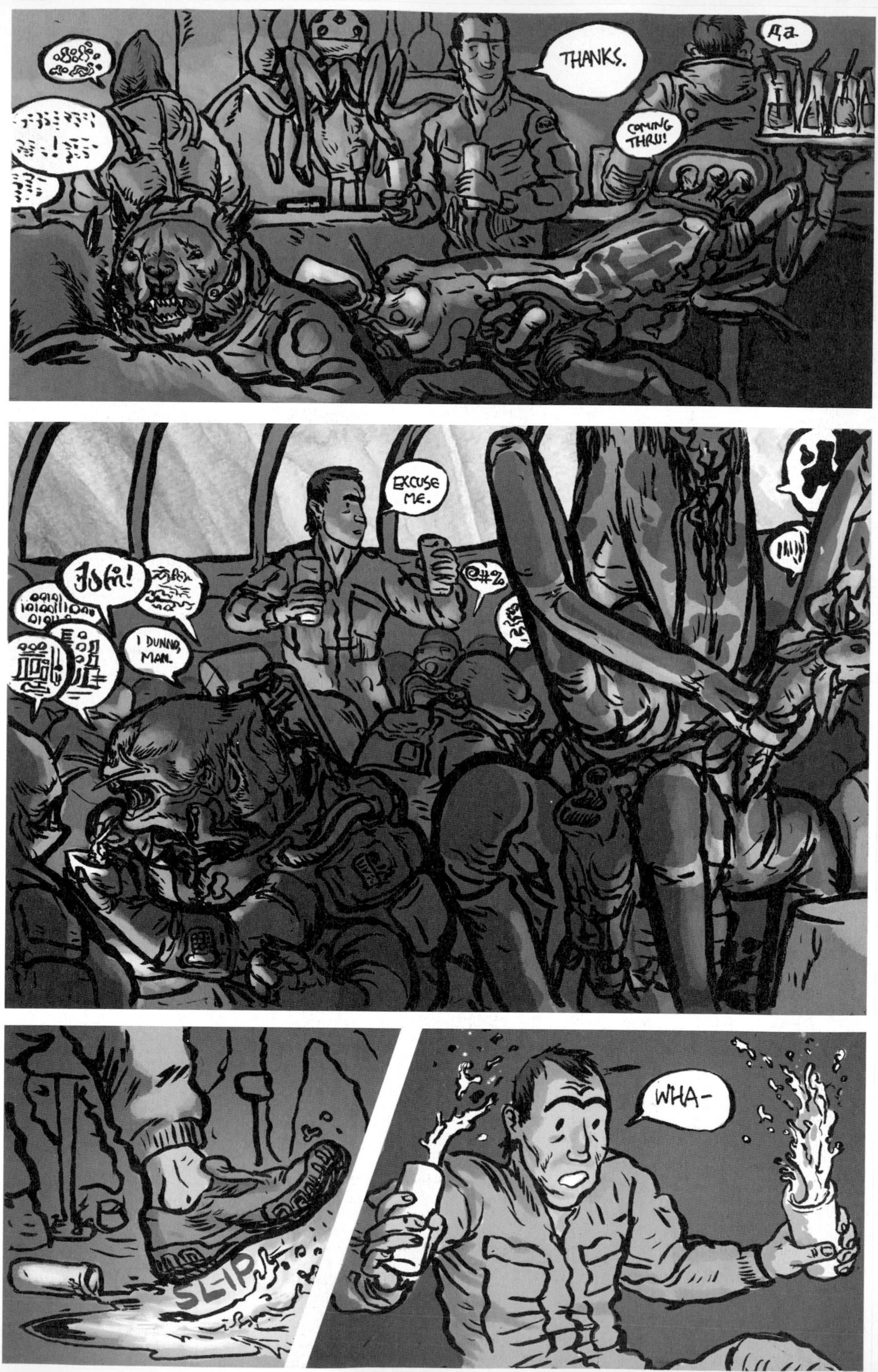

THANKS.
COMING THRU!
Дa.
EXCUSE ME.
I DUNNO, MAN.
@#%
SLIP
WHA-

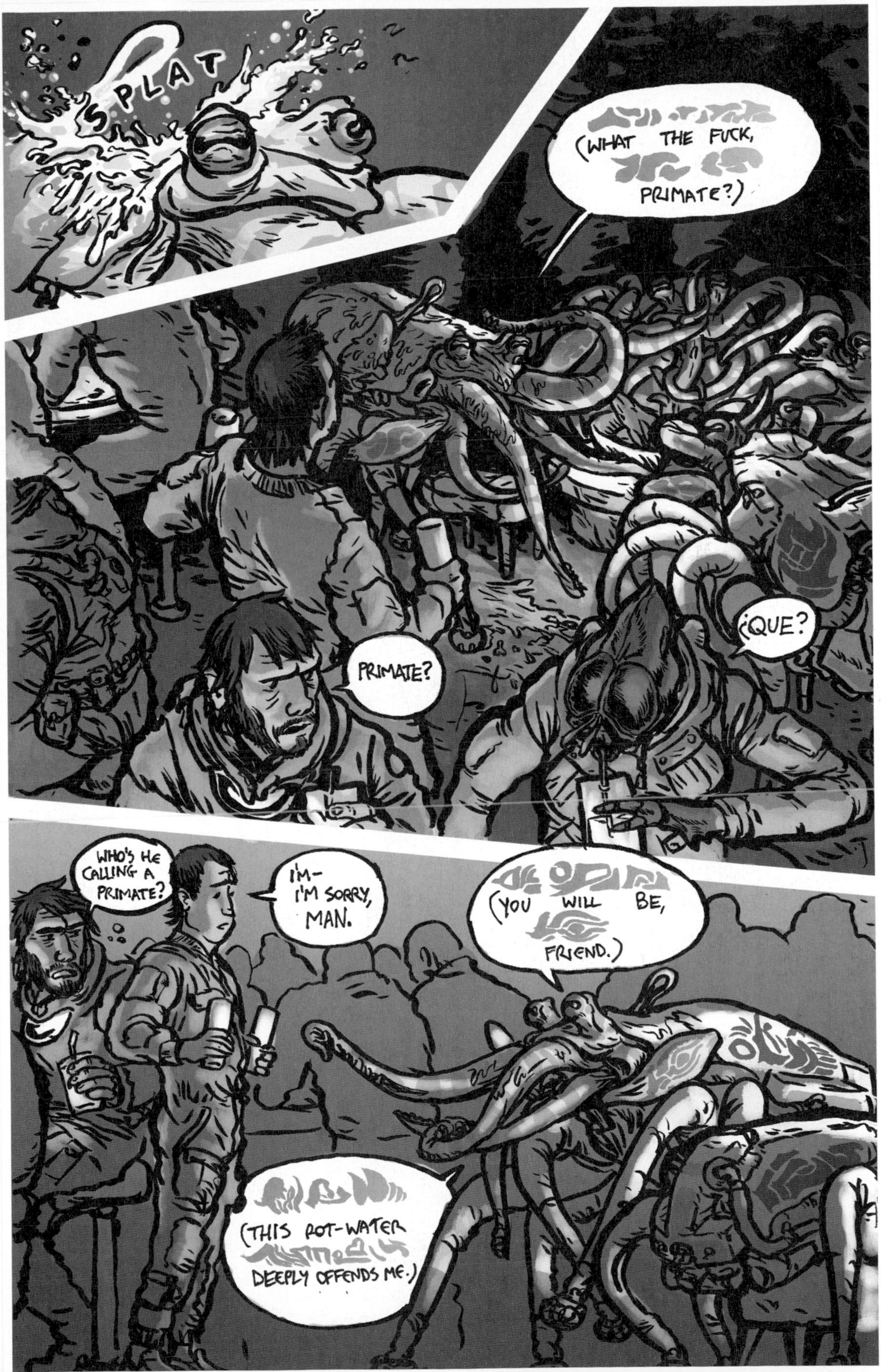
SPLAT
(WHAT THE FUCK, PRIMATE?)
PRIMATE?
¿QUE?
WHO'S HE CALLING A PRIMATE?
I'M- I'M SORRY, MAN.
(YOU WILL BE, FRIEND.)
(THIS ROT-WATER DEEPLY OFFENDS ME.)

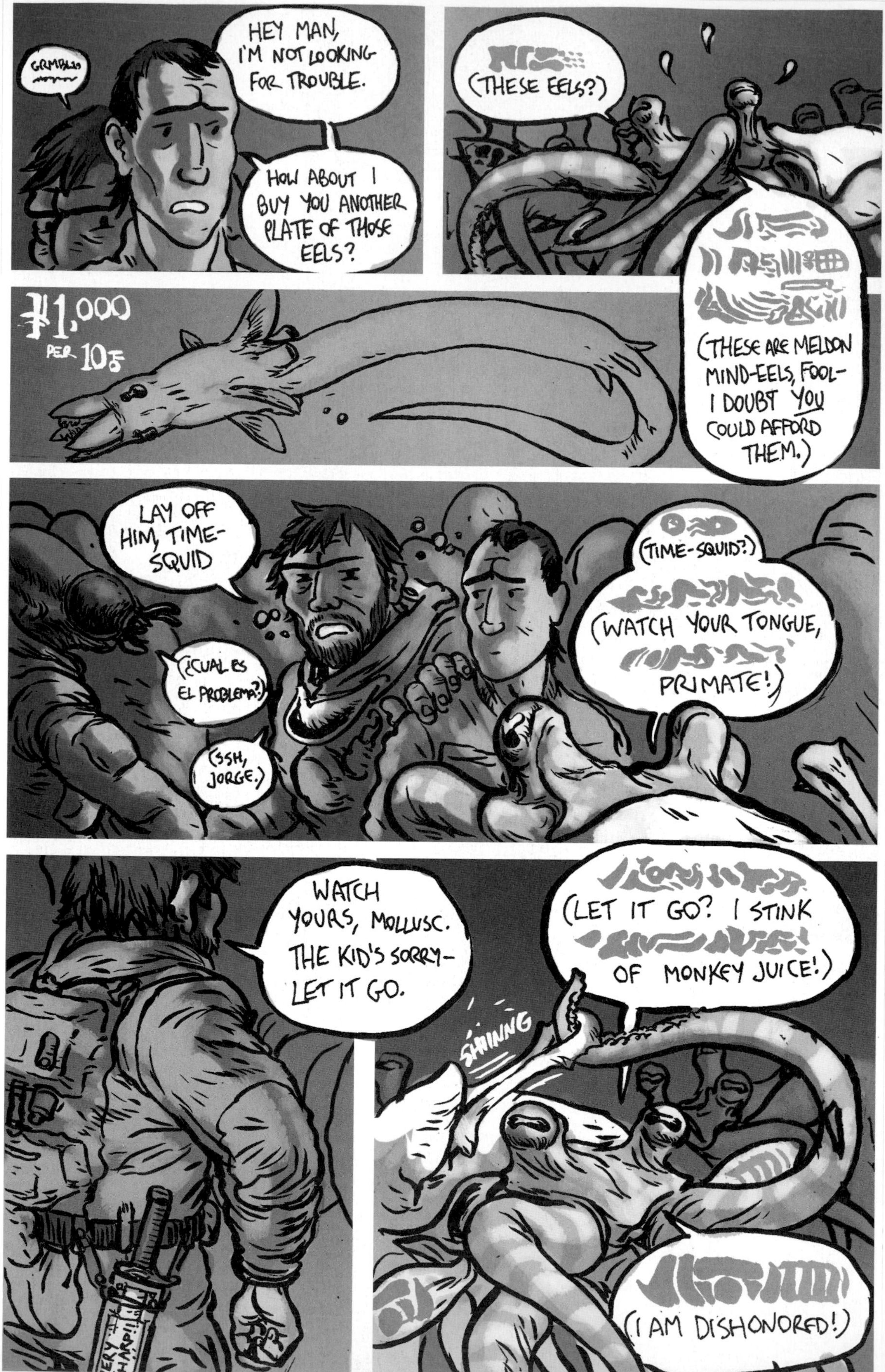
GRMBL
HEY MAN, I'M NOT LOOKING FOR TROUBLE.
HOW ABOUT I BUY YOU ANOTHER PLATE OF THOSE EELS?
(THESE EELS?)
(THESE ARE MELDON MIND-EELS, FOOL- I DOUBT YOU COULD AFFORD THEM.)
₮1,000 PER 10
LAY OFF HIM, TIME-SQUID
(TIME-SQUID?)
(WATCH YOUR TONGUE, PRIMATE!)
¿CUAL ES EL PROBLEMA?
(SSH, JORGE.)
WATCH YOURS, MOLLUSC. THE KID'S SORRY- LET IT GO.
(LET IT GO? I STINK OF MONKEY JUICE!)
SHAKING
(I AM DISHONORED!)
VERY SHARP!!

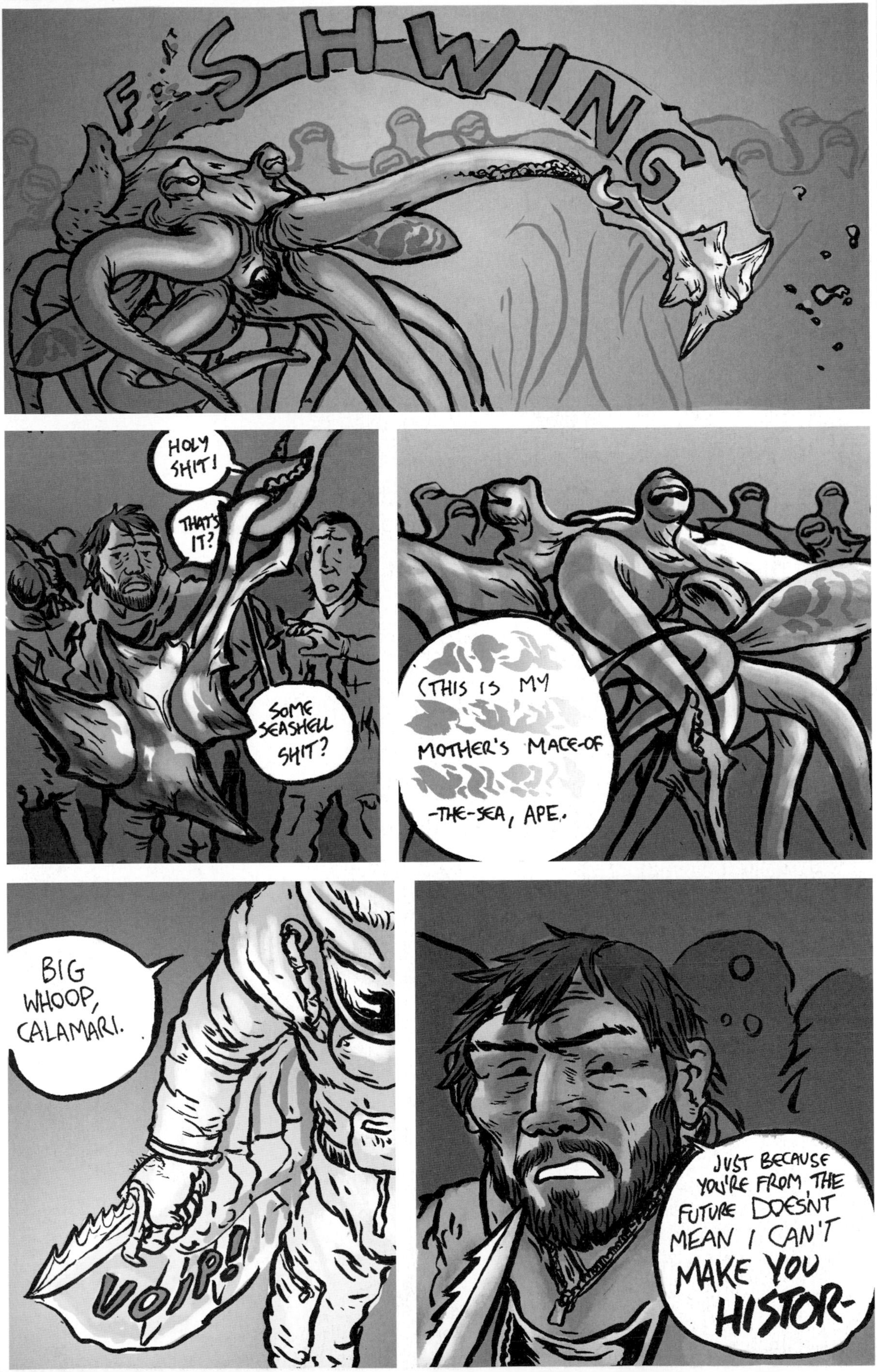
FSHWING
HOLY SHIT!
THAT'S IT?
SOME SEASHELL SHIT?
(THIS IS MY MOTHER'S MACE-OF-THE-SEA, APE.
BIG WHOOP, CALAMARI.
VOIIP!
JUST BECAUSE YOU'RE FROM THE FUTURE DOESN'T MEAN I CAN'T MAKE YOU HISTOR-

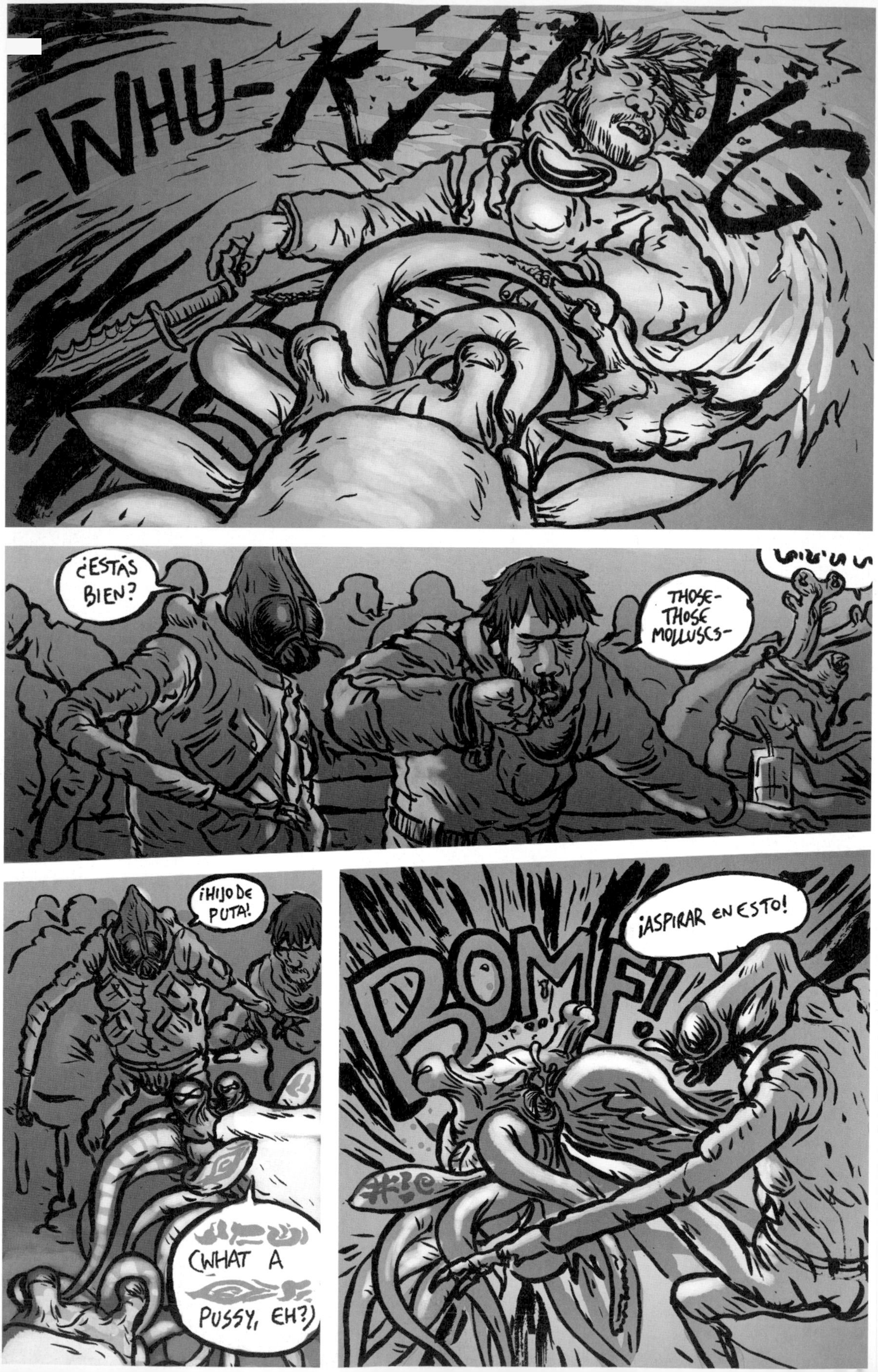
WHU-KANG
¿ESTÁS BIEN?
THOSE- THOSE MOLLUSCS-
¡HIJO DE PUTA!
(WHAT A PUSSY, EH?)
¡ASPIRAR EN ESTO!
BOMF!

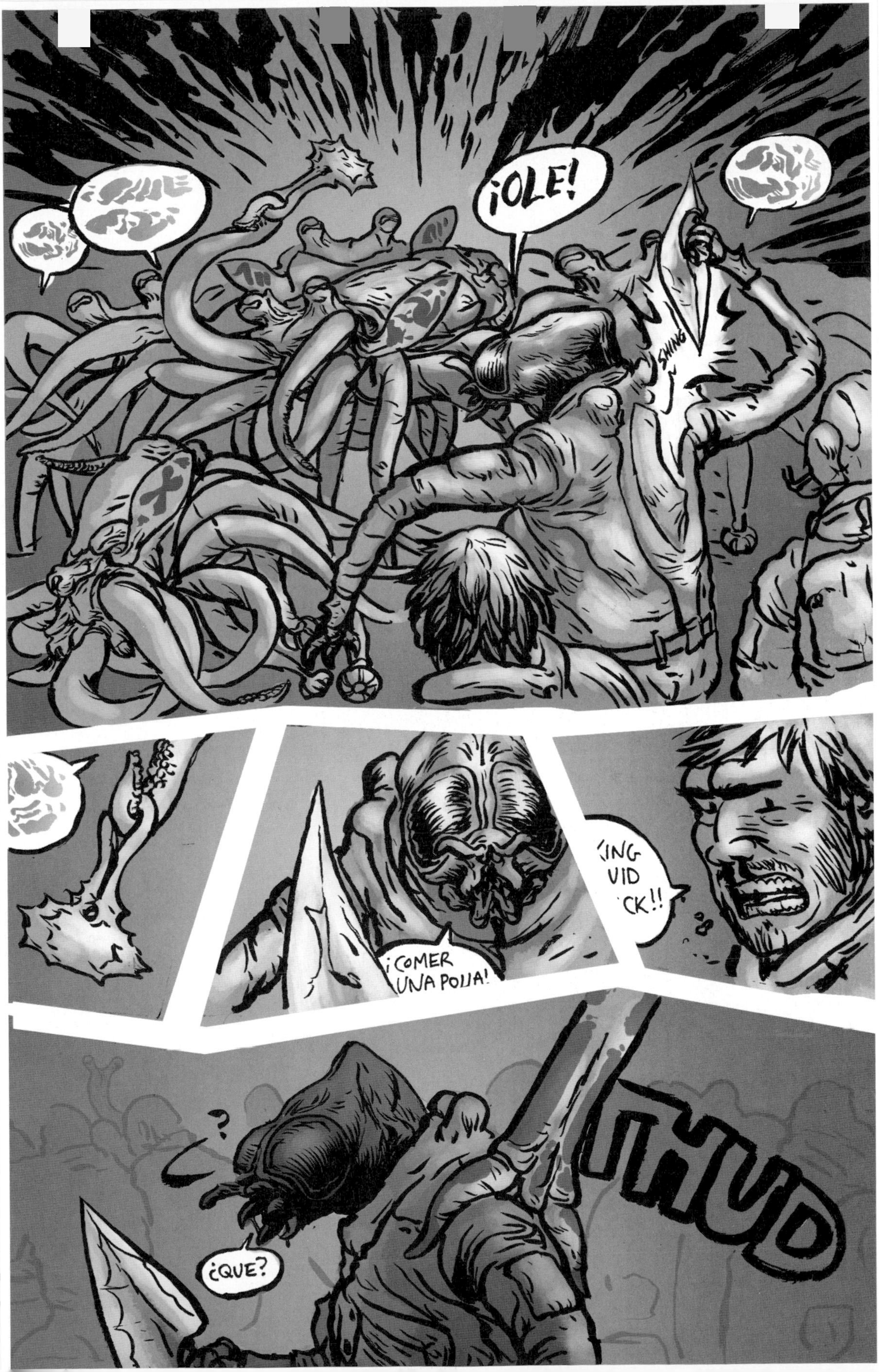
¡OLE!
SHING
ING VID CK!!
¡COMER UNA POLLA!
?
THUD
¿QUE?

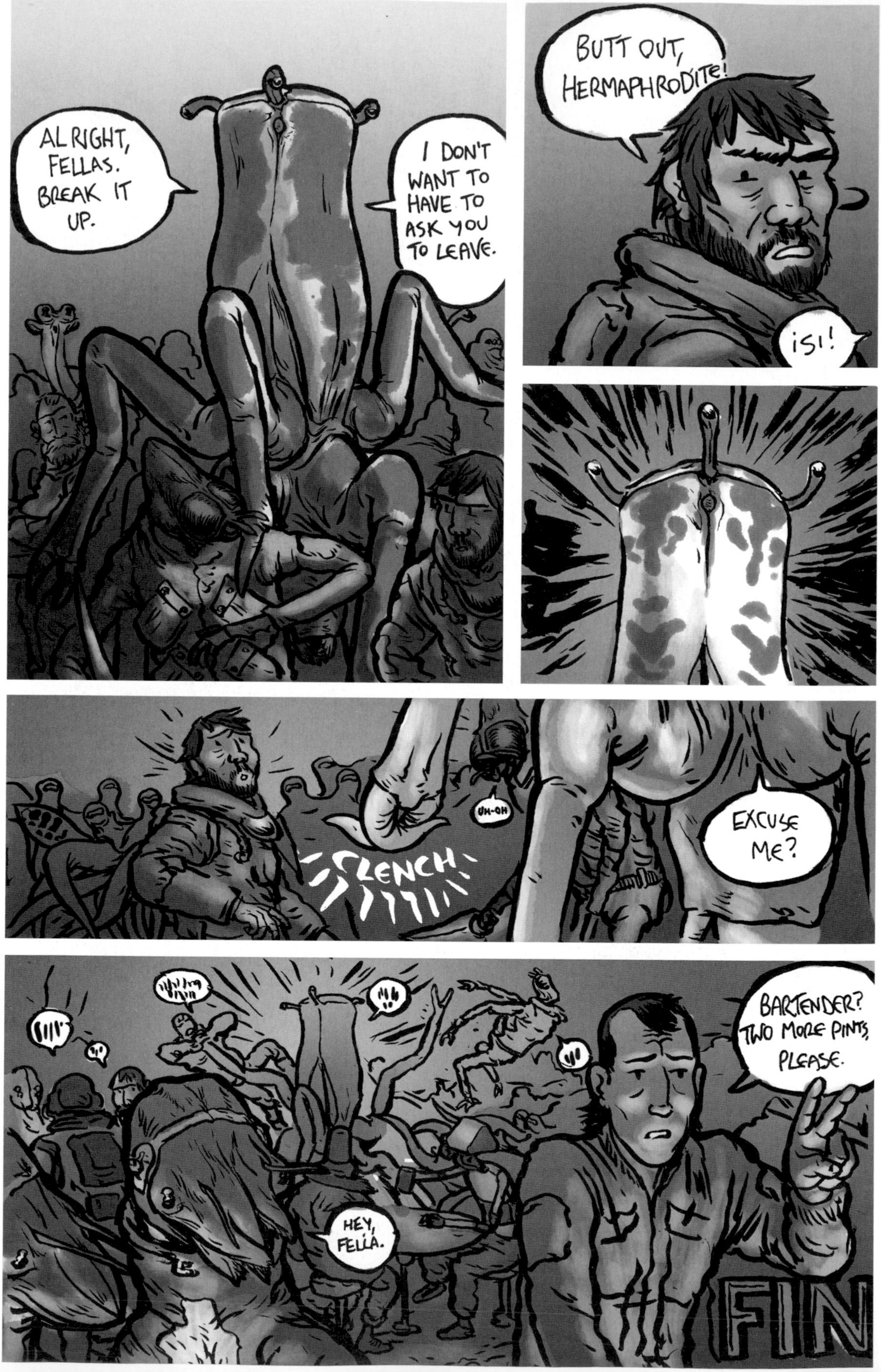

AL RIGHT, FELLAS. BREAK IT UP.
I DON'T WANT TO HAVE TO ASK YOU TO LEAVE.
BUTT OUT, HERMAPHRODITE!
¡SI!
UH-OH
CLENCH
EXCUSE ME?
BARTENDER? TWO MORE PINTS, PLEASE.
HEY, FELLA.
FIN

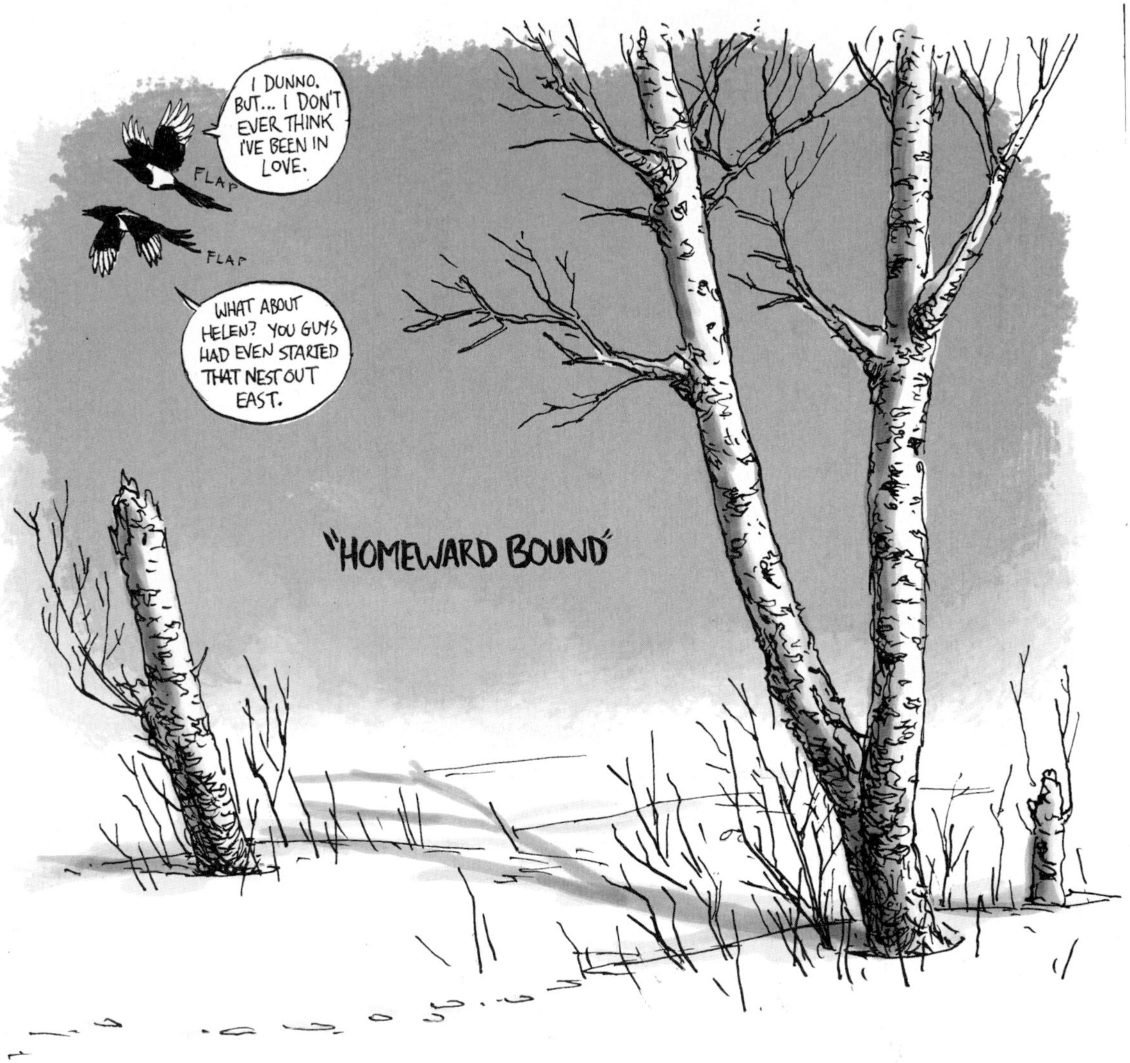
I DUNNO. BUT... I DON'T EVER THINK I'VE BEEN IN LOVE.
FLAP
FLAP
WHAT ABOUT HELEN? YOU GUYS HAD EVEN STARTED THAT NEST OUT EAST.
"HOMEWARD BOUND"

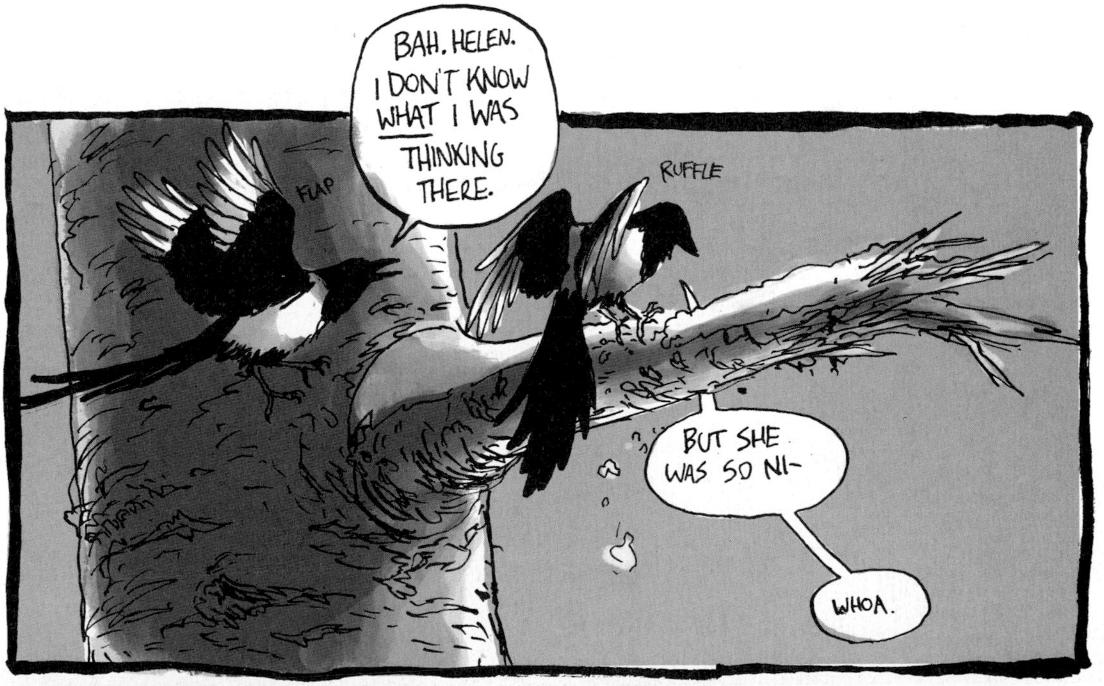
BAH. HELEN. I DON'T KNOW WHAT I WAS THINKING THERE.
FLAP
RUFFLE
BUT SHE WAS SO NI-
WHOA.

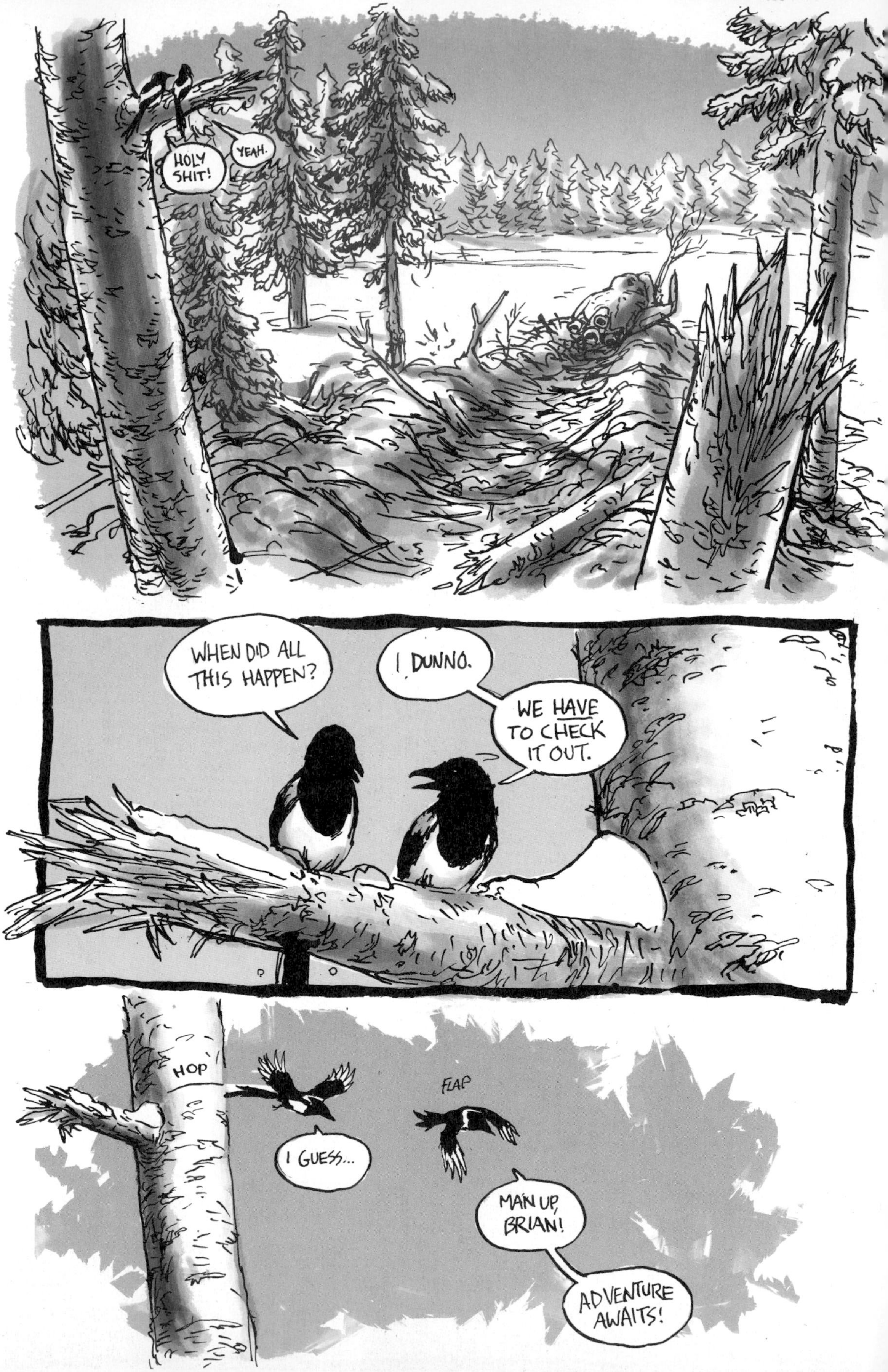
HOLY SHIT!
YEAH.
WHEN DID ALL THIS HAPPEN?
I DUNNO.
WE HAVE TO CHECK IT OUT.
HOP
FLAP
I GUESS...
MAN UP, BRIAN!
ADVENTURE AWAITS!

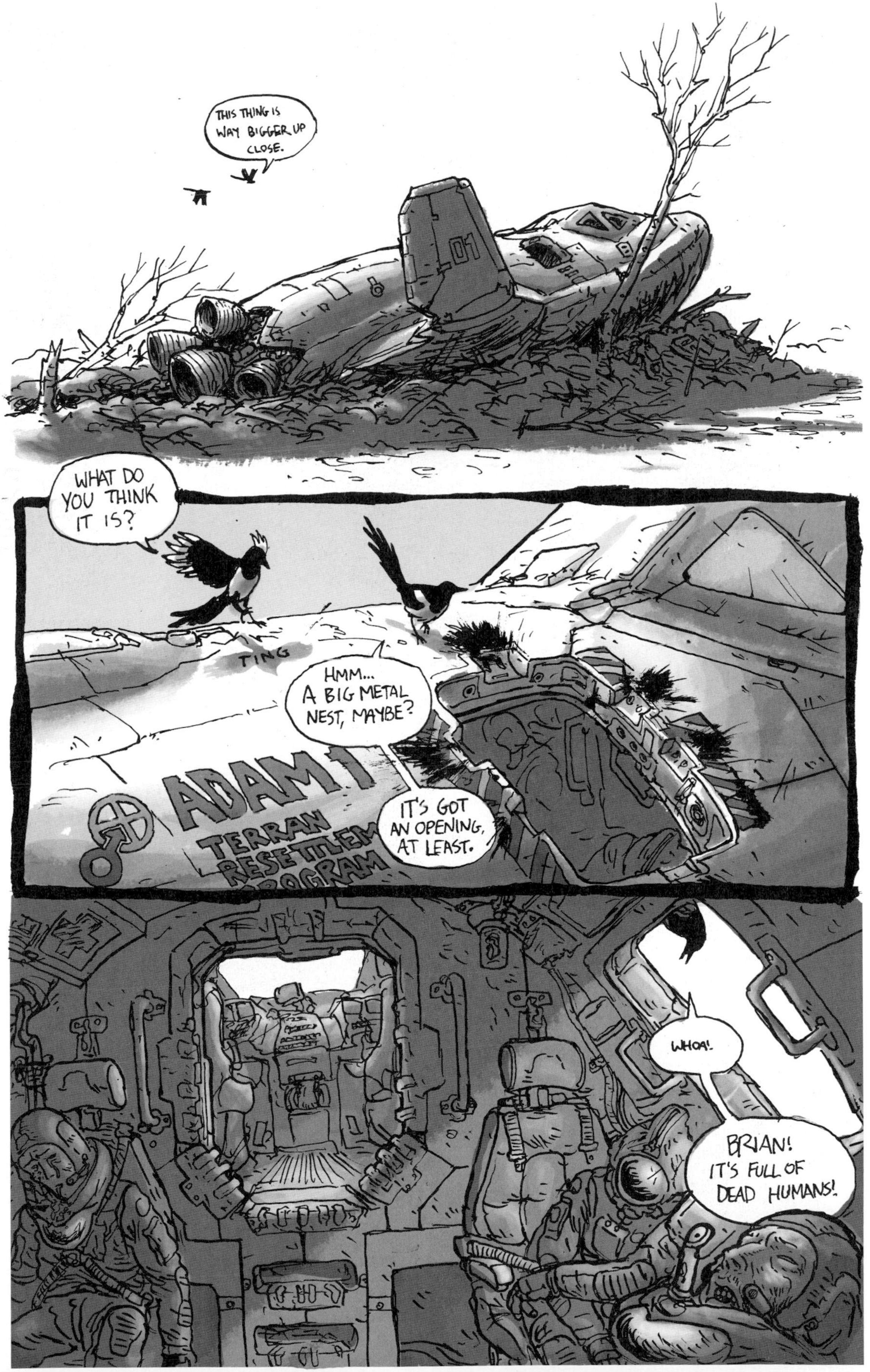
THIS THING IS WAY BIGGER UP CLOSE.
01
WHAT DO YOU THINK IT IS?
TING
HMM... A BIG METAL NEST, MAYBE?
ADAM 1
TERRAN
IT'S GOT AN OPENING, AT LEAST.
WHOA!
BRIAN! IT'S FULL OF DEAD HUMANS!

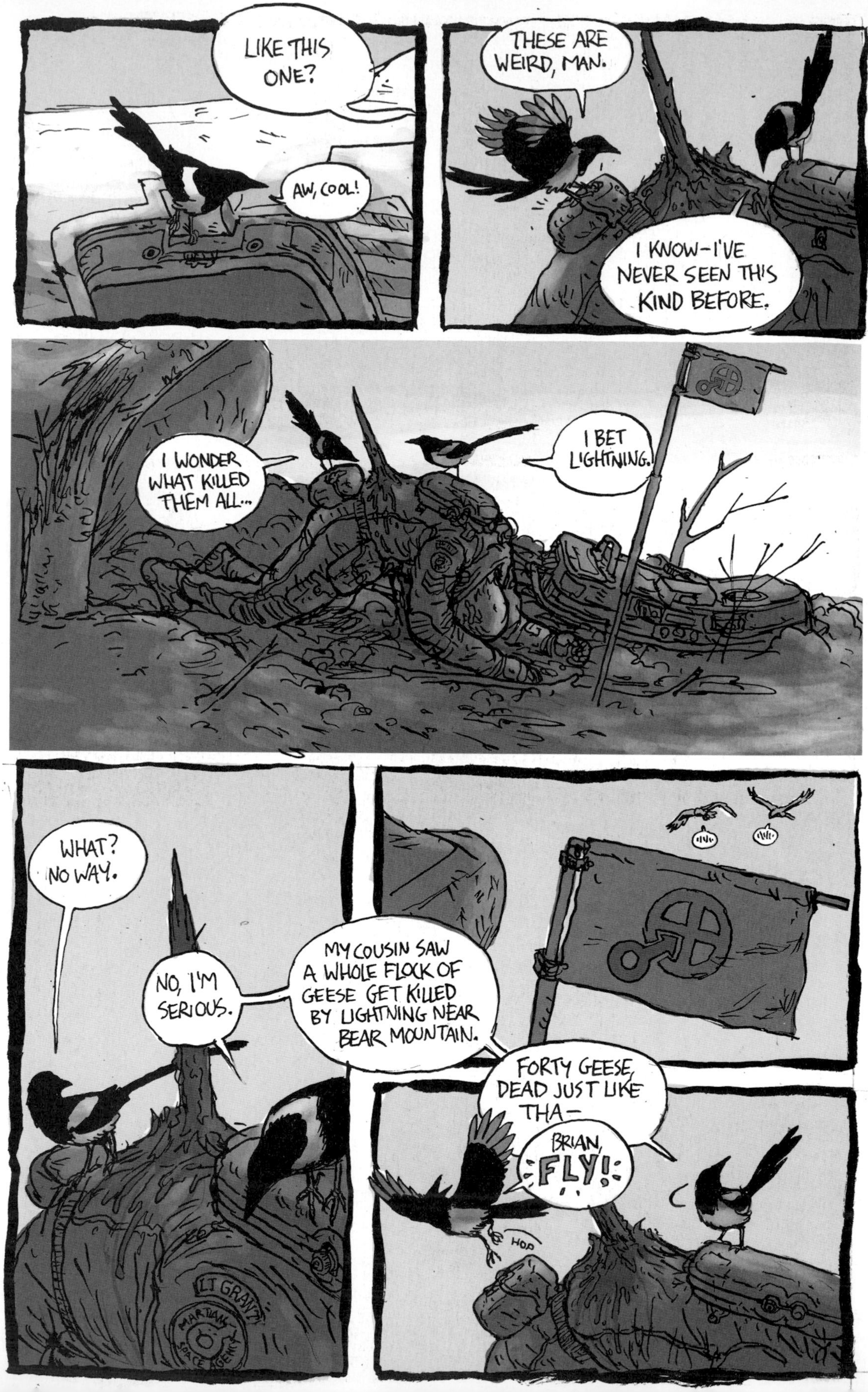
LIKE THIS ONE?
AW, COOL!
THESE ARE WEIRD, MAN.
I KNOW–I'VE NEVER SEEN THIS KIND BEFORE.
I WONDER WHAT KILLED THEM ALL...
I BET LIGHTNING.
WHAT? NO WAY.
NO, I'M SERIOUS.
MY COUSIN SAW A WHOLE FLOCK OF GEESE GET KILLED BY LIGHTNING NEAR BEAR MOUNTAIN.
LT GRANT
MARTIAN SPACE AGENCY
FORTY GEESE, DEAD JUST LIKE THA–
BRIAN, FLY!
HOP

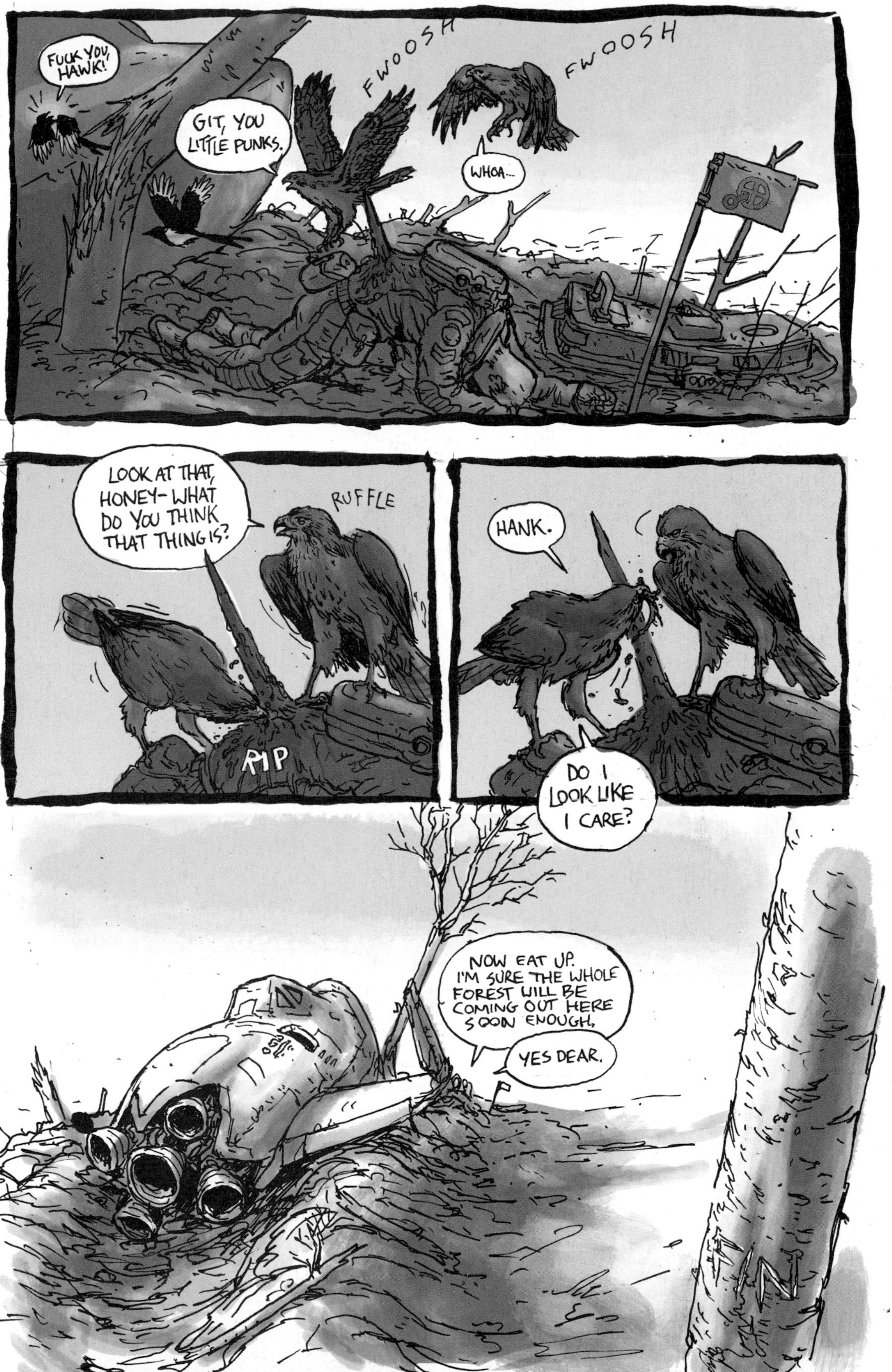
FUCK YOU, HAWK!
GIT, YOU LITTLE PUNKS.
FWOOSH
FWOOSH
WHOA...
LOOK AT THAT, HONEY- WHAT DO YOU THINK THAT THING IS?
RUFFLE
RIP
HANK.
DO I LOOK LIKE I CARE?
NOW EAT UP. I'M SURE THE WHOLE FOREST WILL BE COMING OUT HERE SOON ENOUGH.
YES DEAR.

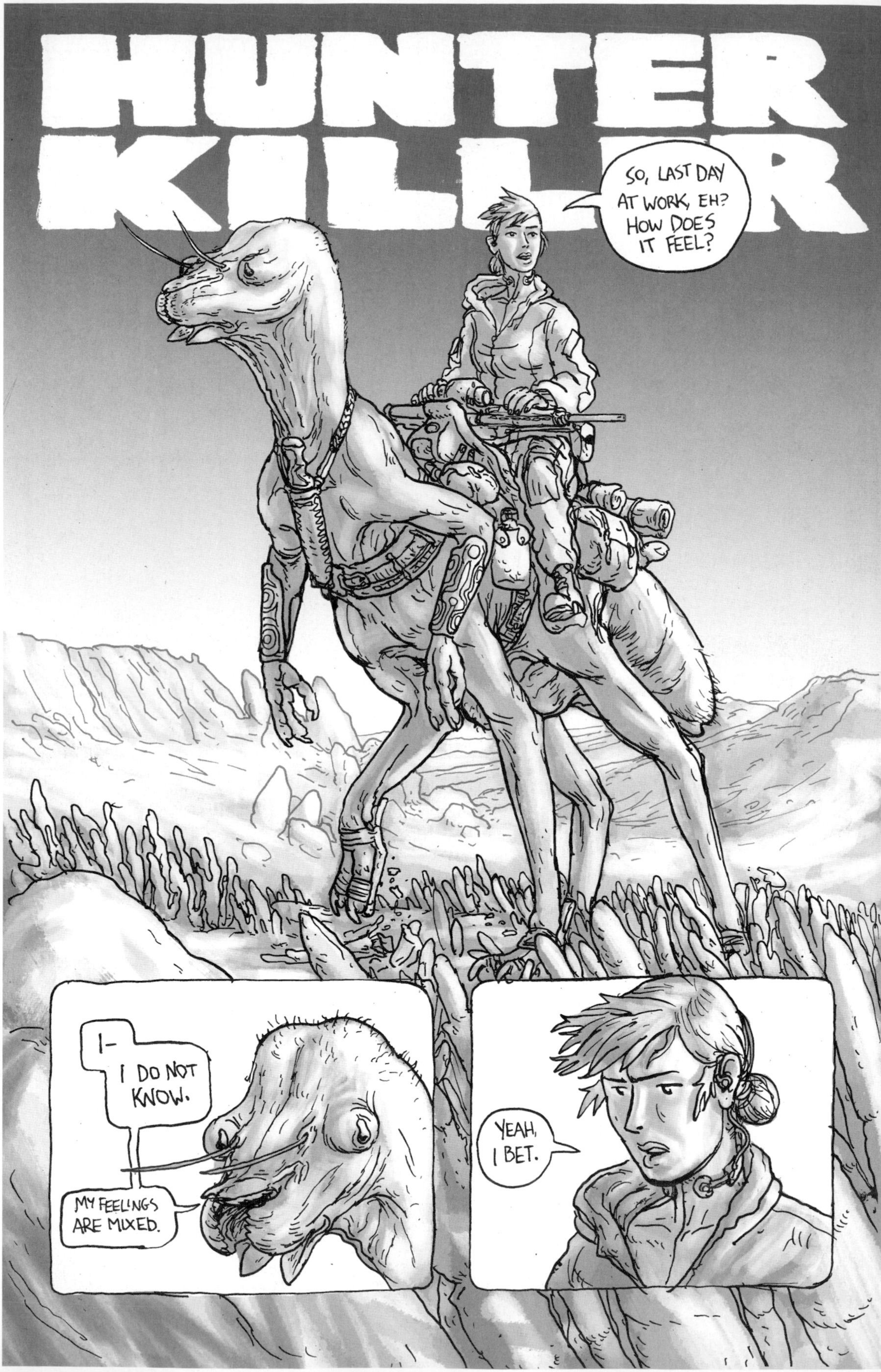
HUNTER KILLER
SO, LAST DAY AT WORK, EH? HOW DOES IT FEEL?
I-
I DO NOT KNOW.
MY FEELINGS ARE MIXED.
YEAH, I BET.

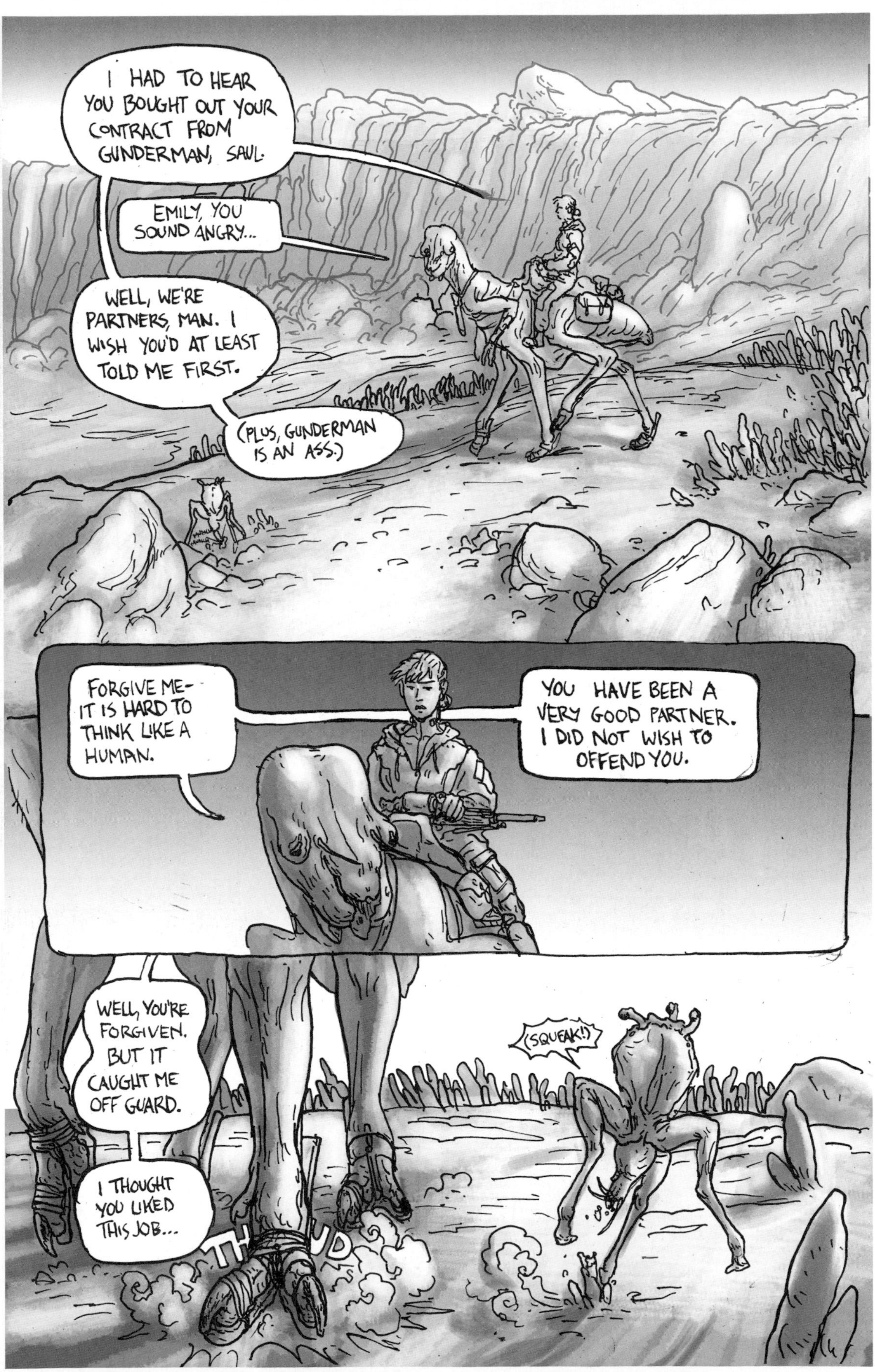
I HAD TO HEAR YOU BOUGHT OUT YOUR CONTRACT FROM GUNDERMAN, SAUL.
EMILY, YOU SOUND ANGRY...
WELL, WE'RE PARTNERS, MAN. I WISH YOU'D AT LEAST TOLD ME FIRST.
(PLUS, GUNDERMAN IS AN ASS.)
FORGIVE ME- IT IS HARD TO THINK LIKE A HUMAN.
YOU HAVE BEEN A VERY GOOD PARTNER. I DID NOT WISH TO OFFEND YOU.
WELL, YOU'RE FORGIVEN. BUT IT CAUGHT ME OFF GUARD.
I THOUGHT YOU LIKED THIS JOB...
(SQUEAK!)
THUD

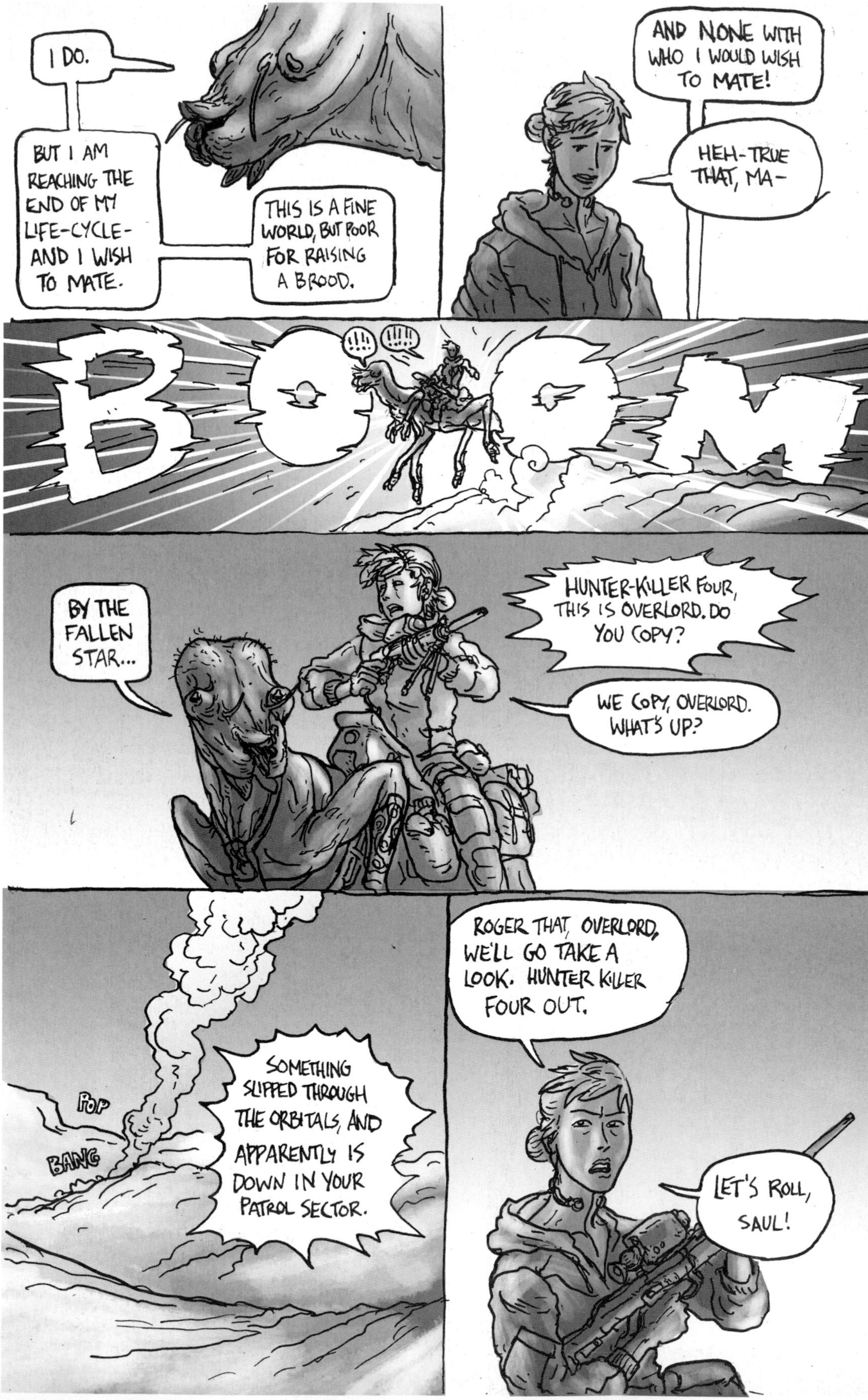
I DO.
BUT I AM REACHING THE END OF MY LIFE-CYCLE- AND I WISH TO MATE.
THIS IS A FINE WORLD, BUT POOR FOR RAISING A BROOD.
AND NONE WITH WHO I WOULD WISH TO MATE!
HEH-TRUE THAT, MA-
BOOM
!!!
!!!
BY THE FALLEN STAR...
HUNTER-KILLER FOUR, THIS IS OVERLORD. DO YOU COPY?
WE COPY, OVERLORD. WHAT'S UP?
SOMETHING SLIPPED THROUGH THE ORBITALS, AND APPARENTLY IS DOWN IN YOUR PATROL SECTOR.
POP
BANG
ROGER THAT, OVERLORD, WE'LL GO TAKE A LOOK. HUNTER KILLER FOUR OUT.
LET'S ROLL, SAUL!

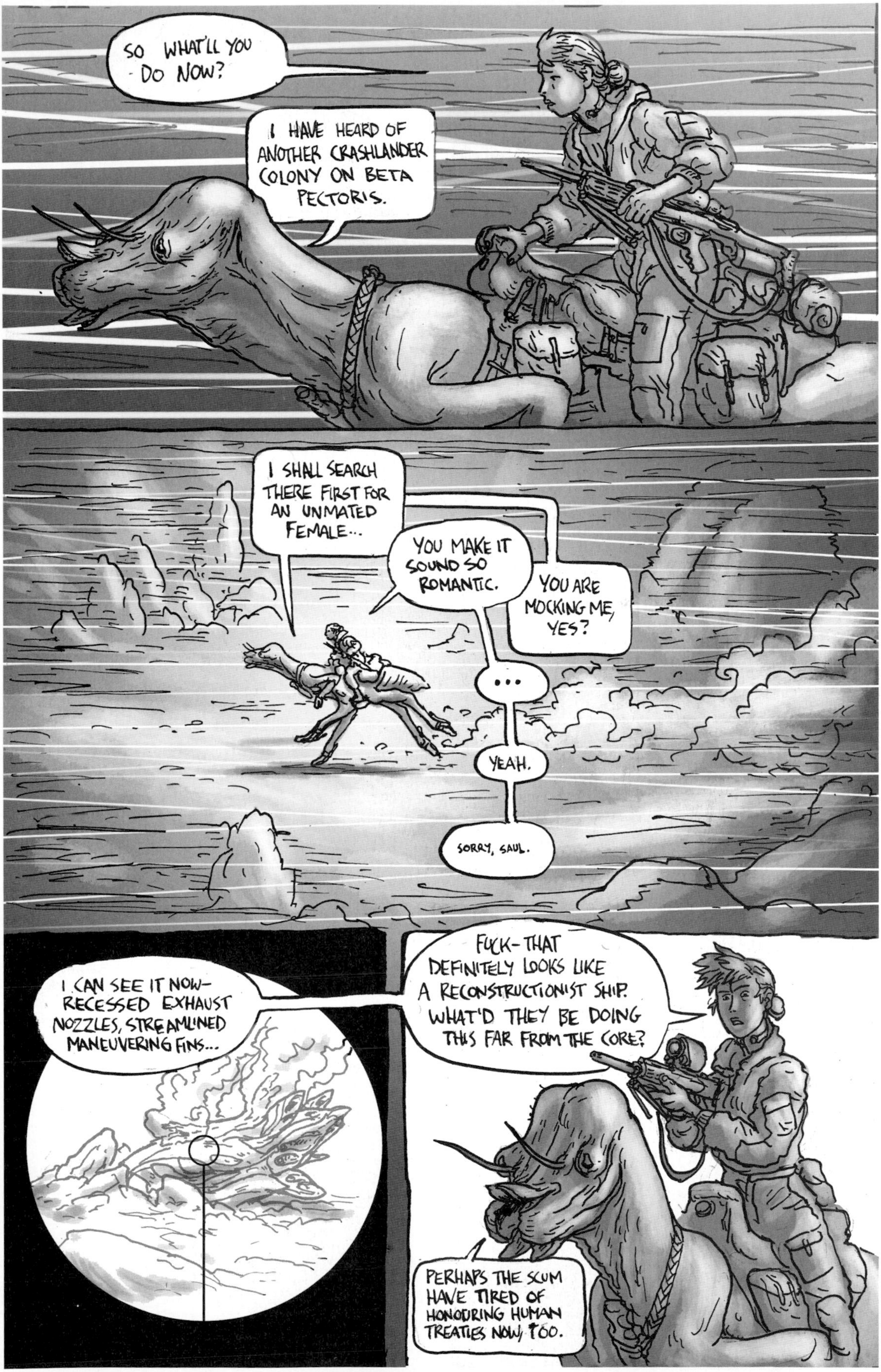
SO WHAT'LL YOU DO NOW?
I HAVE HEARD OF ANOTHER CRASHLANDER COLONY ON BETA PECTORIS.
I SHALL SEARCH THERE FIRST FOR AN UNMATED FEMALE...
YOU MAKE IT SOUND SO ROMANTIC.
YOU ARE MOCKING ME, YES?
...
YEAH.
SORRY, SAUL.
I CAN SEE IT NOW- RECESSED EXHAUST NOZZLES, STREAMLINED MANEUVERING FINS...
FUCK- THAT DEFINITELY LOOKS LIKE A RECONSTRUCTIONIST SHIP. WHAT'D THEY BE DOING THIS FAR FROM THE CORE?
PERHAPS THE SCUM HAVE TIRED OF HONOURING HUMAN TREATIES NOW, TOO.

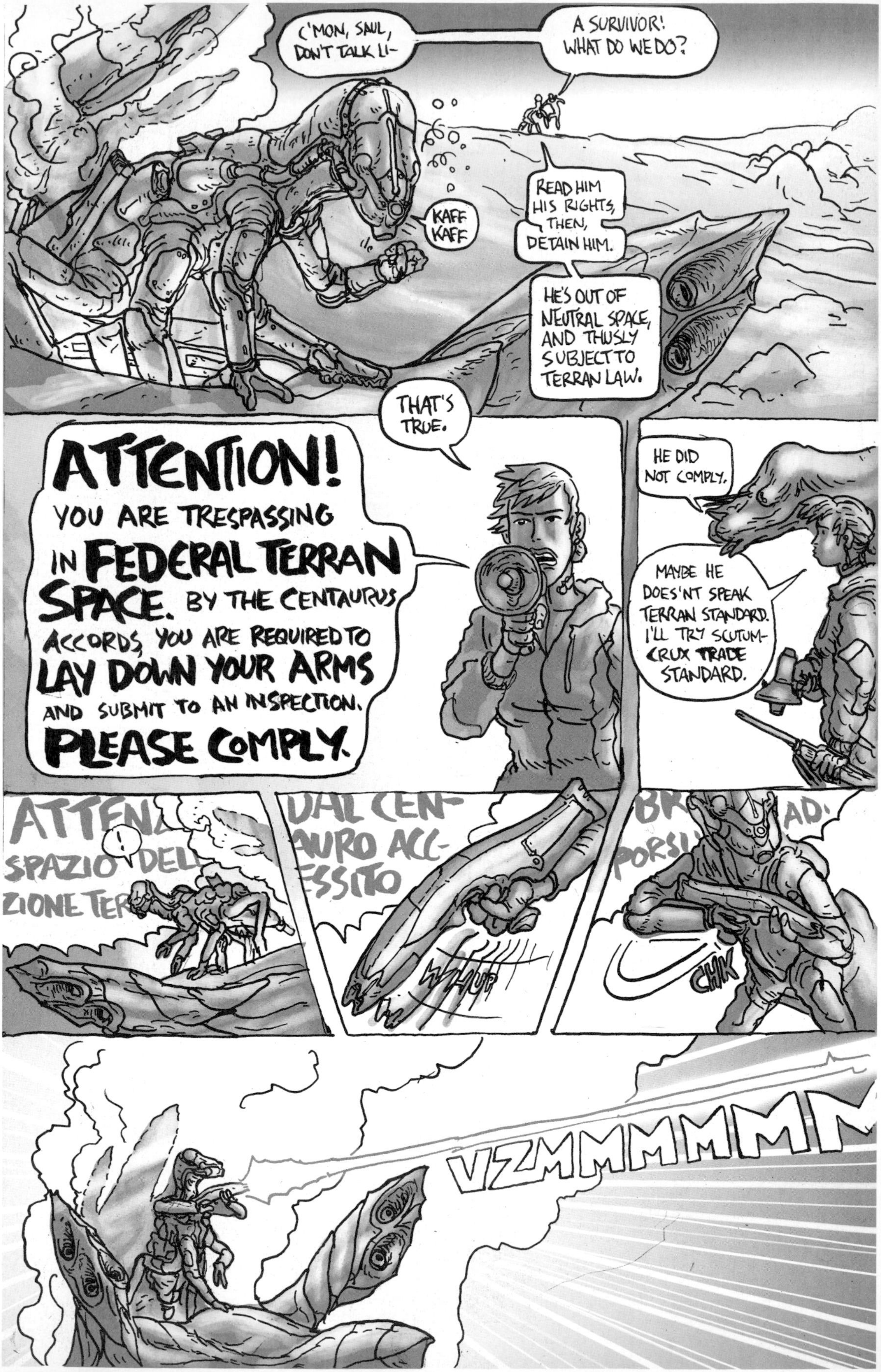
C'MON, SAUL, DON'T TALK LI-
A SURVIVOR! WHAT DO WE DO?
KAFF KAFF
READ HIM HIS RIGHTS, THEN, DETAIN HIM.
HE'S OUT OF NEUTRAL SPACE, AND THUSLY SUBJECT TO TERRAN LAW.
THAT'S TRUE.
ATTENTION! YOU ARE TRESPASSING IN FEDERAL TERRAN SPACE. BY THE CENTAURUS ACCORDS, YOU ARE REQUIRED TO LAY DOWN YOUR ARMS AND SUBMIT TO AN INSPECTION. PLEASE COMPLY.
HE DID NOT COMPLY.
MAYBE HE DOES'NT SPEAK TERRAN STANDARD. I'LL TRY SCUTUM-CRUX TRADE STANDARD.
ATTEN
SPAZIO DEL
ZIONE TER
!
DAL CEN-
AURO ACC-
ESSITO
WHUP
BR
AD
PORSI
CHK
VZMMMMMMM

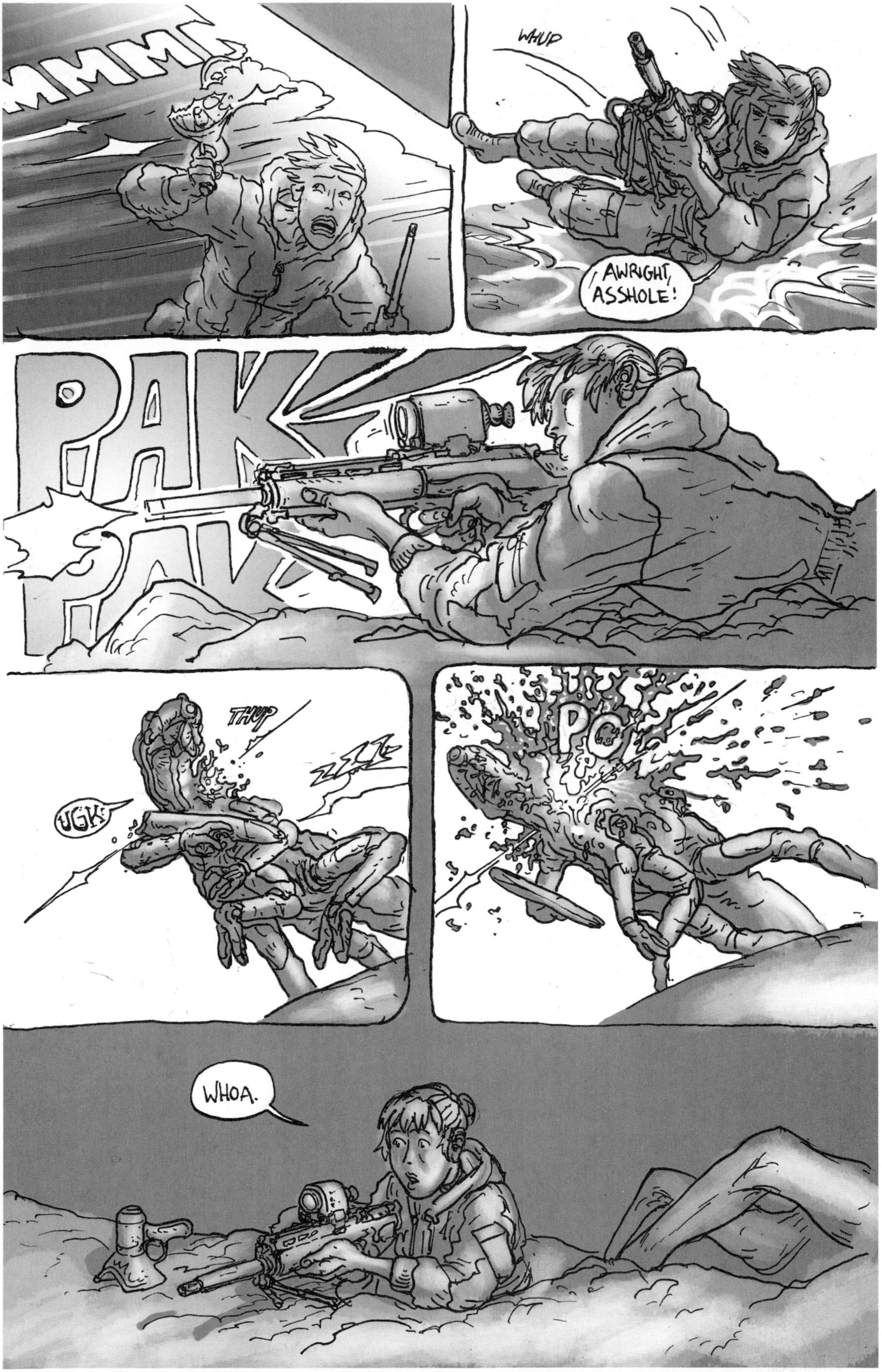
MMMG
WHUP
AWRIGHT, ASSHOLE!
PAK
PAK
THUP
UGK!
PC
WHOA.

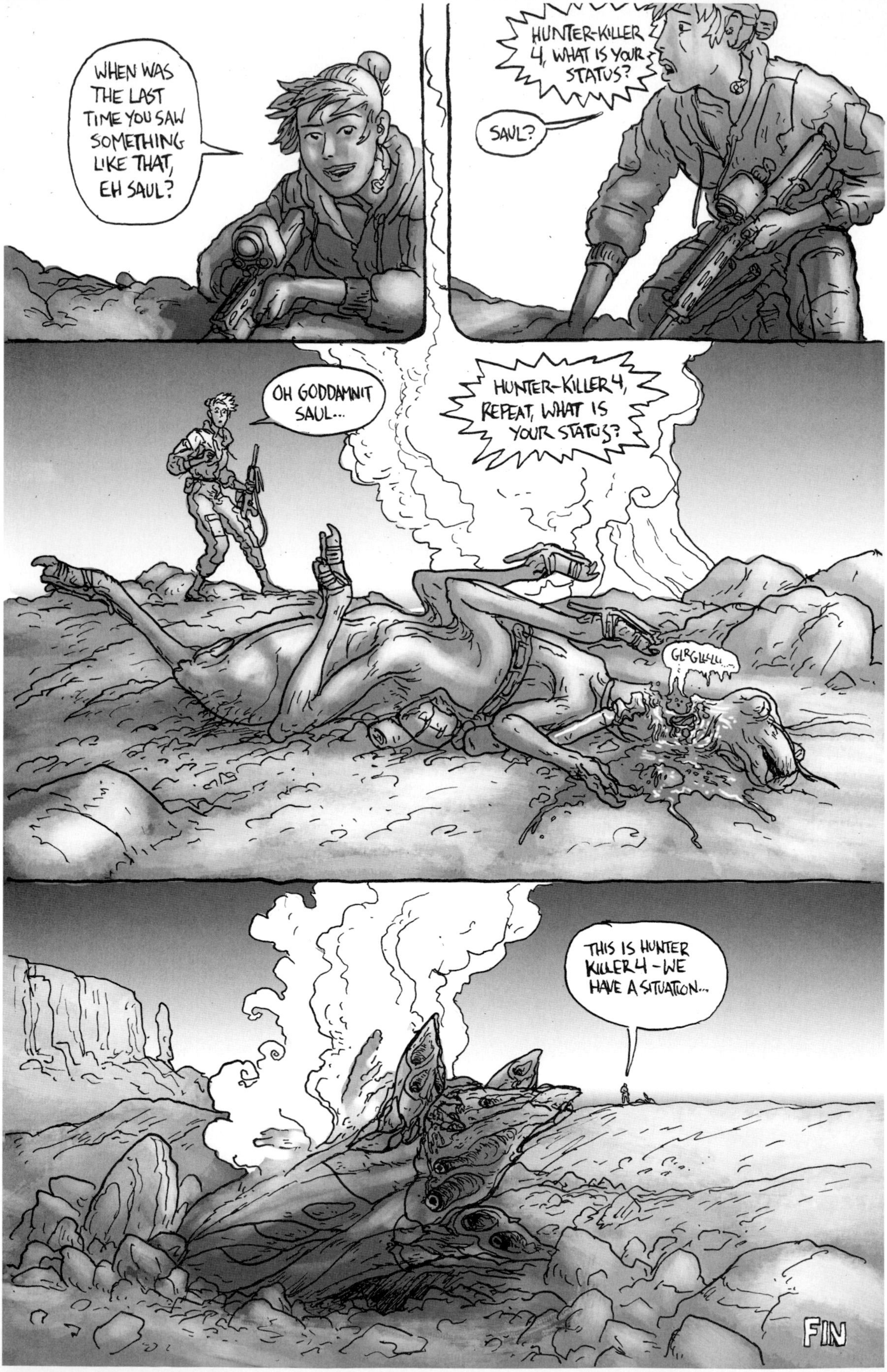

WHEN WAS THE LAST TIME YOU SAW SOMETHING LIKE THAT, EH SAUL?
HUNTER-KILLER 4, WHAT IS YOUR STATUS?
SAUL?
OH GODDAMNIT SAUL...
HUNTER-KILLER 4, REPEAT, WHAT IS YOUR STATUS?
THIS IS HUNTER KILLER 4 - WE HAVE A SITUATION...
FIN

Well, fuck.
Mom, you're embarrassing me in front of the food!
KISS
We'll talk once you pupate, honey.
SIMON FOY 2011

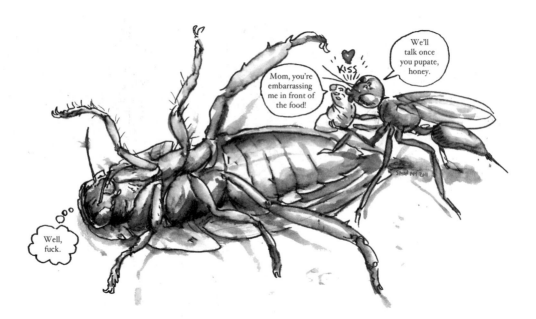